The Church on TV

The Church on TV

PORTRAYALS OF PRIESTS, PASTORS AND NUNS ON AMERICAN TELEVISION SERIES

By Richard Wolff

continuum

2010

The Continuum International Publishing Group Inc
80 Maiden Lane, New York, NY 10038

The Continuum International Publishing Group Ltd
The Tower Building, 11 York Road, London SE1 7NX

www.continuumbooks.com

Library of Congress Cataloging-in-Publication Data
A catalog record for this book is available from the Library of
Congress.

ISBN: 978-1-4411-4109-5 (Hardback)
      978-1-4411-5797-3 (Paperback)

Typeset by Pindar NZ, Auckland, New Zealand

In loving memory of Nancy

Contents

Acknowledgments

The origin of this study into the history of portrayals of the church and its leaders on popular American television programs was in a seminar at Ohio University on the history of American cultural, social and intellectual life. This class, led by noted historian Charles Alexander, served as my first foray into the project — one that would take over a decade to complete. I am thankful to Professor Alexander for sparking my interest in this topic. So too must I thank Patrick Washburn, also of Ohio University, for whose historical seminar in journalism and communication studies I continued this research. To others at Ohio University who encouraged these efforts, including David Mould and Jenny Nelson, I am likewise grateful.

My methodology for researching this book leads me to recognize those scholars without whose work my research would not have been possible. To discover which television programs were relevant to my own study, I relied on standard reference works in television studies. These are Vincent Terrace's *Complete Encyclopedia of Television Series, Pilots and Specials* (New York: Zoetrope, 1986), Alex McNeil's *Total Television: The Comprehensive Guide to Programming from 1948 to the Present* (New York: Penguin Books, 1996), and Tim Brooks and Earle Marsh's *The Complete Directory to Prime Time Network and Cable TV Shows, 1946–Present* (New York: Ballantine Books, 1999). I conducted an entry-by-entry review of all programs listed in these books to find which programs focused regularly and principally on ecclesiastics, and I cannot begin to think how difficult this task would have been had these works not been available. A reference work later appeared which helped verify the comprehensiveness of my research, and identify a few final programs worth including; this volume is Ann C. Paitta's *Saints, Clergy and Other Religious Figures on Film and Television, 1895–2003* (North Carolina: McFarland and Company, 2005).

Once I had a list of programs, I screened every available episode of these shows so that this research would be as comprehensive and exhaustive as possible. The number of episodes screened runs into the thousands and required help from various sources to locate and screen every obtainable episode. For many of the programs, I relied on the resources of three institutions: The Motion Picture, Broadcasting and Recorded Sound Division of the Library of Congress in

Washington, DC; the University of California at Los Angeles Film and Television Archives; and the Paley Center for Media (formerly the Museum of Television and Radio) in New York. To the staffs of these institutions who helped me locate and review relevant programs on multiple visits, I am grateful. In particular I wish to thank Madeline Matz and Zoran Sinobad of the Library of Congress, Mark Quigley of the UCLA archives, and Shu-Lin Lee and Mark Bushman of the Paley Center. For some shows, collections of episodes were commercially available and I simply purchased or borrowed and viewed them. In some cases, I received copies of programs directly from the producers, and I thank their staffs for making the arrangements. Some shows I was able to record directly from television; in this effort I must thank my friend Frank Zagottis, who recorded many programs I could not.

I owe gratitude to the faculty and administration of Dowling College who supported my research and made it possible for me to work on this book during academic years.

Finally my thanks go to my colleague and friend Benilde Montgomery, whose thoughtful comments on drafts of this book helped improve the final product.

1

INVOKING THE IMAGE OF CHURCH LEADERS ON TV

We have watched these people of God for years.

We've watched them help parishioners, solve personal problems and contemplate ethical issues. We've looked on as they debated the direction of the church in the modern world. We've seen their battles to remain relevant in a society which often overlooks them. We've watched some balance family and clerical life. We've seen others run orphanages or missions. Through it all, they have managed to make us think, be thankful and yes, even laugh. These are the ministers of the church. The priests, nuns, pastors and deacons of God. The leaders of the Almighty's church on earth. Yes, we've enjoyed our time spent with them.

Especially when they've also solved murder mysteries, staged outlandish pranks and taken to the sky in flight.

Often larger-than-life, these religious leaders have ranged from conservative to liberal, zany to zealous, novices to veterans, celibates to parents. They've been men and women, as well as Protestants and Catholics. And though some have lived sensational lives because of extravagant hobbies such as crime-solving, or extraordinary abilities such as flying, all have shown devotion to the church and a commitment to their faith and calling. What is more, they all represent a pivotally important institution. The church? Yes. But just as important, they emerge from another vastly significant modern institution: television. From Sister Bertrille to Father Dowling and Reverend Camden, these characters have served the church on TV throughout its history. And while they've come from various denominational backgrounds, they've also spanned the range of television genres, from situation comedies and murder mysteries to family-friendly programs and powerful dramas.

Just as churches have endured their share of public controversies, from priest abuse scandals and the role of women in the church to the church's handling of issues such as abortion, illegal immigration and gay rights, so too have TV churches taken on these matters — usually with dismal results, at least as television ratings are concerned. The successful television church most often is sappy or slapstick, and avoids the sensational. Controversy sells where television's depiction of other social institutions is concerned, from the police and the courts to hospitals and the school system. For the church on TV, its mission had better be to induce a smile or warm the heart, for where the sacred is involved the sentimental and silly sell, while controversy often leads to cancelation.

Given this, a number of questions arise. What has been American pop-ular television's representation of the church and its leaders? What changes have occurred in this representation over the years, and why? How does this representation compare with actual trends in contemporary American church history? Why does television's version of this history read as it does? How do these church-set programs compare with trends in television programming? What does all this tell us of US popular culture and its attitude towards the church and its leaders? These are the questions which guide this study. It takes a historical-critical approach to analyze the representation of the institutional church and its ordained leaders (or ecclesiastics) airing in prime time on those US broadcast network programs which focused regularly and principally on people in service to the church.[1]

Focusing the study in this way, the emphasis is on shows about ecclesiastics, as opposed to programs that only occasionally featured a religious leader or set themselves in the church. For example, The Flying Nun and 7th Heaven regularly and principally focused on the lives of people in service to the church and therefore are featured in this study. Other programs, such as M*A*S*H with its Father Mulcahy, featured a cleric as a member of an ensemble cast but were not principally about the life of a cleric, and so do not receive extended discussion. Nonetheless, M*A*S*H is among a handful of programs that do receive brief consideration here because, although not principally about the church and its leaders, their churchly characters are well known, important or appeared somewhat regularly. Programs that included clerics as only incidental characters are excluded from this study.

Also excluded are programs airing on cable networks or subscription chan-nels, such as HBO's Oz, a program set in a penitentiary and featuring a nun and a priest among its characters. While a study of clerical characters appearing on such cable venues may be worthwhile, cable television stations operate under a different set of regulations and expectations than do broadcast networks, and they have a different history. Comparing broadcast to cable station programming is, to a certain extent, incommensurable. Likewise, daytime serials (or "soap operas") have featured ecclesiastics but these too operate under different expectations and appeals than prime-time programming and are not the focus of this survey. Indeed, an examination of clerics on daytime serials would be rather extensive and merit its own study. Additionally, although television programs featuring angels abound (The Smothers Brothers Show, Highway to Heaven, Heaven Help Us, Touched by an Angel), they are not the focus of this study. Nor are programs about paranormal or miraculous phenomena (such as Miracles) or God speaking to ordinary people (such as Joan of Arcadia and Saving Grace). The spotlight here is only on the church and its ordained and avowed leaders — priests, pastors, nuns, bishops, deacons and rabbis.

---

1. As a shorthand, I may use the expressions "church-set" or "focusing on church leaders" to describe the programs discussed.

In film studies, one finds many titles examining religious themes broadly conceived, including portrayals of Christ on the screen; however, analyses focusing on representations of ecclesiastics on film are far less common.[2] The most noteworthy work which does look at the history of clerics and the church in American movies is the classic *Hollywood and the Catholic Church: The Image of Roman Catholicism in American Movies* by Les and Barbara Keyser (1984)[3], wherein the authors analyze how priests, nuns and faithful parishioners are represented in films running from *Boys Town* (1938) and *The Trouble with Angels* (1966) to *The Exorcist* (1973) and *Saturday Night Fever* (1977). The text is an authoritative source for analysis of films up to its publication date and offers useful approaches for any examination of the church's representation in electronic media, including TV and radio. Notably, the focus in that volume is on one particular church — the Roman Catholic Church — whereas the present study more broadly considers clerics of all faiths and denominations. A similar, more recent book, *Catholics in the Movies*, edited by Colleen McDannell, looks at many of the same films and considers why the Catholic Church is a regular focus of movies set in the church.[4] Another well-focused study is Boswell and Loukides' *Reel Rituals: Ritual Occasions from Baptisms to Funerals in Hollywood Films 1945–1995* (1999).[5] This text focuses on the significant disparity between the meaningful, transformative role rituals play in actual experience and the trivialization of these events as depicted in movies. While it does consider the representation of religious events in popular culture, it does

---

2. Examples of the former include: Joel W. Martin and Conrad E. Ostwalt, Jr. (eds) (1995), *Screening the Sacred: Religion, Myth, and Ideology in Popular American Film* (Boulder: Westview Press); Margaret R. Miles, (1996), *Seeing and Believing: Religion and Values in the Movies* (Boston: Beacon Press); Clive Marsh and Gaye Ortiz (eds) (1997), *Explorations in Theology and Film* (Massachusetts: Blackwell); Albert J. Bergensen and Andrew M. Greeley (2000), *God in the Movies* (New Brunswick: Transaction Publishers); Peter Fraser and Vernon Edwin Neal (2000), *Reviewing the Movies: A Christian Response to Contemporary Film* (Wheaton, Illinois: Crossway Books); Robert K. Johnston (2000), *Reel Spirituality: Theology and Film in Dialogue* (Grand Rapids: Baker Academic); Bryan P. Stone (2000), *Faith and Film: Theological Themes at the Cinema* (St. Louis: Chalice Press); John C. Lyden (2003), *Film as Religion: Myths, Morals, and Rituals* (New York: New York University Press); and Adele Reinhartz (2003), *Scripture on the Silver Screen* (Louisville: Westminster John Knox Press). Examples of the latter include: W. Barnes Tatum (1997), *Jesus at the Movies: A Guide to the First Hundred Years* (Santa Rosa, California: Polebridge Press); Lloyd Baugh (1997), *Imaging the Divine: Jesus and Christ-Figures in Film* (Wisconsin: Sheed and Ward); Richard C. Stern, Clayton N. Jefford, and Guerric Debona (eds) (1999), *Savior on the Silver Screen* (New York: Paulist Press); Richard Walsh (2003), *Reading the Gospels in the Dark: Portrayals of Jesus in Film* (New York: Trinity Press International); and Adele Reinhartz (2007), *Jesus of Hollywood* (New York: Oxford University Press).

3. Les Keyser and Barbara Keyser (1984), *Hollywood and the Catholic Church: The Image of Roman Catholicism in American Movies*. Chicago: Loyola Press.

4. Colleen McDannell (ed.) (2008), *Catholics in the Movies*. New York: Oxford University Press.

5. Parley Ann Boswell and Paul Loukides (1999), *Reel Rituals: Ritual Occasions from Baptisms to Funerals in Hollywood Films, 1945–1995*. Bowling Green, Ohio: Bowling Green State University Popular Press.

not exclusively focus on the role or representation of ecclesiastics.

While such studies may prove useful companions to those considering broadcast media, television and radio are quite different from film in a number of ways, most notably by nature of their being broadcast media and hence more immediately accessible to the widest possible American public. Likewise, broadcast media have a different regulatory history than that of film and this impacts upon the history of television programs in distinct ways. Then complications arise from radio and television as commercial media which need to attract sponsors, who significantly affect what images are presented on broadcast media. Finally, broadcast media have a different programming history, which to date has been all but neglected as it relates to church-set programs. For all these reasons, analyses of the representation of people in service to the church focusing particularly on broadcast media are an important contribution to studies of the church and its leaders as they are represented in US popular culture. In the case of radio, research has revealed that only one prime-time network drama focused regularly and principally on an ecclesiastic: a priest on *The Bishop and the Gargoyle* (1936–42, 1949).[6] The crime drama featured a retired cleric whose sidekick, an ex-con, helped him solve acts of mysterious wrongdoing. As the only radio program of this type, it alone represents the history of network prime-time radio dramas focusing on church leaders.

With the end of the era of dramatic radio programming in the middle of the twentieth century, the representation of ecclesiastics on American broadcast media continued on television. The programs started appearing in the early 1960s and continue through today. Even so, a study focusing on the depiction of fictional clerics featured on television, already accomplished for film and radio, is wanting.[7] This study accomplishes the task. It finds that the relevant shows (that is, those meeting the above outlined criteria) fall into three categories, each fairly well defining an era. These eras are considered in three chapters, each describing the programs, their commonalities and differences and how they depict the church and its leaders. Ultimately, I compare television's portrayal of the church in each given era to church historians' accounts of the church in the same period and consider why television's portrayal reads as it does. While the church's depiction on TV generally follows contemporaneous trends in church history, successful programs avoid focusing on contentious social issues and personal vices faced by church leaders and instead take a cheerful, inoffensive

---

6. Richard Wolff (2000), "*The Bishop and the Gargoyle*: a study of network-produced, prime-time church-set dramatic old-time radio programs." *Journal of Radio Studies,* 72, 428–40.

7. While plenty of books exist on the phenomena of televangelism, religious broadcasters or religious themes in general on secular television, none has focused specifically on an exhaustive study of representations of ecclesiastics on prime-time television shows featuring them. One recent, more focused journal article deserves mention, as it considers the representations of religious characters during one month of network programming in September of 2002: Scott H. Clark (2005), "Created in whose image? Religious characters on network television." *Journal of Media and Religion,* 4, 137–53.

approach to ecclesial subject matter. The overall finding is that those church-set programs that succeed take a light-hearted, sentimental approach to their subject; while depictions of other institutions (such as schools, hospitals and the courts) thrive on showing their servants facing controversial issues and personal vices, the nature of the church and the public's need to preserve its ideal image make such subject matter unacceptable on serial television programs spotlighting the church.

The first theme to emerge in television's portrayal of the church and its leaders depicts the church in conflict with itself. Notably, all of the television programs in this era focused on the Catholic Church. Historically, this is not surprising, given events in that church during this time. In the 1960s and 1970s, when Catholicism was receiving lots of attention for wide-ranging reforms instituted by the Vatican, a series of programs focused on the disputes that erupted between younger, more liberal ecclesiastics who welcomed these reforms and their more conservative, older counterparts who resisted them. The trend includes programs from the earliest church-set drama, *Going My Way* (1962–3), to the most fantastic, *The Flying Nun* (1967–70), and finally Norman Lear's short-lived *In the Beginning* (1978). Chapter 2, "In the Beginning . . . Conflict in the Church," considers these programs, how accurately they reflect their era, why the focus was exclusively on Catholicism, and why these programs were relatively few and far between.

The next category arose principally in the 1980s at a time when the church was facing new challenges in the modern world. The programs which emerge at this time focus less on inner ideological conflicts between church leaders than on their struggles to remain relevant in contemporary society. An early entry into this category is *Sarge* (1971–2), a program focused on a former policeman turned Catholic cleric who uses his investigatory skills to serve the rather worldly needs of his community, more so than the spiritual needs of his parishioners. Better known is the pop culture classic *Hell Town* (1985), a drama starring Robert Blake (former star of the cop show *Baretta*) as an ex-con turned priest who, together with a collection of streetwise nuns, serve a congregation of orphans and city slickers and help them survive the dangers and temptations of life in the inner city. *Sister Kate* (1989–90) does much the same, although her service is to the children of a suburban orphanage. Sister Kate's image is in direct opposition to that of Sister Bertrille of *The Flying Nun*, and a comparison of the two reveals much about the evolution of TV's representation of ecclesiastics. Another program of this era is *Have Faith* (1989), a program which is particularly noteworthy because in it for the first time the younger liberals are in leadership positions in the church. Noteworthy also is *Lanigan's Rabbi* (1977), the only Jewish-set program featuring a cleric; appearing in the late 1970s, this periodic subseries of the ABC Sunday Night Mysteries focuses on a rabbi's efforts to solve crimes. Similarly, *Father Dowling Mysteries* (1989–91) features a tradition-minded priest who enlists a progressive ex-con turned nun to help solve his congregants' criminal, if not spiritual problems. Finally, *Nothing Sacred* (1997–8) is a late entry in this category, and focuses on the featured clerics' dedication to serve the needy of an inner city, and their own congregants, as they struggle with significant modern ethical problems. Along the way, the freethinking bunch re-examine the church's role in society and question their own faith. Chapter 3, "The Church Seeks Relevance in the Modern World," provides an analysis of programs in this grouping, looking at which issues receive most attention and why, how accurately these programs reflect the direction and challenges of American churches at the time, and how these programs were and were not successful.

The age of the family-centered program follows, with a related trend to focus more on the leaders of Protestant faiths and less on the Catholic faith. These programs, generally appearing in the 1990s and 2000s, focus on the challenges of running a parish while raising a family, and also on the church's ability to help resolve everyday family problems. An early program in this category is *The Family Holvak* (1975), a show which follows the everyday life of a Tennessee minister and his family during the Depression. *Amen* (1986–91) comes next, a much more successful program which focuses on the family and church life of a parish's most outspoken deacon (star Sherman Helmsley). Not only is this the first successful Protestant-set program, it is also the first to focus on an African-American congregation, leading the way for a similar program airing years later, *Good News* (1997–8). Patty Duke starred as a female cleric dealing with family and parish problems in the short-lived drama *Amazing Grace* (1995). Another program featuring a big-name actor was *Soul Man* (1997–8), in which Dan Aykroyd plays a widowered father and pastor who must balance family and parish life. In a return to programs focusing on Catholic clerics, *Trinity* (1998) focuses on the lives of three Irish-American brothers, one of whom is a priest. However, by far the most successful program in this category is *7th Heaven* (1996–2007), a program about a pastor and his ever-growing family. The show became the longest-running family drama in television history. Rounding out this category is the edgy comedy *The Book of Daniel* (2006) about an Episcopal minister and his problem-ridden family. Christ himself appears to this Vicodin-addicted minister, offering words of comfort, advice and wry commentary to help the cleric cope with his challenging job and family. In all of these programs the focus is on households headed by people serving the church and how their professional clerical duties influence their family life and vice versa, and is the subject of Chapter 4, "The Church in Family Life."

Throughout these historical chapters, several themes emerge. One concerns the portrayal of the ecumenical movement. The trend begins with a somewhat tentative and limited commitment to ecumenism in programs like *Going My Way*, and moves through more full-hearted depictions of it in later years to include non-Western religions, ultimately treating the ecumenical movement as a foregone conclusion. Another trend concerns portrayals of clerical celibacy and sexuality. Here, the representations range from sentimental to sensational, with the more conservative portrayals found on the more successful programs. Also considered are reflections on clerics' calling, as many question and rededicate themselves to their vocation, even as there is a growing acknowledgment of a crisis in the recruitment of people into ecclesiastic professions, especially for the Catholic Church. Increasingly, issues regarding race and gender are raised, either as these concern the church's response to them, or as concerns the role of women and racial minorities in the life and leadership of the church.

Finally, the last chapter looks at the broad sweep of all the programs considered and draws overall conclusions about the representation of people in service to the church on American popular TV — from flying nuns and sleuthing clerics to priests-as-advocates and pastors-as-parents — and what this suggests about American popular culture and its depiction of the sacred. It finds that those church-set programs that are more successful take a light-hearted approach to depicting the church, whereas those focusing on controversy — no matter how realistic or relevant — fare poorly by television's standards of success, such as ratings and longevity. This differs from shows portraying people serving other social institutions (such as "cop shows", "doc shows" and programs set in education systems), where controversial programs thrive as much as those taking a more jovial approach. The difference concerns the sacred subject matter, where controversy involves not just public policy and social issues but ecclesiastic doctrine, and where audiences assess depictions of human frailty in lead characters not just by standards facing public servants but by ideal expectations of proper clerical conduct. Where the sacred is involved in popular television programs, light-hearted approaches bring more success than controversial ones. Further, these programs focus on external action and conflict, to the virtual exclusion of the spiritual, and focus on generalized discussions of religious belief rather than on the foundations of a particular faith, such as by discussing "God" and God's love and expectations rather than "Jesus" and his example and teachings. What might offend some by invoking too many particulars of religious faith is replaced by more generalized fare in order to achieve broad appeal. What emerges is a popular mythology of the church and its leaders which, while reflecting many contemporaneous trends in actual churches, either waters itself down for mass consumption or faces widespread rejection.

Questions for Reflection

1) What sorts of stories do you expect episodes of television programs about church leaders will focus upon? What aspects of their lives and vocations will TV shows depict, and how will they do so? What sorts of characters do you expect TV ecclesiastics will have?

2) To what extent do you expect church-set programs will reflect historical events, circumstances and issues facing actual churches in the depicted eras? Which kinds of such events and issues do you think TV is more likely to include or avoid? Why?

Suggested Further Reading

Boswell, Parley Ann and Loukides, Paul (1999), *Reel Rituals: Ritual Occasions from Baptisms to Funerals in Hollywood Films, 1945–1995.* Bowling Green, Ohio: Bowling Green State University Popular Press.

Keyser, Les and Keyser, Barbara (1984), *Hollywood and the Catholic Church: The Image of Roman Catholicism in American Movies.* Chicago: Loyola Press.

McDannell, Colleen (ed.) (2008), *Catholics in the Movies.* New York: Oxford University Press.

Wolff, Richard (2000), "*The Bishop and the Gargoyle*: a study of network-produced, prime-time church-set dramatic old-time radio programs." *Journal of Radio Studies,* 72, 428–40.

Sally Field as Sister Bertrille and Madeleine Sherwood as Reverend
Mother Superior Placido in *The Flying Nun.*

2

IN THE BEGINNING . . . CONFLICT IN THE CHURCH

Dramatic series focusing on the church and its leaders first appeared on prime-time network television in the 1960s, when two such programs debuted. Focusing on two urban Catholic priests, *Going My Way* (1962–3) came first, followed by the Caribbean convent-set *The Flying Nun* (1967–70), which focused on a strict Reverend Mother and her most challenging, zany novice. Both series spotlighted the relationship between an older, tradition-minded superior and a younger, progressive counterpart. This premise was also the basis of *In the Beginning* (1978), a program set in an urban mission headed by an older conservative priest but also served by a young, liberal nun. The tensions between these series' featured characters define this early cluster of programs set in the church and focusing on its leaders. They spotlight ideological conflict within the church. The programs were exclusively Catholic and highlighted actual tensions existing in the Catholic Church during the depicted era.[1] Why television focused on Catholicism and how accurately it reflected goings-on in the American Roman Catholic Church are among the subjects considered ahead. Before reflecting on such questions, however, the initial task is to introduce these programs, from the rather traditional *Going My Way* of the early 1960s, to the quirky *The Flying Nun* of later in that decade and finally to the controversial *In the Beginning* in the late 1970s. These programs set the stage, and began — cautiously at first, more sensationally in the end — to push the envelope of how network TV would depict the church in decades to come.

Going My Way

The first network church-set series to appear in prime-time television was the hour-long drama *Going My Way*, a televised version of the 1944 film classic. Airing on ABC from October 1962 to September 1963, the series created an early trend in television's depiction of the church: pitting a younger, more progressive ecclesiastic against an older, conservative counterpart. Gene Kelly played the role of the youthful priest, Father Charles O'Malley, while Leo G. Carroll played the part of his behind-the-times colleague, Father Fitzgibbon.

---

1. Yet another Catholic-set program, *Sarge* (1971–2), also began in this era, but will be considered as part of the next chapter's cluster of programs, as it focused on the church's struggle to remain relevant in the modern world. Nonetheless, it is part of television's early, nearly exclusive focus on Catholicism, which, other than a brief interruption by the short-lived Protestant-set *Family Holvak* (1975), would continue until *Amen* (1986–91).

As in the movie, these priests serve a working-class Manhattan Catholic parish. They work together, despite their differences, to help their parishioners and the church itself. The inner-city setting is established from the program's opening, which shows various images of New York City, ending on one of the exterior of a church. One important regular character added to the television program was Tom Colwell (played by Dick York), the young director of the local West Side Community Center Boys' Club and close friend to Father O'Malley. Colwell holds a master's degree in sociology from Yale University and often helps O'Malley with problems facing his parishioners, especially the church's youth. Notably, York received second billing after Kelly and before Carroll, thus emphasizing the roles of the younger men. Lest Father Fitzgibbon be left without an older, more traditional counterpart, the series included another regular character, Mrs. Featherstone, as the rectory's housekeeper.[2]

In the 1944 movie, the local Bishop sends young Father O'Malley (played by Bing Crosby) to St. Dominic's Church, ostensibly to assist the elderly Father Fitzgibbon (played by Barry Fitzgerald), who has served the parish for 46 years; in actuality, the Bishop's plan is for the younger priest to look after the parish and to help run things from behind the scenes because Fitzgibbon seems too old and ill-equipped to handle the church's problems. Crosby's O'Malley is soft-spoken, articulate, witty and respectful. A man with many secular talents and connections, he plays golf, stick ball and jazz piano, and composes and sings catchy pop songs. His friends include local priests, the Bishop, professional baseball players and a world-renowned opera singer. O'Malley is better able to relate to the parish's young boys than is his older counterpart, and organizes a boys' choir. His success is in part due to his stated commitment to show that religion can be "bright" and "fun." Fitzgibbon's contributions often come from his seasoned wisdom and insight. In fact, upon the Bishop's reassignment of O'Malley to another ailing parish, Fitzgibbon himself articulates the relationship these two priests have together, saying, "We're separated by many years, Father O'Malley, which could be the reason why we haven't seen eye-to-eye in many instances; but though we've had many differences, we never differed in fundamentals; it was only in method . . ." and O'Malley finishes the thought: ". . . but never in our hearts," upon which the younger priest leaves, leaving the older cleric once again in charge.[3]

The premise of the television series is the same as that of the movie. The local Bishop sends Father O'Malley to serve as an "assistant" to the aging Father Fitzgibbon at St. Dominic's Church and Parochial School, but really to help the parish run smoothly without stripping the elder cleric of his dignity by forcing

---

2. A style note is in order: the present tense is used when retelling the storylines of episodes or premises of programs, and the past tense when discussing a program's history or how it relates to historical accounts of the church.

3. *Going My Way*. Screenplay by Frank Butler and Frank Cavett; story by Leo McCarey; produced by Leo McCarey. Released by Universal Studios, 1944. Reviewed off commercial VHS.

him to step down. Fitzgibbon, increasingly unable to handle the problems of the parish, nonetheless remains the official authority figure at the church, sitting behind the desk in the church office and offering "advice" to the younger priest as his "mentor." Most often, O'Malley is the one with perception, insight and wisdom, who effectively handles situations facing the parish, tactfully allowing Fitzgibbon to take credit for *his* ideas. Although they have their differences, the two generally work well together, sharing concerns and ideas over meals in the rectory dining room, while strolling through the parish gardens, or seated in the church office. Even so, despite their common commitment to serve the church, the two are quite different.

Father Fitzgibbon is an Irish-born and -educated priest, with a thick Irish brogue to prove it, who has been a priest at St. Dominic's for over 40 years. Often he is forgetful or inattentive; for example, in one episode he continually inquires about the housekeeper's trip to Pittsburgh, despite constant corrections from others that her trip was to Philadelphia. Many times, Father O'Malley finds him asleep in a chair in his office, Fitzgibbon claiming he is just "meditating." Fond of an occasional nip of spirits but far from being a drunkard, he is a traditionalist who fondly reminisces of his homeland. He can at times be rather naive, as when he is waiting at the church for a couple to return after a date and wonders aloud, "what can a person do in New York City after midnight?"[4] Unaccustomed to modern trends, he often does not understand the colloquial-isms used by his younger counterparts. For example, when he is in Greenwich Village looking for a troubled parishioner in beatnik bars, Tom Colwell remarks there is one club where they might find him, but that the place is a little "far out"; the older priests asks, "how far out: Queens?"[5] Elsewhere, Fitzgibbon tries to use modern lingo with humorous results, as when O'Malley discusses how some local boys got into trouble when they "went ape"; Fitzgibbon inquires as to the meaning of the phrase, and later remarks that he hopes the boys do not once again "go monkey."[6] Bemused by aspects of youth culture, Father Fitz (as he is sometimes called) in one episode arrives at a dance and asks Father O'Malley what the teenagers are doing; when O'Malley explains it is a dance called "The Twist", Fitzgibbon remarks, "If we can live through 'The Big Apple' we can live through this."[7] He is not always intellectually adept, as when he is searching for an appropriate New Testament quotation to share with a couple with whom he is set to meet to discuss their uncertainty as to whether to have a baby. O'Malley suggests a quote from Matthew, "Where two or three are gathered in my name,

---

4. "Florence, Come Home." Written by Richard Baer; directed by Alan Crosland, Jr. Series produced by Joe Connelly. April 10, 1963. Reviewed at the UCLA Film and Television Archives (hereafter, UCLA).

5. "Run Robin Run." Teleplay by Emmet Lavery and Mark Weingart; story by Emmet Lavery; directed by Joseph Pevney. March 20, 1963. Reviewed at UCLA.

6. "Tell Me When You Get to Heaven." Written by Lewis Reed; directed by Felix Feist. January 2, 1963. Reviewed at UCLA.

7. "The Father." Teleplay by Mark Weingart and Joe Connelly; story by Caryll Houselander; directed by Alex March. October 24, 1962. Reviewed at UCLA.

there I am in the midst of them." Fitzgibbon agrees that the quote is fitting since three will be involved in the discussion, requiring O'Malley to point out that the three to which he was referring was the couple and their baby.[8] Even so, the older priest has moments of sheer eloquence, as when a woman challenges Fitzgibbon's clout in the community saying, "Your influence ends the moment you leave the rectory," and the priest quickly retorts, "and yours the moment you enter."[9] Often bungling but harmless, occasionally sharp as nails, Fitzgibbon frequently intones the values of experience and the shortcomings of youth, even as he creates problems that his younger counterpart will have to undo.

In contrast to Fitzgibbon, Father O'Malley (called "Chuck" by his friends) is American-born and -educated. Solemn but friendly, he is as skilled at piano playing, singing and dancing as he is at playing golf, basketball and baseball. In addition to his other priest's duties, he oversees the boys of the parish (most of whom call him "Fadah" with a strong New York accent), hence the reason for his many interactions with Tom Colwell and the boys' club. It is O'Malley who helps organize concerts, dances and tournaments for the church's young members, and becomes involved whenever one of the parish's rambunctious boys gets into trouble with the law. The police in the neighborhood of St. Dominic's allow Colwell and O'Malley a significant degree of latitude in handling what ordinarily would be matters for law enforcement, such as giving them time to locate boys suspected of wrong doing before they step in, leading one police officer to remark, "you know the trouble with this precinct? Too many priests and social workers playing detective."[10] Fitzgibbon frequently remarks about O'Malley's regular contact with the Bishop, a reminder for the audience of O'Malley's actual role in the parish, of which Father Fitzgibbon seems largely unaware. The audience is also reminded of this whenever O'Malley is kind-hearted and gracious enough to allow Fitzgibbon to receive credit for the younger priest's ideas and actions.

An episode titled "The Parish Car" illustrates the relationship between the two priests. The story opens with a boy asking another what to do with a car he has stolen. The thief says he must find someone "who doesn't know much about cars, who trusts people . . . someone who will fall for a hard luck story;" the other boy suggests Father Fitzgibbon. Meanwhile across town, Father O'Malley is surveying the church's damaged roof and discussing an estimate for repairs with two contractors. When O'Malley says he will run their bid by Father Fitzgibbon, one of the contractors says to him, "Oh now look, Father, you don't have to put up a front for us. We know who calls the shots around here." In defense of his older counterpart, O'Malley insists that Father Fitzgibbon

---

8. "Hear No Evil." Written by Richard Baer; directed by Joseph Pevney. April 17, 1963. Reviewed at UCLA.
9. "Custody of the Child." Written by Mark Weingart; directed by Joseph Pevney. April 3, 1963. Reviewed at UCLA.
10. "Shoemaker's Child." Written by Bob Mosher; directed by Robert Florey. January 30, 1963. Reviewed at UCLA.

still is in charge, an assertion which does not convince the contractors. At that moment, Father Fitzgibbon is driving the parish car across town when the breaks fail and the priest crashes the car into a fire hydrant. A newspaper photographer is nearby and snaps a photo of the priest standing beside the smashed vehicle, water gushing from it like a fountain. The next day, Fitzgibbon nervously asks O'Malley if the Bishop subscribes to the newspaper in which the photo has been published, when the Bishop's secretary calls to ask the older priest to come for a visit. When Father Fitzgibbon returns, he mentions that the Bishop said several times how happy he is that O'Malley is at the parish, and adds that the bulk of the conversation concerned Fitzgibbon's health, the accident, and talk of mutual friends — including priests who have retired. O'Malley sees that his older friend is worried about being asked to step down, and assures him that he is not that old, claiming that he himself at times has a hard time keeping up with the elder priest. Before they part, the two make a wager: whether O'Malley will be able to sell the old parish car before Fitzgibbon can buy a new one.

Later that day the two priests are in the office and the older one inquires about the younger priest's day, his ulterior motive being to see if O'Malley has sold the car. O'Malley says he visited a sick parishioner, but managed to sell the car for $150, noting there were problems with the differential and clutch. Father Fitz teases him, saying he was taken advantage of and that there is "no substitute for experience." Of course, when later the older minister meets the young thief to look at the stolen car, it is he who is taken in. Trying to convince the boy that he knows about cars and cannot be duped, he uses words he heard earlier from Father O'Malley, discussing the car's differential and clutch, inaccurately identifying each part. The priest gets the boy to drop his asking price, at which point Father Fitz becomes suspicious. The boy claims he is entering the army and needs money to get married before he leaves, whereupon Fitz says he cannot take advantage of the boy — and insists on paying the full amount. When Fitzgibbon proudly shows the car to Colwell and O'Malley, Tom notes that the price seems fair, leading O'Malley to confide that that is what worries him. The younger priest's suspicions are well-founded, which they discover later when a police officer reveals to Colwell that one of his boys sold Father Fitzgibbon a stolen car. Before Tom can inform Father O'Malley, who is busy hearing confessions, Fitzgibbon takes the stolen car to deposit that week's offering in the bank, wearing only gardener's clothes. As he is en route to deposit the money, a police officer recognizes the license plate and pulls him over. The officer sees a poorly clothed man driving a stolen car with a sack of money labeled St. Dominic's Church and arrests Fitzgibbon. Luckily, someone at the precinct recognizes the priest, and he is released.

O'Malley's efforts to help his aging friend are on display towards the end of the episode, first when Fitz shares his concerns that the police captain will inform the Bishop of the incident, noting that they are cousins. O'Malley handles this worry for him, summoning the captain to the church office and slyly assuring the captain that *he*, O'Malley, does not intend to tell the Bishop about the mix-up, to spare the captain the embarrassment of having his clerical cousin hear that the captain's officers cannot recognize a priest. The grateful captain thanks O'Malley for his discretion. Secondly, O'Malley arranges to boost his colleague's ego by having a car salesman come to Fitzgibbon and offer him a good deal on a used car. Fitz buys the car and proudly shows it to Colwell and O'Malley. Finally, O'Malley protects Fitzgibbon's image by arranging for the boy who stole the car to work off the money he took from the priest by fixing the church's roof with his dad, a contractor. O'Malley, who brokered the deal, nonetheless congratulates Fitzgibbon for having made such a smart arrangement. Later the two original contractors walk up to the church and see the work being done on the roof. O'Malley tells them that Fitzgibbon got a better deal on the repair work and hired someone else. O'Malley does all this to protect Father Fitz. He not only solves the church's problems and helps a troubled boy and his family but does so in a way that maintains the dignity of his friend, the elder priest.[11]

Throughout the series, the producers are careful not to overdo Fitzgibbon's shortcomings, here and there making sure his experience and wisdom receive due attention, even if this is between moments of comic clumsiness. For example, in one episode both priests face several dilemmas, from figuring out who is stealing from the church's poor box to helping a family as it struggles to stay together. Both priests have different ideas about how to proceed, each ultimately contributing in his own way. To deal with the stolen money, O'Malley immediately wants to call the police. In offering an alternative perspective, the older Fitzgibbon demonstrates characteristic wisdom and authority as he explains his ideas for dealing with the problem: "To steal from the poor, whoever he is, the poor man's at his wit's end . . . Poverty breeds pride. Perhaps he'd rather steal than ask for help. We must find the man, save him from himself." The older priest's scheme is to hide in the pews until he catches the thief red-handed, and then try to help him. Comically showing his age, the older priest naps through the next theft. Fitzgibbon's sense of Christian charity is admirable, but his younger counterpart solves the crime when he sees a boy from the baseball team he coaches enter the church. After a momentary hesitation, the priest follows him into the sanctuary and catches him breaking into the poor box.

Over the course of the episode the priests discover that the boy is acting mischievously in order to reunite his parents, who have separated. Realizing this, the priests discuss how they may help the couple with their interpersonal problems, sharing their thoughts at a ball game, over dinner and in the parish office. The older priest recounts for O'Malley the couple's wedding day, years earlier, and how happy they seemed. In a thick Irish brogue, he likens their situation to wind-tossed ships he saw as a boy, when he would remember their happy launchings: "That's the way it is today with the Corbins . . . the broken marriage . . . I can still see the fine launching." The younger priest offers his own wisdom,

11. "The Parish Car." Teleplay by Mark Weingart and Joe Connelly; story by Joe Connelly; directed by Joseph Pevney. October 17, 1962. Reviewed at UCLA.

noting that it is easy to "forget the good and joyful and remember the bad and the bitter," before the two discuss the difficulties of human relationships. At the episode's end, the couple are together with both priests in the parish office. While it has been O'Malley who has done much of the leg-work, visiting the parents at their home and discussing their options, it is nonetheless Fitzgibbon whose wise analysis sizes up their situation as he entreats the parents to realize the effect their disagreements have on their son. As the priests look on, the parents reunite outside the church. The episode ends with O'Malley asking Fitzgibbon "Feel good Father?" to which the older cleric, referring back to the earlier motif, replies, "Always do, Chuck, when I see a fine launching."[12]

The television series taps into a trend in depicting priests that Keyser and Keyser, in their analysis of portrayals of Catholicism on film, term the "clerical melodrama." Unwaveringly set on portraying the priest as a positive, iconic social force in American life, the clerical melodrama offers simplistic stories and solutions in which the emotional response of the audience is assured, eliciting warm associations with religion. This is achieved by their focus on upright, one-dimensional characters that in the end triumph over clear-cut wrongs.[13] The exaggerated emotions and formulaic plots promise the audience sentimental satisfaction when the righteous prevail. Often in the clerical melodrama, this involves social activism on the part of the priest, who must battle and overcome racism, poverty, the sources of juvenile delinquency, family crises or indifference to those in need. The outcome of these struggles usually emphasizes social transformation; helping others achieve some worldly happiness, often to the exclusion of spiritual guidance or the priest's sacramental role in ritual.[14] The emphasis is on the religious figure's role in transforming the secular world.

Like the episodes above, many others concern the priests' efforts on behalf of families in crisis. In one, the priests help the overly cautious parents of a seriously injured boy to accept his situation and approve the medical help that he needs.[15] Another concerns the priests' efforts to help the father of a choir boy reform his dishonest ways, so that his son is not tempted to follow in the father's footsteps.[16] One episode focuses on the priests' assistance in helping an estranged father re-establish a good relationship with his daughter, so that he may attend her wedding.[17] In another, O'Malley and Fitzgibbon help a family resolve a custody battle over a young girl in a manner that makes everyone

---

12. "Ask Me No Questions." Written by Mark Weingart and Joe Connelly; directed by Robert Florey. December 5, 1962. Reviewed at the Library of Congress — Division of Motion Pictures, Broadcasting and Recorded Sound (hereafter LOC).

13. Les Keyser and Barbara Keyser (1984), *Hollywood and the Catholic Church: The Image of Roman Catholicism in American Movies*. Chicago: Loyola Press, p. 95.

14. Ibid., p. 105.

15. "Tell Me When You Get to Heaven."

16. "The Crooked Angel." Written by William Fay; directed by Joseph Pevney. October 10, 1962. Reviewed at UCLA.

17. "Mr. Second Chance." Teleplay by Mark Weingart and Joe Connelly; story by Robert Hardy Andrews; directed by Allen Reisner. November 28, 1962. Reviewed at UCLA.

happy.[18] Several other episodes follow along these lines, focusing on the church leaders' efforts to help families reunite or reform their ways. In this way, the clerics serve as surrogate father figures, akin to other heads-of-household appearing on family programs of the era, with the priests offering sage advice and guidance to families in struggles. Notably, these stories about as often focus on single-parent families as they do on nuclear families. Although both types of families provide unique challenges for the clerics, the priests, nonetheless, are not only sensitive to each family's needs but also effective in responding to them.

Another trend in the series is to emphasize the ethnic diversity of the people and families served by the church. This is just as fitting for a program set in the inner city as it is for one about the Catholic Church, which had to help many of its members assimilate after waves of immigration earlier in the century. Ethnic characters depicted on *Going My Way* are either older immigrants, or first-generation Americans being raised by immigrants. For example, one episode focuses on a Spanish-American family in which the widowered father (born in Spain) is raising an American-born daughter with the help of his immigrant sister. The episode portrays the father's struggle between allowing his daughter to enjoy the freedoms of American culture, such as dating and going to dances, and the stricter behavioral code upon which his sister insists, based upon the more conservative role of women she learned in their homeland. When the daughter stays out too late with a boy, the father assumes what she may have done and disowns her. Largely due to O'Malley's efforts, the daughter learns a lesson about responsible freedom and the father in learning to trust his daughter.[19] The emotion-laden, simplistic story exemplifies the clerical melodrama while also depicting the priest as facilitator of American assimilation.

Other episodes likewise depict people of various racial and ethnic backgrounds, from Polish, Spanish, Jewish and Italians to the ubiquitous Irish. One noteworthy example concerns an African-American family and deals not only with racism but also the challenges of integration in the inner city in the 1960s, and church leaders' role in such struggles. The episode concerns a 25-year-old African-American parishioner and struggling musician named Robin Green, who is prone to getting into arguments and has had trouble with the police. It begins as O'Malley arrives at a police station to bail Robin out of jail for having gotten into a fight with a drunk who called him "Kingfish" (a reference to an African-American character from the old-time radio and television program *Amos 'n' Andy*). When speaking to Father O'Malley at the precinct, an officer asks why the priest keeps helping Robin and whether it is "because he's a Negro," to which O'Malley rhetorically asks "should it make a difference?" Matters intensify when the owner of a local jewelry store identifies Robin as one of the men who recently beat him up, and the police make plans to search for him, agreeing to delay their search for a day so Tom Colwell and Father Fitzgibbon can look for

---

18. "Custody of the Child."
19. "The Father."

the boy first. They speak with the boy's mother, a choir member, who shares that her son was always angry that she and her husband became successful caterers, saying that cooking and serving is degrading; he likewise hates them for being middle-class, and not having the "dignity" of being poor or the "luxury" of being rich. When the priests do find Robin, he questions his mother about the merits of being the "biggest Colored caterer" in the city, whereupon she scolds him for his attitudes about race. She observes that he feels doubly persecuted for being "Negro" and an artist, but that his problem with finding work is not his race so much as his mediocre talent as a musician. In the end, Father Fitz speaks with the jeweler, who admits that he is not certain that Robin was one of his attackers and only made the charge because he resented Robin and his family for being the first African-Americans to move into the neighborhood. He adds that since "their kind" have arrived his business is down. Father Fitzgibbon tells him not to blame Robin because of his own shortcomings as a business-man, and suggests he meet the new neighbors. In the end, the jeweler's actual attackers are caught, and Robin's life is on the mend as he looks for work in the neighborhood.[20] Dealing with issues of race and class, this episode illustrates how stories in *Going My Way* considered issues of diversity facing inhabitants of the inner city, and the role representatives of the church might play in helping to resolve them.

Another area of diversity depicted in the series concerns ecumenism. Throughout, the program labors to specify that Tom Colwell is Protestant; further, Colwell's minister, Dr. Thornton, is a friend and golf partner of Father O'Malley's. Both Tom's and Dr. Thornton's presence in the series illustrates O'Malley's complete acceptance of members of different religions, and others' (including Fitzgibbon's) residual uncertainty about the same. This resonates with actual attitudes of the time. Hence, learning that O'Malley and Colwell are driving to pick up an item being donated to the church, Mrs. Featherstone disapprovingly remarks, "When I was a young girl in Ireland, priests didn't run around in station wagons with Protestants for chauffeurs," to which Father Fitzgibbon observes that times change and that he is surprised that the house-keeper has not developed more liberated attitudes. Even so, the older cleric himself shows signs of hesitancy to associate with members of other faiths, as when Father O'Malley asks Father Fitzgibbon's permission to invite Colwell and Dr. Thornton to dinner at the rectory, so they may discuss building plans for the boys' club. Fitzgibbon remarks that they have never had a Protestant minister over to dinner, and wonders if this is a good idea: "Well, my boy, I have no objection to you serving on committees with young Colwell and Dr. Thornton, but having a minister to dinner! It's just never happened at St. Dominic's. That might be rushing matters a bit!" Father O'Malley explains to the older priest that they must communicate with "our separated brethren" if they are ever again to join together, whereupon Fitzgibbon is reassured and gives his blessing for the

---

20. "Run Robin Run."

meeting. At their dinner, they discuss how the newly renovated boys' club will remain "interdenominational," welcoming "boys of all faiths."[21]

One episode that exemplifies the ecumenical spirit and the role leaders of various religions may play in the lives of their communities is "A Matter of Principle." At the request of the police, Father O'Malley, Tom Colwell and Dr. Thornton decide to hold a basketball tournament involving teams from the Catholic and Protestant churches, and the Jewish temple during a holiday school recess, in part to keep the boys occupied and away from juvenile delinquency. The interfaith competition is almost set, but an obstacle looms: to convince Father Fitzgibbon to approve of the plans. O'Malley reveals that he has already discussed the matter with the other clerics, and Fitzgibbon is riled that his assistant would discuss the matter with other clerics before him, whereupon O'Malley quickly clarifies that he conditioned St. Dominic's involvement upon Fitzgibbon's approval. Fitz refuses to consent until O'Malley emphasizes how likely they are to beat the other teams. He reminds Fitzgibbon of their ace — a talented young athletic parishioner whose involvement should ensure a win for St. Dominic's. Fitzgibbon sweetens to the idea, and agrees — the interdenominational tournament, requested by civic authorities, goes on.[22]

The series also emphasizes the differences among clergy of different denominations, as when Dr. Thornton, who is single, introduces his date to Father Fitzgibbon at a young people's dance at the community center. Committing a minor faux pas, the older priest tells the Protestant minister's girlfriend that she looks as charming as she did at the Christmas party, leading O'Malley to whisper in Fitzgibbon's ear that that was a different girl, whereupon all exchange polite, nervous smiles. To round out the ecumenical gathering at the dance is Rabbi Adler and his wife. The rabbi remarks that when he first saw a boy in a blue suit at the party, "I thought I was at a bar mitzvah." Like Dr. Thornton, Rabbi Adler appears in several episodes, as do other Jewish people, as when a girl from Adler's temple comes to St. Dominic's to speak with Father O'Malley about one of his parishioners, and she remarks that she has never before been in a church, leading O'Malley to explain that she is in the rectory, not the church.[23]

Beyond episodes dealing with ecumenism, another issue facing the church that is depicted in *Going My Way* is its financial needs and the clergy's commitment to fundraising. Indeed, this is another trend of the clerical melodrama, where priests are concerned with achieving financial success for the church, and an enduring theme in many church-set television programs.[24] While Father O'Malley is happy to accept donations from businessmen whom he visits,

21. "A Dog for Father Fitz." Written by Emmet Lavery and Joe Connelly; directed by Herman Hoffman. December 19, 1962. Reviewed at UCLA.

22. "A Matter of Principle." Written by Richard Baer; directed by Fielder Cook. November 21, 1962. Reviewed at UCLA.

23. "My Son, the Social Worker." Written by Richard Baer; directed by Joseph Pevney. January 9, 1963. Reviewed at UCLA.

24. Keyser and Keyser, p. 104.

more often it is Father Fitzgibbon who attends to money matters. For example, when the priests come upon the pledge card of someone whom they have just buried, Father Fitzgibbon remarks as he tears it up: "It's sad when you have to put an old friend in the ground, and it's sad when you have to put a generous one in the wastebasket." In the same episode, Father Fitzgibbon sends O'Malley to recover debts owed to St. Dominic's and one of its parishioners by a now wealthy businessman, instructing his younger counterpart to get the money for St. Dominic's first, and only then recover the funds owed to the member.[25] Elsewhere, Fitzgibbon meticulously prepares the church's quarterly financial statement for the diocese, having much difficulty making the statement balance. When he thinks the report is finally finished, he realizes he should include money that has just come into the parish. O'Malley suggests that he simply carry it over to another quarter, leading Fitz to lavish praise on the young priest, saying, "Boy, you have the makings of a fine pastor!"[26] In another episode, a down-on-his-luck gambler wins the preliminary round of a lottery and has a chance to win the Irish Sweepstakes. He promises half of his prize money to the church should he win. However, the man begins to live an opulent lifestyle and flaunt his wealth. One nun from St. Dominic's parochial school voices her concern to Father O'Malley that the sisters are receiving parishioners' requests to pray for the man to win. She notes that the distortion of values in the parish has led the nuns to one conclusion: they must pray that the man does not win. The priest remarks that they should not "rock the boat" just yet, since "this is the first time we've had 50 percent of the action."[27] Notably, the clerics of *Going My Way* are most often focused on serving others and less so on raising money on behalf of the church — a balance that would change with forthcoming television programs focusing on ecclesiastics.

One aspect of church life touched upon less than in other programs is the church's ritual life. Whereas other programs would include scenes inside a church, such as worship services, sermons, baptisms, weddings and confessions, *Going My Way* rarely includes such imagery. To be sure, the priests discuss the weekly schedule of Masses. Occasionally they discuss or prepare sermons, mentioning only that they are doing so, without going into detail on the content. References to the confessional are restricted to explaining why one of the priests is not available for a meeting. While the priests do perform weddings and baptisms, the television audience only sees the joyful participants outside, on the church steps after the events. They deal more with secular problems than spiritual ones. Even when one parishioner considers entering the priesthood, Father O'Malley helps the man realize that his is not a true spiritual calling but a way of running

---

25. "A Memorial for Finnegan." Written by Malcolm Stuart Boylan; directed by Alan Crosland, Jr. January 16, 1963. Reviewed at UCLA.

26. "A Saint for Mama." Written by Emmet Lavery; directed by Joseph Pevney. December 26, 1962. Reviewed at UCLA.

27. "Cornelius, Come Home." Written by James O'Hanlon; directed by Joseph Pevney. March 6, 1963. Reviewed at UCLA.

from facing problems with his fiancée.[28] True to the social activist agenda of the melodrama, the emphasis of *Going My Way* is on the non-ritual, non-spiritual roles of the priests as they strive to help parishioners face problems, negotiating the differences in their own styles and approaches in order to do so.

Thus, the portrayal of the Catholic Church emerges as one of an institution firmly interwoven with other social institutions — the police, school system, family, even other churches — and working together with them for the common good. With a decidedly conservative image, *Going My Way* depicts the church as a respected and revered institution, a source of traditional authority, at the nexus of civic-minded organizations. It views the Catholic Church as vital, compromising, and secure — an organization to be relied upon for providing direction and stability. This would change in programs of coming years. Thoroughly "masculine," with a sporty young cleric and priests who resolve conflicts with rational discussion and impart fatherly advice, the series' pairing of two male clerics would give way to a duo of female ecclesiastics in a program of the late 1960s, and the friction of a radical woman paired with a tradition-minded man in a show of the 1970s.

Going My Way ran for one year, during which it struggled in the ratings, in part because it was scheduled opposite the number one rated comedy hit of the season, *The Beverly Hillbillies*. This may explain why, despite its light-hearted, uncontroversial approach, the show did not last longer than one season — it could not compete with such competition. Reportedly, the ratings greatly improved once the show was in summer re-runs, but by then the decision had already been made to discontinue the production.[29] A dramatic program with touches of humor, *Going My Way* set the stage for other television programs featuring ecclesiastic characters. What audiences saw in the relationship between the older, traditional Father Fitzgibbon and younger, progressive Father O'Malley and their efforts to work together despite differences would seem mild compared to those of programs to come, wherein such differences between ecclesiastics would be much more exaggerated.

The Flying Nun

Four years after the priests of *Going My Way* left the airwaves, an order of nuns made their debut in a TV series that set a young, progressive novice in conflict with an older, conservative Reverend Mother Superior in the classic sitcom *The Flying Nun*. Cheery and not particularly controversial, the show was successful enough to last three seasons. Airing on ABC from 1967 through 1970, the series was set in a convent in Puerto Rico. Starring Sally Field as the bright, energetic Sister Bertrille and Madeleine Sherwood as the often stoic, sometimes

---

28. "Not Good Enough for My Sister." Written by Richard Baer; directed by Bernard Girard. November 21, 1962. Reviewed at UCLA.

29. John Douglas (1992), "Dick York — a farewell interview." *FilmFax*, April/May, 57.

stern Reverend Mother Superior Placido, the show was a vehicle for executive producer Harry Ackerman to develop a new series for the star of his short-lived sitcom *Gidget*, in which Field had appeared from 1965 to 1966. In the new series, Field played the newest member of a teaching order. Formerly named Elsie Etherington in civilian life, Sister Bertrille had come to the Convent San Tanco to serve as the new kindergarten teacher. There she would meet Sister Jacqueline, a good-humored nun who was Sister Bertrille's confidant, and provided the narration for the series. She would also meet and befriend Carlos Ramirez, the local playboy and owner of a discothèque and casino.

While the series was primarily a situation comedy, it was also on occasion a musical. In some episodes the characters — most often Bertrille and the children — would burst forth in song and sing about everything from happiness and painting pictures to the difficulties of eating with chopsticks. Clearly intending to draw upon the success of films like *The Sound of Music* (1965) and *The Singing Nun* (1966), and recording star Soeur Sourire (the Belgian "Singing Nun", whose songs were popular in the 1960s), the central idea behind the TV sitcom came from a young adults' novel by Tere Rios titled *The Fifteenth Pelican* (1965). In this book, a nun comes to a convent in San Juan to become the new Reverend Mother Superior. From the beginning, the contrast between Sisters Bertrille and Placido is clear: Rios describes the latter as "very serious, very strict" and as having "Definite Ideas (sic) on everything, most of them beginning with, *Sisters don't.*"[30] In contrast, Sister Bertrille is very open and friendly, even playing cards with the sailors on the ship on which she arrives and waving to them as she departs the dock, much to the disapproval of the nuns who come to greet her — particularly Sister Placido. But there is something else different about this new nun: as Rios explains, "of all the nuns in the world, Sister Bertrille was probably the smallest"[31] and when on the day she arrives strong Puerto Rican winds blow and she has to run to keep up with the other nuns, Sister Bertrille discovers the principles of flight firsthand:

> People who know about airplanes and why they stay up say that if *lift* + *thrust* is greater than *load* + *drag*, a thing will fly. Sister Bertrille's wide white coronet, folded like a paper airplane with a point at the front, was a perfect airfoil (an airfoil is anything like a wing that gives *lift*); she was running to keep up, which gave her *thrust*; her tiny body was very little *load*, and practically no *drag*. So when she skipped up over the highest hill in San Juan and turned the corner and lifted her head and ran a bit to catch up, that gust lifted her right into the air.[32]

---

30. Tere Rios (1965), *The Fifteenth Pelican*. New York: Doubleday & Company, p. 8.
31. Ibid., p. 7.
32. Ibid., p. 16.

The novel explains that Sister Bertrille learns how to fly and does so nightly with a flock of 14 pelicans (hence the book's title). When she inadvertently lands inside a high-security army base, she is caught and accused of being a communist spy. Eventually, the initially wary officials accept her explanation of how she got there and drop their charges. Sister Bertrille promises never to fly again, sewing fishing weights into her habit to keep her word.

The hour-long pilot for the television series drew upon many elements of Rios' novel and, as *Going My Way* did for its priests, emphasized the contrast between the Reverend Mother Placido and Sister Bertrille — the conflicts between whom would be central to this Catholic-set TV show. It opens with two nuns, Sisters Jacqueline and Sixto, walking to the harbor to greet their new novice, who would serve as the convent's kindergarten teacher. Before they arrive, strong winds blow Bertrille off a steamboat and into the water. She swims to a nearby yacht, where she climbs aboard to find playboy Carlos romancing one of many women on the deck. By the time the older nuns reach the harbor, they find Sister Bertrille in a soaking-wet habit playing gin rummy with Carlos' bikini-clad harem. As Bertrille leaves the boat, one of the women explains to Carlos that she can no longer see him that weekend: "The sister blitzed us," she explains to a disappointed Carlos, adding, "we agreed if we lost we'd attend Mass every Sunday." When the nuns greet Sister Bertrille, Sister Jacqueline inquires as to whether the young nun often plays cards. "No, I just learned about three weeks ago," Sister Bertrille explains, ". . . helped pass the time when I was in jail." "Prison?!" exclaims a concerned Sister Jacqueline. "Yeah," continues Bertrille, "I was arrested at a free speech protest rally." In her voice-over commentary, Sister Jacqueline then confides to the audience: "It was at this point I had the feeling the Convent San Tanco would never be the same again. That turned out to be the biggest understatement of the year."

On her first sight of the convent, Sister Bertrille is left breathless by its beauty. The older nuns agree that the convent is delightful on the outside, but complain that it is plagued by problems caused by its old age and the inability of the order to afford repairs. They enter the convent, where Sisters Bertrille and Jacqueline later hang laundry on a balcony, while the wind picks up. They gaze at seagulls flying overhead and, just as Sister Bertrille admits to having had fantasies of being a bird, the wind catches her coronet and she hovers a few feet off the floor. "Have faith, sister, have faith, I'll get you down!" Sister Jacqueline reassures the flying nun, just before Sister Bertrille falls back to the ground. They wonder about this unusual event until breakfast the next day, when Bertrille shares with the other members of the order her theory on why she was able to fly. Citing a principle she found in a book in the convent's library, and noting her weight and the shape of her coronet, she explains that, "when lift plus thrust is greater than load plus drag, well, anything will fly." The nuns at breakfast suggest she put more starch in her diet . . . or at least in her coronet.

Continuing their breakfast, Sister Bertrille notes how anxious she is to meet the Reverend Mother Superior, who is away, and inquires what she is like. Sister

Jacqueline cautiously chooses her words as she warns Sister Bertrille about their Reverend Mother:

> Sister Jacqueline: You must understand that when the Reverend Mother entered the order, profession was reached by discipline — discipline which destroyed all traces of self will or rebelliousness. At least, that was the idea. I suppose what I'm trying to say is that her ideas are rather . . . traditional.
>
> Sister Bertrille: Oh, but sister, times are changing so fast.
>
> Sister Jacqueline: I know, and the Reverend Mother tries very hard to understand but for her sometimes it's difficult.
>
> Sister Bertrille: Well, thank you for the advice but you don't have to worry. I'm sure the Reverend Mother and I will get along just fine.
>
> Sister Jacqueline: You think so?
>
> Sister Bertrille: Of course! We young sisters may approach things differently but our aims are still the same.

As it would turn out, Sister Bertrille may have been too optimistic.

On seeing the conditions of the classrooms and hearing of the convent's other problems, Sister Bertrille tries to fix everything she can and overcome the convent's financial problems. She gets everyone involved, including the orphans and nuns at the convent; as Sister Jacqueline explains: "She managed to infect the other sisters with her enthusiasm" and "managed to create quite a stir, even with her feet planted firmly on the ground." Bertrille even leads the children into town where they sing, march about and get new clothes. As Sister Jacqueline explains: "she introduced a new word to the convent: credit." Finally, while Bertrille, the children and other nuns are singing in the town square in an effort to solicit donations for the needy convent, a taxi pulls up — and out steps the very upset Reverend Mother. Back in her office, Placido scolds Bertrille for having caused such disruption at the Convent San Tanco. Bertrille defends her actions, saying that when she saw all the convent's problems she had to do something. This irks the Reverend Mother, who offers the young novice some perspective:

> Reverend Mother: For twenty years I have been fighting a losing battle against inadequate space, not enough books, bad plumbing and not enough money. For twenty years, sister. And you spend one week here and tell me what is needed.
>
> Sister Bertrille: Forgive me, Reverend Mother. Sometimes I speak first and think later.
>
> Reverend Mother: You are young with young attitudes and I am trying to take all that into consideration.

The older nun finally gives a word of advice to the young novice: "Sister Bertrille, you are new here, so I am willing to overlook your breach of conduct, but in the future, please remember: dignity."

Sister Bertrille later pays Carlos a visit to ask about some land he owns. She enters his discothèque in her habit and, amidst the go-go girls and couples dancing, becomes inspired and begins to dance herself. Realizing she is calling attention to herself, she stops and goes to Carlos' office. Their exchange gives a glimpse of her inner maturity and religious devotion:

> Carlos: I don't believe it! How can you come here like this? There's dancing and drinking and gambling out there. Aren't you afraid of being contaminated? You are a sister!
>   Sister Bertrille: All the more reason I should set an example.
>   Carlos: At a discothèque?!
>   Sister Bertrille: To show that the Christian life can flourish in the land of reality.
>   Carlos: Boy, you are some nun, you know that?! When I was a child the sisters never would . . .
>   Sister Bertrille (interrupting): Excuse me, señor, I wish you wouldn't talk about "the sisters" as if we were all turned out on an assembly line. We're all different, with different personalities. We're really like everybody else, señor!

She inquires about the land. Carlos says he will not sell it. She reveals she had hoped he would *donate* it and adds that she believes he is a good man who wants to do the right thing, whereupon Carlos asks her to leave and not return to his disco (a request she will ignore time and time again). Eventually, he succumbs and donates the land after he and the nuns see her fly.

By the episode's end, Sister Bertrille is sad because she is not sure what the Reverend Mother Superior intends to do with her and fears the older nun will send her back to the mainland. The Reverend Mother summons the novice to her office, where she asks the young nun if she would like to continue to fly. Bertrille says yes — a little too enthusiastically at first, then in a more appropriate, reserved manner. The Reverend Mother tells Bertrille: "I understand you believe in responsible freedom. I also know that you do not wish to bring any undignified attention to the Convent San Tanco. Therefore, I leave the problem of your flying to your conscience." In keeping with the book, Sister Jacqueline suggests Bertrille sew fishing weights into her habit so she will be too heavy to fly — a suggestion the young nun would not heed, since the series required that Bertrille fly in every episode. By the pilot's end the rest of the premise was also apparent: that a younger nun with modern ideas would serve the church in ways that set her in conflict with an older, traditional Reverend Mother Superior.

Thus, the premise of the series emerges as one focused on the balance between the worldly, wise and conservative Reverend Mother and an innocent, childlike, wide-eyed activist — politically naïve and ultimately respectful of the traditions of the institutional church. That the program arose during a time of change in the church and the concurrent rise of the feminist movement helps contextualize its depiction of women in general and nuns in particular. Sisters at the time were represented in the media, from films to magazines and newspapers, as privileged representatives of the feminist movement. As figures who existed apart from the now questioned norms of the domestic sphere, and who joined with other women to effect change in society, nuns held an important place in the public consciousness.[33] As such, "the convent operated in popular culture as a privileged symbolic space for women, somewhere between the private and public," where "women's roles, religious authority and the space between the two" were publicly mediated.[34] In this context, Bertrille's idealism, independent spirit and rather tame liberalism would serve as a safe exploration of how young feminists would sometimes be at odds with older women who had invested in maintaining the social order and, with it, their status.[35]

Another episode which serves as a good introduction to the themes that would evolve over the course of the series is "The Hot Spell."[36] The story involves the usual clash between Sister Bertrille and the Reverend Mother, as Bertrille tries to solve problems caused by the convent's poverty and inadvertently shows up the Reverend Mother. The episode begins as San Juan is suffering through a hot spell. At a meeting of the sisters (from which Bertrille is absent) the sweltering nuns ask the Reverend Mother to purchase air conditioners for the convent; they are particularly concerned about having cool air for the dispensary. The Reverend Mother notes that they cannot afford such expensive items, but rather need to buy medicine for the dispensary. Sister Bertrille arrives with a delivery man, announcing she has air conditioners for the convent. She explains that Carlos was getting new ones for his casino and she convinced him to donate the old ones to the sisters. Placido is concerned and sternly remarks, "Sister Bertrille, Carlos Ramirez is a man of questionable character. I do not like the idea of the Convent San Tanco being continually in his debt." Eventually, she reluctantly concedes to the wishes of the sisters and accepts the air conditioners to use in the dispensary and hottest classrooms. The Reverend Mother's concerns, however, will prove prophetic and wise.

Sister Bertrille visits the casino to thank Carlos for the donation. Just before she enters, however, Carlos learns that mobsters are coming to take the casino from him. He asks Sister Bertrille to express her gratitude with a "tangible" favor. When the mobsters arrive and demand to speak with the manager, they are surprised to find the rosy-cheeked Sister Bertrille sitting at Carlos' desk, in full

---

33. Rebecca Sullivan (2005), *Visual Habits: Nuns, Feminism, and American Postwar Culture*. Toronto: University of Toronto Press, p. 10.

34. Ibid., pp. 10–11.

35. Ibid., pp. 206–7.

36. "The Hot Spell." Written by James Henerson; directed by Matt Bing. Series executive produced by Harry Ackerman. January 18, 1968. Reviewed off broadcast television and commercial DVD.

habit and coronet. Carlos' assistant explains that they have signed the casino and discothèque over to the sisters of the Convent San Tanco. The Reverend Mother is shocked to discover that her convent owns an establishment that caters to gamblers and go-go dancers. When Sister Bertrille explains it is "just until the heat is off," the older Reverend Mother (much like Father Fitzgibbon) fails to understand the younger sister's use of vernacular, and inquires what the heat has to do with the matter. Bertrille seems unable to avoid street slang, saying Carlos "took a powder" while the mob puts "the squeeze" on him so they do not "rub him out." Unable to follow along, Reverend Mother Placido suggests the young novice spend time in chapel and "pray for a less vivid imagination." Nonetheless, the mobsters come to the Reverend Mother to make her a "deal" to take the casino from the sisters. The mobsters get nervous when they realize they are "being watched," after they notice Sister Bertrille keeping an eye on the Reverend Mother through a window. Bertrille calls the Reverend Mother on her phone and asks if she should call the police, to which the Reverend Mother repeats aloud "call the police?!" The mobsters, thinking this is a threat instead of a question, admit defeat and leave.

When the mob boss comes to the casino, Carlos' assistant explains he "gave up his worldly possessions" to "live a life of religious contemplation" and that the sisters own the casino now. The gangster requests that the house limit be waived so he can play for high stakes. The assistant explains that only the new owners can authorize the request and that the "Holy Sisters" are asleep. When the gangsters threaten him, however, he calls Sister Bertrille, who comes to his aid. Wearing her habit, she plays the mobsters for ownership of the casino. She wins the hand on a bluff, but when the gangsters overhear the assistant speaking to Carlos on the phone, they realize his claim of being on a religious retreat is a fraud. Fearing they will harm Carlos, Sister Bertrille flies to the gangsters' boat, where she hovers overhead, calls for the boss, and asks him to leave Carlos alone. Thinking he has seen a vision, the mob boss leaves in a hurry. Near the episode's end, the Reverend Mother receives a phone call from a monsignor. She begins to explain the disturbing situation, but is surprised when he asks to speak with Bertrille to hear how she "coffee housed" the mob boss. The young nun takes the phone and, using lots of cardplayer's jargon, excitedly explains to the monsignor how she duped the underworld king.

The episode illustrates a number of trends in the series: Bertrille's quickness to act on behalf of the convent, often in well-intentioned but problematic ways; the Reverend Mother's more cautious manner and the conflicts that result from the nuns' different approaches; the generation gap between the hip, streetwise young novice and the stoic, wise Reverend Mother Superior; the sensational but comic scenarios that arise in many episodes (a considerable number of which involve the convent becoming involved with the mob — a running theme in Catholic-set films and television programs); and the young nun's attempts to apply her entrepreneurial talents to help the poverty-stricken convent. As with *Going My Way*, her success is often measured in worldly ways, in terms of her ability to raise cash to support the convent's social outreach programs — such as a school, hospital and its programs for the poor — and much less on her efforts to provide spiritual guidance.

Many of Sister Bertrille's contributions to the Convent San Tanco arise from her business-mindedness — a trait church historians also attribute to the Catholic Church itself.[37] The first glimpse of her business sense comes in the pilot, where Bertrille organizes efforts to raise funds for the convent and introduces the sisters to the use of credit. Many other episodes continue this trait, perhaps most notably "Days of Nuns and Roses," wherein Sister Bertrille convinces the nuns to make use of a local resource, and bottle and sell sea grape juice.[38] Showing surprising knowledge of the product development process, Bertrille asks Carlos and another businessman to invest in the business, offering them "distribution rights." When negotiating with grape farmers, who expect their money up front, Bertrille matter-of-factly explains, "it's obvious you've never dealt with big business before" and that in "big business" everyone gets paid on the tenth of the month. When Carlos discovers the sisters' product is sea grape juice, he pulls his backing, leading Bertrille to protest, asserting they had a "verbal contract." Carlos refuses to reconsider, and so Bertrille scolds him, saying, "Naturally, this means you no longer have exclusive distribution rights!" With the sea grape juice bottled but having no one to distribute or purchase it, the sisters are excited when they hear some people have arrived at the convent to discuss their product. They rush out to the courtyard, only to find the farmers waiting for their payment, it being the tenth of the month. When Bertrille is asked who these people are, she smartly replies, "I think you call them creditors." The nuns strike a deal with the farmers to hold off on payment, in exchange for a share in the business.

The inevitable encounter between the Reverend Mother and Sister Bertrille occurs when the older nun summons the younger to her office to discuss the matter. Not so much angry as concerned, Placido compliments the impulsive, optimistic novice on her "valiant effort" but advises her that "the time has come to face reality: we were just not meant to be businesswomen." Disappointed, Bertrille grumbles about losing their chance to be independent and not rely on charity. The Reverend Mother solemnly reminds the young sister of what Saint Paul wrote in his Epistle to the Corinthians, that among faith, hope and charity, the greatest of these virtues is . . . "Charity," Sister Bertrille finishes the Reverend Mother's sentence with a smile, accepting her superior's wisdom and comfort. Although their business venture fails, the episode is noteworthy for Bertrille's entrepreneurial spirit, familiarity with business terms and processes, and willingness to use the convent's resources and name to produce a product.

----

37. See for example John Tracy Ellis (1970), "American Catholics and intellectual life." In *Catholicism in America*, edited by Philip Gleason. New York: Harper & Row.

38. "Days of Nuns and Roses." Written by Austin and Irma Kalish; directed by E. W. Swackhamer. November 2, 1967. Reviewed off broadcast television and commercial DVD.

That Bertrille drives a hard bargain on behalf of the convent is made clear in several other episodes as well. In "Candid Commercial," the convent washing machine is on the fritz and Sister Bertrille unwittingly steps into a candid commercial for laundry detergent. Having first asked Carlos to buy the convent new washing machines as a tax write-off, her wealthy friend instead directs her to a new laundromat. There, she speaks to an undercover producer about how much she loves his product, and when he reveals that they have taped her and would like to use her on their commercial — in exchange for a new washing machine and a year's supply of detergent — Bertrille remarks, "You're the answer to all my prayers!" She pressures him to donate enough detergent for the whole convent, not just herself, leading the producer to remark, "You drive a hard bargain, sister," and her to confess, "Well, they've told me that before." The young nun signs a release and rushes to the convent to give the nuns the good news. True to form, the episode takes a turn when the Reverend Mother hears of the matter and is displeased with Bertrille's actions, saying, "I do not believe that anyone in religious life should appear on television recommending a commercial product," and "the Convent San Tanco is not available for testimonials." She instructs Sister Bertrille to speak with the producer and cancel their deal. Accepting the Reverend Mother's wisdom, the novice tries to explain why she cannot honor their contract, saying, "When you're a nun you can't do things ordinary people can do because you're a representative of the church." When the producer refuses to succumb, Bertrille mutters, "wait till the Vatican hears about this . . . you know they have some pretty good connections." After much scheming that ultimately gets Bertrille released from the contract, she nonetheless persists in nagging the producer to give the convent the much-needed washing machine and detergent. He agrees.[39]

Many other episodes involve Bertrille and the nuns scheming to make money in one way or another. In one, the Mother General visits the convent and when the nuns realize she had been a famous silent film star before entering the order, they arrange a screening of the Mother General's movies for her many fans, using the proceeds for their school fund. In another, the sisters arrange to scour the casino's daily intake to search for rare, valuable coins to raise funds for the convent. Then there is an episode that depicts what will become a common association running through the history of church-set programs, connecting the Catholic Church with bingo and its receipts. Notably, a number of episodes which focus on raising money also involve music in some manner, making a connection with the singing nuns and priests of movies (The Sound of Music, Going My Way, and others). For instance, Bertrille is offered the chance to sing and play guitar on a television show. She is reluctant to accept the opportunity until she hears it pays $200, which she can donate to the needy convent. When Bertrille later signs a long-term contract to appear on the program and then

---

39. "The Candid Commercial." Written by John L. Greene; directed by Harry Falk. March 6, 1970. Reviewed at LOC.

reconsiders her decision, she once again shows business savvy by insisting on approving the show's sponsors (something she knows the producer will never accept) and that each episode start with a sermon and end with prayers. She makes enough of a pest of herself with unacceptable demands that the producer himself asks her to break the contract — which she only agrees to do if he will make a sizable donation to the convent.

One episode that not only highlights Bertrille's ability to make money for the church but also features the generation gap between her and the Reverend Mother is "Song of Bertrille."[40] It opens with the sisters contemplating the usual litany of problems facing the convent: plaster falling off the walls, electrical problems, bad plumbing. While listening to the radio, Bertrille hears that Sunny and the Sundowners, a popular rock group, will appear at Casino Carlos and asks the Reverend Mother's permission to go visit them, explaining that she went to school with the lead singer. At the casino, Sunny at first does not recognize Bertrille in her habit; when he does, he gives her a big hug (as one concerned onlooker makes a sign of the cross). When he notes that he never realized religion was "her thing," she responds, "it is and I'm really happy." Sunny further explains why he is surprised, noting that their yearbook named her "Miss Far Out of 1965," to which Carlos responds, "she still holds the title." After introducing Bertrille to the rest of the rock group (as "one of the grooviest chicks I know . . . knew"), he and Bertrille sing and perform a soft-shoe dance. Marveling at her talents, Sunny surmises, "that convent really must have something," to which the novice responds, "it has everything . . . including poverty." It is then that Sunny invites her to write a song for his group to record, offering her the rights to donate the royalties to the convent. Bertrille later flies about the island to gain inspiration, and writes a sweet song about the wonders of nature and the miracles that abound every day. All the nuns gather at a table at the casino to hear the group's debut live performance of the song. They are all proud of Sister Bertrille's effort — until the Sundowners play her song in a heavy rock style, burying her words and eliciting drug references from what had been innocent lyrics. A most displeased Reverend Mother Superior eyes Sister Bertrille, who slowly sinks into her chair.

Back at the convent, the Reverend Mother offers a telling observation, saying: "Sister Bertrille, I am aware of the generation gap between us, but I didn't think that it was quite that wide." Bertrille tries to explain that the song as it was performed was not the same as the one she wrote. She faces an uphill battle until the manager of the Sundowners offers Bertrille a check for $500, and she refuses it. Then the Reverend Mother begins to understand how upset the novice is. Out in the courtyard, Bertrille and the children sing the song as she wrote it. A reassured Reverend Mother walks up to Bertrille and smiles. In the end, the rock group's manager scolds them for tampering with such beautiful

---

40. "Song of Bertrille." Written by Michael Morris; directed by Murray Golden. September 26, 1968. Reviewed at LOC, and off broadcast television and commercial DVD.

lyrics and offers to have Bertrille's song recorded by his only other client: the Salt Lake City Boys Choir.

The impression left by this episode regarding the relationship between the older, traditional Reverend Mother and the young, progressive Sister Bertrille is not unlike that of other episodes, where clear tension gives way to collegial understanding. As the Reverend Mother says of the novice to a visiting Bishop, who has just witnessed Bertrille skating through the convent halls: "Sister Bertrille is somewhat unorthodox but her intentions are good." Sometimes, however, it is not just unorthodoxy that resides at the heart of their conflict. Occasionally the Reverend Mother takes offense at Sister Bertrille's youthful enthusiasm, especially when it causes the novice to push for reforms that her older counterparts already have tried. For example, on one occasion the young nun works with an older adult who cannot read, trying to teach him in the same class as the orphans. Bertrille argues with the Reverend Mother that the nuns should be allowed to teach adults as well, leading the Reverend Mother to admonish her for not realizing that those who have served the convent longer already have made such proposals to the Bishop. The Reverend Mother notes she has learned to accept that the Bishop has other priorities for the sisters. Nonetheless, Bertrille convinces Placido to try a pilot program to present to the Bishop. For their part, in this and other episodes, the other nuns seem energized by Bertrille's exuberance while also respectful of the Reverend Mother's wisdom and experience. In fact, in one episode Sister Jacqueline, who is Sister Bertrille's confidant and closest friend, notes how she has always idolized the Reverend Mother despite her old-fashioned approach and authoritarianism. One by-product of the series' focus on the two contrasting nuns is that it presents the bulk of the sisters, those in between the extremes and somewhere between the featured nuns' ages, as followers rather than independent-minded. Charmed by the young nun's activist enthusiasm while respectful of the older nun's more tempered approach, the majority of the sisters of *The Flying Nun* are easily influenced, neither innovative nor complacent, but responsive to the direction of others among them. Of no concern to those who feared radicalism in the church or society, the nuns of the Convent San Tanco were rather tame, open to change without the predilection to fight for reform.

This touches on the subject of another episode where a surprising twist causes the younger nuns to reject innovation and modernization. "New Habit" finds the order faced with an edict from the Mother General stating that they will adopt new habits that are modern, stylish, and skirt-length. This episode is historically accurate in that the Second Vatican Council called for, among other reforms, modernization of religious wear. Whereas the order's old habits were loose-fitting, ankle length and either all-white (for novices) or white with a blue scapular (for avowed sisters), with black socks and shoes, and a wide-arched coronet, the new habits are blue and knee-length with a white sash and a blue bonnet-style coronet. The response to the new habits is predictable: the younger nuns are excited (at first), Bertrille calling them "super" and "cute."

A less enthusiastic Reverend Mother notes that "a habit should be comfortable, respectable, and show us to the secular world with restraint and dignity." When Sister Bertrille realizes that the new design is not aerodynamic, the other nuns' initial enthusiasm for the modern attire fades. Sister Jacqueline suggests that the Reverend Mother get special dispensation for Bertrille to wear the old-fashioned habit, but the novice will have none of that, not wanting to be treated differently from the other sisters in the order. When the Mother General arrives to inspect the new habits, Carlos — in a scheme to convince the visiting Mother to return to the old attire — arrives with a girlfriend (a dress maker) who is wearing a secular outfit she has designed to look very much like the new habits. Seeing the outfit, the Mother General voices her concern, noting that an order's habit should be "distinctive." She ultimately issues an edict that the order should return to the use of their old habits. By the episode's end, Sister Bertrille has informed the Reverend Mother that she has figured out yet another way to raise money for the convent — she has sold the new habits to Carlos' girlfriend, who plans to alter and sell them as secular dresses.[41]

To resolve the problem with the new habits, Sister Bertrille at one point offers to give up flying for the sake of the unity of the order — that is, so they will all be able to wear the same, modern habit. Throughout the series, Bertrille has opportunities to declare her devotion to the church and the order, explaining why they are important, what kind of service is involved in her calling, and why serving the order makes her happy. Her calling is presented as a joy, not a burden. She says how pleased she is with her vocation when the leader of the Sundowners looks surprised at her choice; she explains she is very happy as a novice and that the convent "has everything." She makes similar declarations to others who seem surprised by her calling. What is more, she clearly defines what serving the church as a nun entails. In one episode she tries to explain what is involved in being a nun to an actress who is too casually considering joining the order. Explaining that "it isn't something you decide just like that" and that the decision is not only up to an individual, she elaborates on the sacrifices novices and nuns must make, such as giving up "all worldly goods and earthly considerations, to give up all thoughts of self." On another occasion, a boy considers revealing that Bertrille can fly until she convinces him to reconsider. She explains how the publicity would obstruct the nuns from doing the work they are called to do: "We teach the children, we look after the old people, we take care of the sick, we try and help the poor." She notes that if the people came to the convent to see her, it would disrupt that important work. Even the Reverend Mother has opportunities to discuss her willingness to go wherever her calling takes her in an episode titled "With love from Irving," wherein she nearly leaves the convent to become dean of women at a college. Throughout the episode, antics at the convent threaten to compromise the Reverend Mother's standing as a viable candidate for the

41. "The New Habit." Written by Burt Styler; directed by Jerry Bernstein. November 19, 1969. Reviewed at LOC.

new job. In a touching moment at the episode's end, Sister Bertrille finds the Reverend Mother in the convent chapel, arranging flowers, making the sign of the cross and kneeling before the altar. Sister Bertrille is there to comfort her because she did not get the position. The Reverend Mother tenderly remarks that she would go wherever the church directs her to, but that she is pleased she will be staying at the Convent San Tanco where she is truly needed.[42]

One episode that not only deals with a nun's vocation but also is one of several to involve Jewish characters is "The Reconversion of Sister Shapiro."[43] In it, Carlos agrees to watch a girl named Linda while her parents go on a trip, until he himself is called away and leaves her with Sister Bertrille at the convent. Together they read to a blind man, help children, take care of babies for a busy mother, pick flowers to bring to hospitalized children and generally make others happy. Linda enjoys all they do together, and when Carlos arrives at the Reverend Mother's office to pick up the girl, all are surprised when she enters wearing a makeshift white habit. When Carlos exclaims "Linda!", the girl politely insists, "Please call me Sister Shapiro." At a loss for a response — especially since Linda's family is Jewish — Bertrille suggests they allow the girl to see what being a nun is really like by putting her on the duty roster. To the surprise of all, Linda gladly performs all her duties. In fact, when asked if she ever plans to leave the convent, Linda thoughtfully responds: "Well, maybe for my brother's bar mitzvah." Finally, Sister Bertrille has the idea to show Linda home movies of her own past, before she became a nun. Bertrille shows footage of her surfing, singing with a rock band, and working as a mechanic, and notes she gave herself plenty of time to explore who she was and what career she wanted to pursue. In the end, Linda learns a lesson, saying, "I'll always want to be like you and help people, but I think I'll start by being myself." When the two later say goodbye, Linda tells Bertrille, "Goodbye, Sister Bertrille. God bless you," to which Sister Bertrille responds, "Shalom."

Another episode that sees the nuns in relation to Jews is "The Rabbi and the Nun."[44] The episode serves not only as a primer on Judaism but also a case study in ecumenism. Sister Bertrille receives a trunk from the estate of her recently deceased aunt, and the nuns gather to watch her go through the items. When Bertrille finds a menorah, she explains the religious function of the item to the others, saying that Jewish people use it to light candles on Hanukah and adding that she thinks her aunt received the relic as a thank you during religious brotherhood week. Bertrille decides to donate the item to Rabbi Mendez at Temple Beth Shalom. Seeing the antique, the Rabbi proclaims it a "menorah of menorahs" and tells the nun it will one day grace their new, larger synagogue.

---

42. "With Love from Irving." Written by Dorothy Cooper Foote; directed by E. W. Swackhamer. November 9, 1967. Reviewed off commercial DVD.

43. "Reconversion of Sister Shapiro." Written by Austin and Irma Kalish; directed by Jerry Bernstein. February 29, 1968. Reviewed at LOC, and off broadcast television and commercial DVD.

44. "The Rabbi and the Nun." Written by Michael Morris; directed by Jerry Bernstein. October 10, 1968. Reviewed at LOC, and off commercial DVD.

He explains that the congregation has outgrown the current temple and is raising money to build a new one. The two then discuss a more immediate problem facing the Rabbi — that a wedding he is set to perform involves a party that will not fit into the present temple. Bertrille expresses her sympathy, saying the temple "might be small in square feet but it's big in tradition," to which the Rabbi wryly responds, "Tradition: it doesn't hold a hundred friends and family." He laments the thought of having the wedding in a Chinese restaurant rather than in a sacred space. They agree that, above all, a marriage is a "sacred union between a man and a woman," and discuss whether or not it is important where the union takes place. This gives the young novice an idea.

After discussing the matter with the Reverend Mother, Sister Bertrille offers the Rabbi the use of the convent garden for the ceremony. "A Jewish wedding in a convent!" the Rabbi repeats several times, as Bertrille notes, "There's nothing denominational about grass or hedges." They discuss the theology behind the idea, the Rabbi observing, "there is nothing in the Old Testament that forbids it," the nun replying, "and I don't think there's anything about it in the New Testament either!" And so the sisters of the Convent San Tanco excitedly plan the Jewish wedding, donating flowers and decorations and arranging rented chairs and tables on the lawn. (One overly enthusiastic nun offers to bake a ham for the occasion, to which Sister Bertrille says, "Boy, have you got the wrong wedding!") As they prepare, the Rabbi explains aspects of the Jewish wedding tradition to the nuns, such as the significance of the chuppah (the wedding canopy) and the breaking of the glass. Finally, amidst men wearing Yamacahs and nuns in their habits, the couple is married. When all yell "mazel tov", a quartet of nuns begins singing "Hava Negelah", and the guests — a bit surprised at first — begin to sing along and do traditional Jewish circle dances. All enjoy the happy moment, including Bertrille and the Rabbi, who dance together, the novice adding some funky moves to the dance. In the end, the Rabbi sees a Star of David cloud formation floating in the sky. Wanting to contribute to the occasion in her own special way, Bertrille had managed to fly unnoticed and create the Jewish star in the sky using the spray from a fire extinguisher. Seeing it, the Rabbi exclaims, "It's a miracle!" The Reverend Mother, knowing Bertrille, suggests perhaps it is just "an interesting cloud formation," but the Rabbi has none of it, saying, "Don't be so scientific, Reverend Mother. I believe God had a finger in it!"

Despite the delicately balanced portrayal, the producers of *The Flying Nun* were concerned with how Catholics would accept a nun as whimsical as Sister Bertrille. Catholic Church officials were consulted about the series prior to its production. In a concession to them, the producers made one important change from the Rios novel. Whereas Rios depicted Bertrille as a professed nun in line to be the Reverend Mother's successor, the producers of the TV series made it clear that Sister Bertrille was a novice who had not yet taken her vows.[45] In another

---

45. Rosalind Wyman, former Vice President of Screen Gems, telephone interview with the author, February 20, 1991.

effort to avoid criticism, the church was involved as a consultant. The National Catholic Office for Radio and Television (NCORT) received on-screen credit for serving as an advisor. NCORT had been created by the Catholic Church a few years earlier, after the Second Vatican Council, to promote more positive relations between the national media and the church. NCORT supplied a nun as an on-set consultant to advise about matters such as how to wear a habit and what a nun's room should look like. Beyond this, officials at NCORT also reviewed scripts and made suggestions for revisions. One NCORT director described the agency's role in these matters as "damage control," offering the example of a script that called for a visiting Bishop to arrive with his wife. "You had to nip that stuff in the bud," he commented, declaring "Catholic priests were not to be married!"[46] Using consultants allowed the producers to avoid conflict with the church; every effort was made to correct problems before they arose. The producers' efforts to satisfy any concerns of the Catholic Church in part allowed *The Flying Nun* to air without challenge and become television's first church-set situation comedy. The stoic Reverend Mother and airborne novice worked through their differences each week, always finding a balance by the episode's end. More upbeat than daring, the show did relatively well, producing 82 episodes over three seasons. This would be very different from the next television program to focus on a clash between a younger liberal and older conservative ecclesiastic, both in its approach to depicting conflict and in the response of the church and television audience.

In the Beginning

Airing eight years after *The Flying Nun* ended, *In the Beginning* (1978) became the next program to feature conflict in the church. The CBS show centered on a clash between an older, conservative priest and a younger, liberal nun as they ministered to a poor, inner-city community. While reflecting contemporaneous issues in the church at the time, the show was also edgy, and lasted only a handful of episodes. The program was a creation of Norman Lear, who was not involved with the show beyond its conception. His hope was that *In the Beginning* would "explore the social problems of the inner city"[47] and consider "the tension between institutionalized religion and the creative forces of reform, renewal and social awareness."[48] The show was to deal with these issues in the politically-informed comic fashion Lear made famous in the classic TV series *All in the Family* and its spin-off *The Jeffersons* (which was the lead-in program to *In the Beginning* on CBS's Wednesday night lineup). The "creative force of reform"

---

46. Charles E. Reilly, former Executive Director of the National Catholic Office for Radio and Television, telephone interview with the author, February 7, 1991.

47. Jeanette Abi-Nader, HM, (1978), "Beyond *The Flying Nun*." *National Catholic Reporter*, September 8, 13.

48. Elizabeth Thoman, CHM, (1978), "What went wrong with *In the Beginning*." *National Catholic Reporter*, November 24, 14.

was represented by Sister Aggie (played by Priscilla Lopez), while the old order was embodied by Father Daniel Cleary (played by McLean Stevenson). The nun and priest ministered and bickered in a Baltimore mission serving the needy of the inner city, from drunks and hookers to troubled youths — an assignment which delighted Sister Aggie but irritated Father Cleary. In fact, the priest regularly tried to secure another placement away from the mission and Sister Aggie, whom he called "Attila the Nun."[49] In one episode, he even complains of his treatment by the diocese, which he concludes must have it in for him: "Why else would they have dragged me out of my lovely little parish and stuck me down here with you?" he asks Sister Aggie, before apologizing to her.

Sister Aggie is an outspoken, insightful, quick-witted young nun who regularly wears jeans and a sweater or shirt; this is in contrast to the mission's other nun, Sister Lillian — an older woman who regularly wears a traditional habit. Aggie relates to the young people of the mission, speaking their language, playing their games (such as when she demonstrates her skill with a hula hoop) and understanding their problems. That Aggie would provide dramatic conflict for an older, more traditional Father Cleary is clear from the series' opening sequence. Her words unheard under the theme music, Sister Aggie speaks in an impassioned manner to Father Cleary, the two of them facing each other with a statue of the Virgin Mary behind them. As Aggie speaks, Cleary places his fingers in the statue's ears. (To establish her vocation in the first shot of the opening, Sister Aggie wears a traditional habit; later in the sequence, she dresses in casual, secular garb.) The series theme song also establishes their conflict, playing with the double entendre of an unlikely romantic couple — appropriate for the first opposite-sex pairing of ecclesiastics in a church-set TV series:

> In the beginning, we were not a very likely pair, but I guess you never know.
> In the beginning, there was not one point of view we shared, and that's not so long ago.
> It makes me smile to think of how it all began.
> Mission improbable was what they called our plan.
> In the beginning, we could've used a miracle or two, never thought we'd see it through,
> In the beginning.

Throughout the opening, the two are shown occasionally laughing together, more often squaring off against each other.

In "Father Cleary's Crisis" (the only episode available for review), the primary storyline focuses on Father Cleary's possible promotion to monsignor.[50] Rumor

---

49. Tom Brooks and Earle Marsh (2003), *The Complete Directory to Prime-Time Network and Cable TV Shows 1946–Present*, 8th edn. New York: Ballantine Books, p. 574.

50. "Father Cleary's Crisis." Written by Lenora Thuna; directed by Doug Rogers. Series

has it that the Bishop has narrowed his search to two priests, and his final decision just happens to fall on Father Cleary's 47th birthday. It opens with Sister Aggie directing the mission's youth as they prepare for the priest's birthday celebration, hanging balloons and a sign reading "Happy birthday Father Cleary." Cleary enters holding a box, which he says contains a birthday surprise from himself: a putter. When Sister Aggie humorously asks what kind of surprise that is, Cleary responds: "Big. I was gonna get a driver." They then discuss the possible promotion, and Sister Aggie cautions Cleary about prematurely getting his hopes up. But he is excited and certain he will receive the promotion to monsignor. Eventually, Monsignor Barlow visits the mission to tell Cleary that the Bishop has decided to promote someone else. Cleary responds immaturely, poking fun at the new Monsignor's ability to lead church ceremonies, like marriage, saying, "With that cock-eye of his, you can't tell if he's looking at the bride or the groom." He pouts about his misfortune for the rest of the episode, refusing to speak at community events or participate in any activities with fellow priests.

In the episode's subplot, Father Cleary goes out of his way to help a deaf African-American teenager, Jerome, get a job. Cleary has arranged for an interview with a car dealer. Apprehensive, Jerome agrees to meet the salesman. One of the episode's best comic moments comes when Father Cleary confronts Jerome about missing the interview. The youth is not interested in what Cleary has to say. As Cleary speaks, Jerome looks away, eventually turning 180 degrees to avoid reading the priest's lips; in an effort to have his say, Cleary bends into the youth's eyesight, desperately encircling him as the youth spins away. The priest makes a final plea: "Would you just stand still and look at what I am saying!" Sister Aggie tells Jerome he owes Father Cleary an explanation, but Jerome insists his reasons are his own.

The two storylines dovetail throughout, in several significant moments. In one, Jerome refers to Cleary as "Father Honky," and Cleary asks why Sister Aggie is not "Sister Honky," since they are both white. Jerome responds that "honky" does not refer to a color but a state of mind — an indication that the older, traditional cleric is more out-of-touch and less able to minister with teenagers than his younger, more liberal counterpart. Jerome asks if the promotion to "Monsignor Honky" is a big deal, to which Cleary responds at first in religious terms, then in his best attempt at hip lingo: "I could tell you that it was nothing at all. You'd think I'm being modest, which is a virtue. But I'd be lying, which is a sin. So to tell you the truth, becoming monsignor is an absolute boot in the buns." Another moment comes at the episode's end, when Sister Aggie is in Cleary's office listening to him confide about his disappointment with being passed over for monsignor. She catches him sneaking a drink to forget his problems, a vice for which she scolds him. Jerome enters and explains why he did not go to his job interview. Since he is deaf, and cannot read or do math, he figures he is

executive produced by Mort Lachman; developed by Norman Lear. Unknown date, 1978. Reviewed off VHS copy provided by Lear.

wasting his time pursuing any meaningful employment. Among his past failed ventures, he explains, is a job at a diner, from which he was fired: "They had a tall counter and a short cook. I couldn't read his lips." Cleary rebukes Jerome for all of his complaining, telling him he has to make the most of his situation. Noting that the young man has skills in auto repair (Jerome earlier fixed Cleary's car), the priest convinces him to pursue that line of work. After the youth leaves, Cleary confides to Sister Aggie that he felt bad for coming down on the teenager. Sitting cross-legged on his desk, she responds:

> I don't blame you, Father, you did what you had to. He had it coming. Why you saw the way he was moping around and feeling sorry for himself, and blaming others, and jealous of others. Why you'd think he hadn't made monsignor or something. Oh boy, the way some people act. He ought to be ashamed. You know what I mean?

The nun grins and looks over at Father Cleary, who says, "Sister Agnes, nobody likes a smug nun." They both smile, as the program ends.

One episode finds Father Cleary and Sister Aggie offering a sex education class for the youngsters at their mission, while in another Sisters Aggie and Lillian win a poker game to raise money for the mission's youth program (a similar scenario to *The Flying Nun*'s pilot).[51] Only a handful of episodes of *In the Beginning* aired before the show was canceled. Critics called the series "tired" and "formulaic",[52] with jokes that were "coy attempts at blasphemy," citing as an example Sister Aggie's outburst in a moment of frustration, "Damn, I wish I could swear!"[53] Another critic agreed, stating that the jokes were "tiringly biblical," as when Father Cleary complains of Aggie, "If it were up to her, God's commandments would be called the ten suggestions."[54] One critic summed up the series' shortcomings in Biblical parlance, writing, "On both religious and secular subjects, its stupidities passeth understanding."[55]

Controversial aspects of the program likely also influenced the decision to cancel the show. Sister Aggie's character reportedly had been in jail, had lived with a man before taking her vows,[56] and in one unaired episode felt guilt-ridden after becoming attracted to a young man she met at the mission.[57] To help the producers create a show that was both accurate and avoided controversy with the church, members of the National Sisters Communication Service were involved behind the scenes, making suggestions for the scripts and sitting in on rehearsals. Their assessment was that the program excelled when focusing

---

51. Thoman (1978), p. 14.
52. James Lardner (1978), "The new season: I." *The New Republic*, October 7, 27.
53. Frank Rich (1978), "The 1978–79 season: III." *Time*, September 16–25, 75.
54. Abi-Nader (1978), p. 13.
55. Martin Mayer (1978), *American Film*. November, 16.
56. Abi-Nader (1978), p. 13.
57. Thoman (1978), p. 14.

on the mission activities of the ecclesiastics, and faltered when it placed the church leaders in situations one might find in most any television comedy. They also criticized the producers for not heeding their suggestions about some episodes — for example, to allow Sister Aggie to face her attraction to the young man, rather than simply feel guilt and deny it — or for failing to understand new directions in the Catholic Church that had arisen since Vatican II, citing Father Cleary's concerns with status over service.[58] Obviously, church leaders were concerned with how accurately television represented them, the church they served and the issues they faced.

In the end, the program faired as well as other church-set shows that pushed the limit. Whereas Sister Bertrille's childlike innocence, watered down feminism and ultimate respect for authority allowed *The Flying Nun* to avoid controversy and become a TV classic, Sister Aggie's sassiness and politically informed iconoclasm led the show into popularly unacceptable territory. Sister Aggie challenged traditional gender norms. Despite her petite and pretty physical appearance, she was not demure and yielding, but tough and anti-authoritarian. Her competitiveness with Father Cleary, and even her costuming (wearing jeans), constructed her as more masculine than the girlish Sister Bertrille. Hers was a more challenging portrayal of nuns for popular consumption, one that was more radical, more transgressive — and ultimately, one which did not survive.

Discussion

The earliest cluster of television programs featuring ecclesiastics focuses on conflict within the church. Assessing how these programs depict the church and its leaders leads us to look to church historians to provide historical accounts for comparison. One striking trend of popular, prime-time television programs in the 1960s and 1970s is the focus on the Roman Catholic Church. Indeed, prime-time American television's focus on the Catholic Church in series focusing principally on ecclesiastics would remain almost absolute (save for one rather short-lived Protestant-set show) until 1986, when *Amen* began its run. This virtually exclusive focus on the Catholic Church may seem surprising, given that Catholics represented just under a quarter of the US population in the same period.[59] Nonetheless, this trend makes sense for a number of reasons.

For one, Catholicism was in the public eye, and there was an explicit public interest in this religion. The visibility and impact of two leaders of the early 1960s, one of them a politician and the other a churchman, saw to this. John F. Kennedy was the first Catholic to be elected US president. His Catholicism was an issue in the campaign, and his election in 1960 proved once and for all

---

58. Ibid., p. 14.

59. Center for Applied Research in the Apostolate (CARA), Georgetown University, "Frequently requested Catholic Church statistics," available at http://cara.georgetown.edu/bulletin/index.htm (accessed May 22, 2007).

that attitudes about Catholics in America had changed. Indeed, church historian Martin Marty notes that with Kennedy's inauguration came a symbolic end to "Protestant America"; historian Jay P. Dolan, citing this observation in his own work, adds that Kennedy's popularity "enabled Catholics to stand a little taller."[60] The other leader was Pope John XXIII, whose call for an ecumenical council (what would become the Second Vatican Council, or Vatican II) drew the world's attention to Catholicism. The Pope's charge that the council should bring the church into the modern age, with reforms in the liturgy and the church's relationship with society, drew a great deal of attention, including much criticism and praise. Just as important as these two leaders in a discussion of Catholics and television programming was a prominent figure whose fame was forged by television itself — Bishop Fulton J. Sheen, whose one-man TV show *Life is Worth Living* aired in prime-time on network television in the 1950s (and later in syndication in the 1960s). Basically a half-hour sermon, the program was hugely popular and showed that an explicitly religious program — a Catholic one at that — could be a successful prime-time venture.[61] Indeed, that popular culture was ready to focus attention on Catholicism is reflected also in the movies of the era, from *The Sound of Music* (1965) to *The Trouble with Angels* (1966), *Where Angels Go, Trouble Follows* (1968) and *Change of Habit* (1969). The success of the earlier movie version of *Going My Way* (1944) (and its sequel *The Bells of St. Mary's* (1945) made the development of a television program based upon these characters a bit less risky.

Another reason for television's exclusive focus on Catholicism in shows of this era concerns the need of dramatic programming to focus on conflict. Conflict is the heart of drama and producers need to develop programs based on situations that will ensure ongoing tension. Given this, the focus on Roman Catholicism seems natural, especially considering the time at which these programs arose. Catholic leaders of this era were involved in well-publicized battles for the direction of the church. Hence, television programs set within a Catholic institution (be that a parish, convent or mission) could focus on internal battles between religious leaders within one church for the direction of that church. While disputes certainly existed within Protestant churches of the time, the existence of various denominational choices within Protestantism, even within particular traditions, allowed for relatively like-minded Protestants to join specific denominations. For example, within American Lutheranism of the 1960s and 1970s, several denominations covered the spectrum from conservatism to liberalism, allowing Lutherans of a particular point of view to join appropriate church bodies. Whereas highly publicized conflicts within Protestant denominations have arisen in more recent years, particularly regarding issues

---

60. Jay P. Dolan (2002), *In Search of an American Catholicism: A History of Religion and Culture in Tension*. New York: Oxford University Press, p. 192.
61. Christopher Owen Lynch (1998), *Selling Catholicism: Bishop Sheen and the Power of Television*. Kentucky: University Press of Kentucky, pp. 7–8.

from homosexuality (such as gay marriage, commitment ceremonies and ordaining homosexual people), similarly well-publicized conflicts were not as present within individual Protestant denominations of the 1960–70 era. Even for those issues that did arise, for example regarding the ordination of women, these typically were not as contentious within denominations, and certainly not as widely publicized as conflicts in Catholicism. Hence, the struggles between progressive and traditional Catholic priests and nuns for the direction of the church seemed ready-made for television programming.

The single most important reason that conflicts in Catholicism were so widely publicized in the 1960s and 1970s concerns the Second Vatican Council and its wide-ranging reforms of the Catholic Church. While a growing awareness of the need to reform had been in development during the 1950s — reforms that probably would have come about in some form with or without a formal council — it was nonetheless by means of Vatican II that the Catholic Church addressed the issues and obliged a response from its members.[62] The conflicts that would be unleashed by the council upon the American Catholic community were, as one historian wrote, "unprecedented" in scope.[63] Held from 1962 to 1965, the Second Vatican Council addressed issues such as the liturgy, the relationship of clergy and laity, religious freedom, ecumenism and the relationship of the church to modernity. In short, Vatican II sought to modernize the church. It made the liturgy more accessible by using local languages and inviting the deeper participation of the laity. It called for a more open relationship between Catholics and those of other religions. It sought to modernize the church in many ways, such as in its structure, means of interpreting the scriptures, and by openness to involving the laity in the life of the church. The significance and depth of this change is dealt with by most every major Catholic Church historian, from John Tracy Ellis, Jay P. Dolan and Philip Gleason to Andrew Greeley and James Hennesey, but it is a Protestant theologian (himself quoted by Dolan) who puts it best; in characterizing the profundity of changes, Langdon Gilkey notes that whereas Protestantism had on the whole kept abreast of changes in the modern world, Catholicism after Vatican II:

> . . . really for the first time tried to absorb the effects of this whole vast modern development from the Enlightenment to the present in the short period between 1963 and 1973! Thus all the spiritual, social and techno-logical forces that had structured and transformed the modern history of the West have suddenly, and without much preparation, impinged force-fully on her life, and they have had to be comprehended, reinterpreted and dealt with by Catholicism in one frantic decade.[64]

---

62. Jay P. Dolan (1985), *The American Catholic Experience: A History from Colonial Times to the Present*. New York: Doubleday & Company, p. 428.

63. Dolan (2002), *In Search of an American Catholicism*, p. 195.

64. Dolan (1985), *The American Catholic Experience*, p. 428 (quoting Gilkey, Langdon [1975], *Catholicism Confronts Modernity*. New York: Seabury Press, pp. 34–5).

The result, as church historian James Hennesey aptly puts it, was that "American Catholics had now to cope with the staggering reality of dissent, change and diversity at the highest levels of the church" leaving many to adopt change with "varying degrees of enthusiasm" while "others less sanguine busied themselves patrolling the battlements of defensive strongholds."[65] Fodder for dramatic conflict, indeed! The changes instituted by Vatican II found some Catholics excited by them and others opposed, exposing conflicts in the church. This left those who were inspired or disaffected to fight for the direction of the church. Often, these conflicts centered on church leaders, the younger ones excited by Vatican II and its reforms, the older less enthusiastic about change.

The relationship between older and younger church leaders and their attitudes towards change certainly were depicted in televised programs of the 1960s and 1970s; in fact, these are their central focus. With one program spotlighting two priests (*Going My Way*), one two nuns (*The Flying Nun*), and one a priest and a nun (*In the Beginning*), television shows in this grouping offered an interesting range of pairings with which to explore conflicts in the leadership of the Catholic Church in the post-Vatican II era. Much of the particulars on these programs ring true to what church historians say was going on in the ranks of the Catholic Church's leadership, and this is true from the first pairing in the form of the priests of *Going My Way*. For instance, whereas Catholics of the early twentieth century were squarely involved in the age of immigration, either as immigrants themselves or as leaders who helped their fellow countrymen and women assimilate, Catholics of the late twentieth century were largely American-born. This meant their identity was more influenced by American culture than that of their parents' or grandparents' homeland. This set off an identity crisis within Catholicism during the 1960s, the older generation looking to the church for tradition, the younger unsure of what identifying as Catholic meant for them.[66] *Going My Way* reflected the tensions between immigrant and native-born Catholics, not only in the persons of Fathers Fitzgibbon (an immigrant from Ireland) and O'Malley (who was American-born), but also in episodes that focused on families coming to terms with different attitudes held by foreign-born parents and American-born children, wherein the church helped resolve these differences. For example, recall the episode focusing on the Spanish-born father and his difficulties accepting his daughter's involvement in American youth culture ("The Father") and the priests' role in helping reunite them, and the episode ("A Saint for Mama") in which the Italian-American businessman's resistance to marrying his Italian fiancée (so he can keep an American mistress) leads her to feign illness and turn to the priests for help.

Another matter reflecting the priests' different backgrounds is their attitudes

---

65. James Hennesey (1981), *American Catholics: A History of the Roman Catholic Community in the United States*. New York: Oxford University Press, pp. 314–5.

66. Philip Gleason (1970), "The crisis of Americanization," in *Catholicism in America*, edited by Philip Gleason. New York: Harper & Row.

towards those of other religions. O'Malley is perfectly comfortable with any and all interactions with those of different religions, as evidenced in his relationship with Dr. Thornton, the Protestant minister, and Rabbi Adler. O'Malley thinks nothing of socializing with them — at parties, on the golf course, at dinner — and of working together with them on projects involving the youth center. Fitzgibbon's openness to such interactions is a bit more cautious, as evidenced by his surprise that O'Malley would invite a Protestant to the rectory for supper, and his self-conscious awareness of the religious background of those with whom O'Malley works. Interaction with those of other faiths is natural for the American-born priest, and something of an adjustment for the foreign-born, although Fitzgibbon's ultimate acquiescence to such ecumenical interactions is noteworthy. This certainly rings true to the era. One of Vatican II's primary contributions was an ecumenical spirit, which was "a major thrust of the Council;" the "dramatic[. . .] move toward ecumenism" in the 1960s ushered in a "new attitude" and "reshaped relationship between Catholics and Protestants and brought an end to the long cold war of hostility and suspicion."[67] This transition is reflected both in the traces of "suspicion" occasionally shown by Father Fitzgibbon (and Mrs. Featherstone), and the entirely open attitude of Father O'Malley. By the end of the decade, *The Flying Nun* would be so open to the ecumenical spirit that a Jewish girl left in Sister Bertrille's care would consider becoming a nun ("The Reconversion of Sister Shapiro"), and all of the nuns of the Convent San Tanco (including the older, traditional Reverend Mother) would enthusiastically help plan and participate in a Jewish wedding held on the convent grounds ("The Rabbi and the Nun").

From differing attitudes about institutional change and ecumenism, to varying degrees of Americanization and effectiveness at dealing with modern problems, the priests of *Going My Way* certainly reflect what John Tracy Ellis describes as:

. . . [the] mounting tension in many places between the younger and older priests, the different concept of the apostolate that divided the two age groups, as well as the widening gap between them on the subject of ecclesiastical authority in general and their mutual relationships in this matter in particular.[68]

Ellis goes on to discuss how the situation facing the changing church was aggravated by "elder clergy who have stubbornly adhered to rules and regulations badly in need of being either abolished or modernized."[69] Father Fitzgibbon certainly was set in his traditional ways, often grumbling that youthful inexperience and

---

67. Dolan (1985), *The American Catholic Experience*, pp. 425, 433–4.
68. John Tracy Ellis (1969), *American Catholicism*, 2nd edn, rev. The Chicago History of American Civilization series, edited by Daniel J. Boorstin. Chicago: University of Chicago Press, p. 245.
69. Ibid., p. 245.

new ideas could not compete with his years of practice and wisdom. Even so, his awareness of his limited ability to adapt to change came through in some of his remarks about retirement or Father O'Malley's greater abilities in various areas, or in his laughably inept attempts to relate to the young or modernize, such as in his efforts to use modern lingo. He was alternately defensive and defeated, resistant and resilient. Nonetheless, *Going My Way* provided a hopeful look at Catholicism, showing an affection (however occasionally strained) between the two emblematic characters, ultimately suggesting that while the church's present lay in the hands of older traditionalists on their way out, its future lay in the hands of those more young and progressive and capable of adapting to the modern world.

The same may be said for the convent-set program which followed *Going My Way* in TV's line of programs focusing on ecclesiastics. In *The Flying Nun*, audiences saw a similar relationship as that which existed between Fathers Fitzgibbon and O'Malley, now played out by Sisters Placido and Bertrille. One important difference is that the rift between an older, traditionalist and a younger, progressive was more exaggerated in *The Flying Nun*, and Sister Bertrille, more so than O'Malley, embodied more of the "authority to dissent" invited by Vatican II.[70] The words of caution offered to Bertrille by the other sisters (in the pilot episode) after she professed her excitement at changes in the world, but before she met the Reverend Mother, aptly set up this difference, as Sister Jacqueline warned her that the Reverend Mother's ideas were "traditional", and the result of years of "discipline" that "destroyed all traces of rebelliousness." Bertrille's optimistic response, that younger nuns "approach things differently" but since their "aims are still the same" her superior would understand this, also helped establish the conflict. The novice's overconfidence that good intentions would outweigh any of her elder superior's concerns about the use of new, unconventional methods to serve the church would be challenged throughout the series, as her older supervisor continually made clear her concern or disapproval. In the end, the younger nun's youthful enthusiasm and open acceptance of popular culture and modern ways often met with the chagrin of her older, traditional counterpart, who preferred a more solemn, conservative approach.

The gap between the two characters does capture something of what transpired in the sisterhood after Vatican II, at least in American convents. As one observer wrote at the time, "Within each separate community of nuns, efforts to modernize are accompanied by strong ideological differences. And within each convent, the gap between the older and younger generations is a pronounced one."[71] Ellis' account of the situation facing women's religious communities in the 1960s echoes this assessment. He notes that "an older generation" of nuns could be too "wedded to traditional ways," while the younger ones greeted change with

---

70. Dolan (1985), *The American Catholic Experience*, p. 426.

71. Edward Wakin and Father Joseph F. Scheuer (1965), "The American nun: poor, chaste and restive." *Harper's Magazine*, August 1965, 35.

"joy and fresh hope" and based their decision to remain in the community on the likelihood that promised reforms would be implemented.[72] The conflicts between Bertrille and Placido certainly resonate with such descriptions. Nonetheless, the series' focus on these two characters does obscure attention to what one sister writing at the time called the "salt-of-the-earth majority group," who were more moderate.[73] Noting that most attention after Vatican II was focused on nuns at the extremes, whom she called "the 'die-hards' (who resist change) and the 'far-outs' (who, finding change a heady draught, want more and more of the same)," this sister regrets that the more temperate in the ranks were overlooked, noting specifically that they were "unheralded by the press" and "unprogrammed by TV."[74] To be sure, as much as the Reverend Mother might appropriately be called "die-hard" (the sister who used this term even noted the die-hards' resistance to modernized habits) and Sister Bertrille "far-out", the remainder of the nuns at the Convent San Tanco often were little more than followers who acted on Bertrille's enthusiasm, and later yielded to Placido's wisdom.

One area in which the sisters of the convent faithfully followed their flying nun is in her fundraising efforts — efforts in which the young novice's business-mindedness was on full display. From her leadership in starting a winery at the convent by working with investors and creditors ("Days of Nuns and Roses"), to her ability to drive a hard bargain with television producers to make deals that would benefit the convent and then use her cunning to break the contracts ("Candid Commercial" and "My Sister, the Star"), she was quite capable of using business sense to make profit for the church. Sister Bertrille was, in fact, as apt to speak in sacrificial terms of how contented she was to serve the church as she was to speak in contractual language and use terms like "exclusive distribution rights" and "product demand." Ellis attests to this Catholic proclivity for business. He compares Catholics' contributions in business to other areas of American life (such as intellectual and political) and, while finding Catholics not having made significant advances in other areas by the 1960s, highlights their influence and abilities in business. In this area, he concludes, Catholics' contributions were more in keeping with their numbers and had been steady, saying that by the 1960s Catholics had "attained more distinction in the business world than they have in any other sector of American life."[75] Ellis notes that since this had been a strength of Catholic laity, religious leaders had been apt to be assessed in terms of their own abilities in this area, noting "it is no exaggeration to say that the Catholic Church of the United States has become 'big business' in the typical American meaning of that term" and religious leaders were expected to possess abilities necessary to help the church achieve financial success.[76]

---

72. Ellis (1969), *American Catholicism*, p. 234.
73. Sister Bertrande Meyers (1967), "Raise your voice: cast your vote." *Vital Speeches of the Day*, 33 (August 15), p. 662.
74. Ibid., pp. 661, 663.
75. Ellis (1970), "American Catholics and intellectual life," p. 123.
76. Ibid., pp. 124–5.

Bertrille comfortably brought the high status of the church to her negotiations, at times even using the term "big business" when wheeling and dealing on behalf of the institution she represented. Although not as inclined to scheme in a fashion similar to Bertrille in order to help the financial success of the church, Father O'Malley nonetheless regularly obtained donations from business leaders on whom he called, whether or not solicitation of monetary support was the reason for his visit. This identification of Catholics with business, and clerics' success with their ability to raise money for the church, would in fact continue to be a focus of Catholic-set television programs, noticeably more so than programs focusing on Protestant clerics.

Another topic unique to the Catholic setting of the television programs of this era concerns the modernization of the habit and the loosening of restrictions on nuns' attire. While it is true that the attire of Catholic ecclesiastics made possible distinct costumes for characters in church-set series, just as interesting (and potentially sensational) was the move to secularize religious garb or abandon it altogether. Following the Second Vatican Council nuns were allowed to "retain the traditional habit" of their order, adopt a "modified habit," or, as one cultural historian noted by quoting Vatican II documents, "adapt any style of dress that was 'simple and modest, [and] at once poor and becoming'."[77] The issue came up in *The Flying Nun* when (in "New Habits") the Mother General of Bertrille's order tried to modernize the sisters' habit. Looking much more modern than the full-length robes traditionally worn by the order, the contemporarily styled skirt-and-blouse attire the Mother General selected came with less aerodynamic headwear. Ordinarily, as Ellis recounts, it was the younger nuns who were excited by modernized attire and the older ones who resisted such change.[78] In an unusual twist, Sister Bertrille and her associates in the order, after a period of excitement over the new habits, ultimately reject them and return to their old attire so that Bertrille might continue to take advantage of the traditional habit's wind-channeling coronet. The ending of this episode, where Bertrille manages to have the new habits altered and sold as secular dresses to raise money for the convent, is yet another example of her business-mindedness.

Ultimately, it was Sister Aggie of *In the Beginning* who was the first television nun to make the most of the loosened restrictions on nuns' attire, appearing in jeans and sweaters or shirts (while her older counterpart, Sister Lillian, fit the bill of Ellis' older nuns, preferring to wear the traditional habit). While Aggie's choice was certainly "simple", "modest" and "poor", as the Vatican documents permitted, some may wonder whether jeans and sweaters met the documents' criteria of being "becoming." Certainly, this was intended to contribute to Sister Aggie's progressive character and set her in contrast to the traditional-cleric-wearing Father Cleary. Indeed, since Aggie worked in an inner-city mission, her more

---

77. Mark S. Massa (1999), *Catholics and American Culture: Fulton Sheen, Dorothy Day, and the Notre Dame Football Team*. New York: The Crossroad Publishing Company, pp. 184–5.
78. Ellis (1969), *American Catholicism*, p. 234.

secular attire corresponded with Ellis' observation that younger religious women in the United States "had taken tremendous strides towards putting themselves au courant with the world in which they lived and worked."[79] Dolan also notes that changes in nuns' dress were part of a larger movement in women's communities to move beyond the "cloister culture" and more and more allow sisters to serve outside of the convent setting, thus "dissolving the boundaries that set women religious apart from the rest of society."[80] Noting that the women's movement in the United States had as much influence on this trend as did the Vatican Council, Dolan notes that the end result was occasional conflict with authorities in such areas as "the dress of women religious, [and] the political involvement of sisters."[81] While he notes such trends began in the 1960s, they certainly picked up over the course of the following decade, placing Sister Aggie's outspoken, politically aware, socially active character in the correct historical moment when this depiction would ring true to an emerging reality in the Catholic Church.

While many aspects of popular television's representation of the church in this era bore semblance to historic accounts of Catholicism, there are noteworthy historical trends which were not in evidence on television. For example, Vatican II called for greater participation of the laity in the life of the parish and national church, and while historians attest to the developing reality in the 1960s and 1970s, this trend is not illustrated on television.[82] Focusing the dramatic conflict on ideologically different church leaders, as the three programs in this cluster did, allowed for a much more even and pointed juxtaposition of combatants in these church-set dramas. Ironically, the rise of the laity's involvement in the Catholic Church corresponded with what most historians call a momentous crisis in the church: that is, the dwindling numbers of people entering religious orders and the priesthood. While popular dramatic programs are of course not expected to depict all contemporaneous aspects of the institution in which they are set, these oversights are nonetheless noteworthy because these very matters would arise as central issues in later network programs focusing on clerics, as would another immensely important issue emerging in this era: that of saying the Mass in the vernacular of the people, as opposed to Latin. Of the programs appearing in the 1960s and 1970s, the only one for which this might have appeared as an issue was *Going My Way*, because it is set in a parish where worship would take place; but since this show was produced before the institution of this reform (in the mid-1960s), this burning issue for many Catholics would wait years before being depicted on later programs set in the church. Notably, while many later programs would feature rituals and worship services, *Going My Way*, showed

---

79. Ibid., p. 231.

80. Dolan (2002), *In Search of an American Catholicism*, p. 232.

81. Ibid., p. 234.

82. Dolan (2002), *In Search of an American Catholicism* pp. 437–40; Dolan (1985), *The American Catholic Experience*, pp. 204–7; Gillis, Chester (1999), *Roman Catholicism in America*. Columbia Contemporary American Religion Series. New York: Columbia University Press, p. 27.

the priests and congregants only lingering on the church steps after services.

Another matter associated with Catholicism that developed over the coming decades of television programming was an association with urban ministry. This connection began in shows of the 1960s and 1970s, with two of the three programs set in American cities: *Going My Way* in New York City, and *In the Beginning* in Baltimore. Television's depiction agrees with historians who note that American Catholicism has had a "pronouncedly urban character," particularly in comparison with Protestant churches.[83] Having ministered to waves of city-bound European immigrants over the years, many of whom were joining the middle-class and fueling a move of Catholic parishes to the suburbs, Catholic churches remained in their historic urban strongholds later in the twentieth century in order to minister to Hispanic immigrants arriving from Puerto Rico and Mexico, and an increasing number of African-Americans joining the Catholic Church.[84] For this reason, the Catholic Church maintained more of its urban parishes for longer periods of time than occurred with Protestant churches.[85] Even so, Catholic city parishes no longer needed to focus so much attention on Americanizing their members and helping them acculturate. The result, as Dolan writes, was that:

> City parishes took on a new look in the 1960s and 1970s. Breaking out of narrow parochial concerns, they began to redefine their mission. As one priest put it, they were "groping for relevance." Many became community institutions committed to serving the needs of all people regardless of race or religion.[86]

This transformation was reflected in a rather interesting way over the course of this era of television programs focusing on the church and its leaders: from the early 1960s' *Going My Way*, which depicts mostly first- and second-generation European immigrants, with an occasional nod to African-American parishioners (such as in the episode "Run, Robin, Run"); to the late 1960s' *The Flying Nun*, which was set in a locale (Puerto Rico) from which many new immigrants to America were coming; and finally to *In the Beginning* of the late 1970s, with its focus on an urban ministry no longer focused on Americanization, and now fully groping for relevance in the modern world by responding to social issues. This corresponds with actual trends in Catholic parishes of the era, which began to focus on issues of urban renewal and social justice, much in the way portrayed in *In the Beginning*, with its focus on matters ranging from teenage sex to welfare bureaucracy and women's liberation. Of course, *In the Beginning* dealt with these emerging concerns of the church while still maintaining the focus on

83. Ellis (1969), *American Catholicism*, p. 164.
84. Ibid., pp. 168–9; Dolan (1985), *The American Catholic Experience*, pp. 356–62.
85. Ellis (1969), *American Catholicism*, pp. 170–1.
86. Dolan (1985), *The American Catholic Experience*, p. 449.

the clash between younger, progressive and older, traditional ecclesiastics, the common theme of most church-set television programs airing in the 1960s and 1970s. The coming era of television programs, emerging mostly in the 1980s, would continue to depict the church's struggle to remain relevant to concerns of the modern world, but without the focus on conflicts between different-minded church leaders struggling for the direction of the church.

Questions for Reflection

1) Harry Ackerman (1912–91), executive producer of *The Flying Nun*, is known for working with programs associated with a particular kind of lead female character. He served as executive producer for *Hazel* (1961–5), *Gidget* (1965–6), and *Bewitched* (1964–70), and helped develop *Our Miss Brooks* (1952–6) and *I Love Lucy* (1951–7). Explore some of these programs. How does Ackerman's disposition towards leading women characters fit together with the portrayal of the young novice, Sister Bertrille?

2) Famed producer Norman Lear, who developed *In the Beginning*, is well-known for his work on a collection of American classics: *All in the Family* (1971–9); *Maude* (1972–8); *Sanford and Son* (1972–8); *Good Times* (1974–9); *The Jeffersons* (1975–86); and *One Day at a Time* (1975–84). How does *In the Beginning* bear Lear's stamp? Lear also founded the organization People for the American Way in 1981. Look into it. How do Lear's politics influence his programs — *In the Beginning* in particular?

3) The programs in this chapter all focus on two contrasting lead characters. Imagine if they focused only on one of each pair. How would the programs and their depictions of the Catholic Church of this era change?

4) Each of the programs in this chapter focuses on a different pairing: two men (the priests of *Going My Way*); two women (the nuns of *The Flying Nun*); and a man and a woman (the priest and nun of *In the Beginning*). How do they compare? What role does gender play in these depictions?

5) Read the speech by Sister Bertrande Meyers, listed below in the suggested readings. How does her perspective compare with the depictions of church leaders — nuns in particular — in this chapter's TV programs?

6) Compare the portrayal of Catholic church leaders on TV shows with that on films of this era, such as *Satan Never Sleeps* (1962), *The Sound of Music* (1965), *The Trouble with Angels* (1966), *Shoes of the Fisherman* (1968), *Where Angels Go, Trouble Follows* (1968), *Change of Habit* (1969), *The Exorcist* (1973), *The Omen* (1976) and *The Sentinel* (1977). What similarities and contrasts do you see between the way the two media portray . . . priests and nuns? . . . spiritual versus worldly concerns? . . . sensational versus sentimental imagery? What do the contrasts suggest about the difference between television and film and their relationship with audiences?

7) Speak with someone who recalls watching these programs when they were

first broadcast. What impressions stand out most in their mind? How do these compare with the discussions in this chapter?

Video Sources

Going My Way. "Florence Come Home." Available on VHS from Hollywood's Attic (www.hollywoodsattic.com).

The Flying Nun. Seasons 1 and 2 available on DVD. Sony Pictures.

Individual episodes are available for screening at the following locations (Library of Congress, Washington, DC [abbrev. LOC]; Paley Center for Media, New York and Los Angeles [abbrev. PCM]; UCLA Films and Television Archives, Los Angeles [abbrev. UCLA]):

Going My Way — LOC, PCM, UCLA

The Flying Nun — LOC, PCM

Suggested Further Reading

Ellis, John Tracy (1969), *American Catholicism*, 2nd edn, rev. The Chicago History of American Civilization series, edited by Daniel J. Boorstin. Chicago: University of Chicago Press.

Meyers, Sister Bertrande (1967), "Raise your voice: cast your vote." *Vital Speeches of the Day*, 33 (August 15), 661–4.

Sullivan, Rebecca (2005), *Visual Habits: Nuns, Feminism, and American Postwar Popular Culture*. Toronto: University of Toronto Press.

Whitney, Dwight (1968), "I didn't want to play a nun." *TV Guide,* March 16–22, 21–5.

Tracey Nelson as Sister Stephanie, or "Steve," and Tom Bosley as Father Dowling in *Father Dowling Mysteries.*

3

THE CHURCH SEEKS RELEVANCE IN THE MODERN WORLD

As the 1970s drew to a close, popular American network television's spotlight on ideological debates within the church faded. With greater distance from Vatican II, the focus on conflicts between younger liberals and older conservatives gave way to efforts to show how the church struggled to remain relevant in the modern world — how in an increasingly secular society the church could still respond to contemporary problems. Television programs featuring church leaders which focused on this struggle for relevance began with one program in the 1970s, increased in numbers in the mid-1980s and continued through the 1990s, to include programs such as *Sarge*, *Hell Town*, *Sister Kate*, *Have Faith*, *Father Dowling Mysteries*, *Nothing Sacred* and *Good News*. In addition to these, several programs including church leaders as members of an ensemble cast arose.

Foremost of these is the classic Korean War sitcom *M*A*S*H* (1972–83). Although not set in the church and not focused on clerics, the series included William Christopher playing chaplain Father Francis Mulcahy, one of the best-known clerical characters in American television history. As the sole ecclesiastic among the characters, his presence was not to battle with other clerics but to demonstrate the church's struggle to be relevant in times of crisis. In fact, Mulcahy's ideological proclivities are never as clear as is his drive to serve those around him. Along these lines, he assists the doctors in and out of the operating room, counsels troubled soldiers and colleagues and works on behalf of the children of the local orphanage (run by a nun). Not unlike Sister Bertrille, Father Mulcahy works on behalf of the orphans, often raising funds for them by applying determination and craftiness. He regularly persuades his already financially strapped colleagues to donate to the orphanage. He holds rummage sales to raise money, and occasionally when playing poker with the officers, promises to donate his winnings to the orphans. In one episode, for example, he agrees to represent the 4077th in a cross-country race against a much younger and physically fit competitor from another M*A*S*H unit, promising his winnings to the orphanage if he is the victor. Along the route he mentions to his rival the overwhelming needs of the orphanage and convinces the younger runner to throw the race. Then as he nears the finish line the priest threatens not to cross it unless his fellow company members promise to donate all their winnings to the orphanage. Knowing their desire to beat their rival will outweigh their personal stakes in the race, his good-natured threat entices his fellow M*A*S*H members to agree, and at the last moment (his challenger coming up behind him) Father Mulcahy runs to victory.[1]

Mulcahy's role as a religious leader is made very clear throughout the series. He wears a silver crucifix and is frequently in the operating room wearing a purple stole and carrying a small black ritual prayer book. As the sole cleric in camp, he is by necessity ecumenical. He can perform services and rites of most any denomination. In one episode, he must perform a brith (circumcision ritual), a Jewish chaplain talking him through the ceremony by shortwave radio.[2] He also explains a Buddhist wedding to the others in camp as it takes place.[3] Most often, however, the rituals he performs are Christian, if not specifically Catholic. He performs Major Margaret Houlihan's marriage, a ritual cut short by the arrival of wounded soldiers, which forces the bride — still wearing her gown — to attend to bleeding patients.[4] He leads poorly attended church services, held in the mess tent. He blesses new camp sites and buildings. He issues last rites and hears confessions. Throughout, Father Mulcahy takes his sacramental duties very seriously. When stricken with hepatitis, for example, his first concern is that no one else can administer the sacraments and last rites, and insists that something be rigged so he can at least continue to hear confessions, declaring to Captain "Hawkeye" Pierce "their souls are in my care!"[5]

Father Mulcahy also counsels troubled doctors and patients. One remarkable example occurs in an episode wherein a soldier suffers a mental breakdown because of the many Koreans he has killed. He tells the doctors he is Jesus Christ. Although Mulcahy and a psychiatrist counsel the young man, the soldier's identity crisis persists and he is sent home.[6] In another episode, an AWOL soldier seeks sanctuary in the tent in which Father Mulcahy holds worship services. The priest is at odds with the military police who come to arrest the man. He argues that no matter how improbable a church the tent might seem, it is nonetheless a place of worship and entitles the soldier to sanctuary. The priest counsels the young man. When the military police receive permission to enter the tent to arrest the young man, the distressed soldier pulls a gun, leading Mulcahy to rebuke him for at first seeking refuge in the Lord's house and then defiling it by drawing a weapon. Showing courage, Father Mulcahy rushes the young soldier and grabs his gun, leading the soldier to cry into the priest's arms and ask

1. "Run For the Money." Written by Mike Farrell, David Pollock and Elias Davis; directed by Harry Morgan. Series executive produced by Larry Gelbart, Burt Metcalfe and Gene Reynolds. December 20, 1982. Reviewed off commercial DVD.

2. "Life with Father." Written by Everett Greenbaum and Jim Fritzell; directed by Hy Averback. October 29, 1974. Reviewed off commercial DVD.

3. "Ping Pong." Written by Sid Dorfman; directed by William Jurgensen. January 18, 1977. Reviewed off commercial DVD.

4. "Margaret's Marriage." Written by Everett Greenbaum and Jim Fritzell; directed by Gene Reynolds. March 15, 1977. Reviewed off commercial DVD.

5. "Hepatitis." Written by Alan Alda; directed by Alan Alda. February 8, 1977. Reviewed off commercial DVD.

6. "*Quo Vadis*, Captain Chandler." Written by Burt Prelutsky; directed by Larry Gelbart. November 7, 1975. Reviewed off commercial DVD.

forgiveness.[7] Another example of Father Mulcahy's bravery, and his struggle to remain relevant, appears in an episode where the priest counsels a soldier who has shot himself in the foot to avoid being returned to combat. The counseling goes well until the soldier discovers that the priest has never been on the front lines and has no idea what soldiers endure. Concerned with gaining this young man's respect, Mulcahy defies his commanding officer's orders and sneaks out of camp, driving to the front to pick up wounded. In the end, Mulcahy returns to the soldier he was counseling, saying perhaps now he has the right to speak with him. The soldier agrees and they begin to talk.[8] This last episode decisively demonstrates the priest's concern with being relevant in any given situation.

Father Mulcahy often shares with others his concern about whether his contributions are as important as those of the doctors, who save lives every day. In one episode he reveals his concerns in a heart to heart discussion with Hawkeye, where he confides: "For some time now, I've been comparing the disparity of our callings, doctor versus priest. You fellows are always able to see the end result of your work. I mean, you know immediately if you've been successful. For me, results are far less tangible. Sometimes . . . most of the time . . . I honestly don't know whether I'm doing any good or not." Hawkeye notes that he believes God plays a role in surgery — a comment that seems proven when the doctors are not able to get a response from a patient on the operating table until Mulcahy holds the patient's hand and makes the sign of the cross.[9] Nowhere are Father Mulcahy's feelings of inadequacy confronted more than in an episode wherein Mulcahy narrates a letter he is writing to his sibling, a nun . . . or as he puts it: "my sister, the sister." Beginning to write after a church service that no one attended, he begins: "When you're faced with such overwhelming physical misery it just doesn't seem enough to offer spiritual comfort. I keep wanting to do more, but more is never enough." He later continues the letter, writing, "I'm almost desperate to be useful, sis." His attempts at having an impact progress with varying degrees of success throughout the episode until he gathers with the members of the 4077th for a Christmas celebration. Still a bit melancholy, he is surprised when Hawkeye raises his glass of eggnog, calls for everyone's attention, and says, "I'd like to propose a toast: to someone who's too modest, too utterly simple a man to know how much strength he gives us just by the decency of his life among us . . . Father John Patrick Mulcahy." In the end, the priest offers the following observation as he concludes his letter: "You know, sis, it doesn't matter if you feel useful or not when you're moving from one disaster to another. The trick is to just keep moving."[10] This expresses

---

7. "A Holy Mess." Written by Elias Davis and David Pollock; directed by Burt Metcalfe. February 1, 1982. Reviewed at UCLA, and off commercial DVD.

8. "Mulcahy's War." Written by Richard Cogan; directed by George Tyne. November 16, 1976. Reviewed off commercial DVD.

9. "Showtime." Teleplay by Robert Kline and Larry Gelbart; story by Larry Gelbart; directed by Jackie Cooper. March 25, 1973. Reviewed at UCLA, and off commercial DVD.

10. "Dear Peggy." Written by Jim Fritzell and Everett Greenbaum; directed by Burt Metcalfe.

the struggle for relevance experienced by Father Mulcahy and all clerics in this grouping of television programs.

The series' spin-off, *AfterMASH* (1983–4), finds Father Mulcahy serving as a hospital chaplain in Missouri, working with former wartime colleagues Colonel Potter and Corporal Klinger. Here, Father Mulcahy remains insightful and sensitive. For example, he realizes an African-American patient is not adapting to his prosthetic leg for other than physiological reasons; once the cleric paints the prosthetic leg black, the patient is able to walk.[11] He continues to put people before rules. In one episode, he sneaks in a depressed patient's young son against regulations, declaring "call me an outlaw, but *this* is your best medicine" as the patient smiles and hugs the boy.[12] Likewise, he continues to display realistic faith and well-placed righteous anger, as when a "freelance" preacher-and-used-car-salesman tries to convince a crippled patient that if he believes strongly enough, God will let him walk again. Mulcahy confronts the "preacher" for building up false hope; he helps the patient accept that he will never again walk and find new ways to lead a full life.[13]

AfterMASH also followed broad trends in television programs focusing on clerics. For one, it presented an ecumenical spirit. To this point, the head of the clerical staff at the hospital is Protestant, and Mulcahy works well with him. Colonel Potter tells his friend the hospital's patients are only ten percent Catholic, leading the priest to comment, "Ten percent! Well, we're a young firm but we're growing!"[14] Similarly, when Father Mulcahy is preparing the hospital chapel for Catholic services, a patient inquires about the altar centerpiece, which Mulcahy explains is three-sided so it can be turned to accommodate all services held in the chapel: for Jewish services, one side has a Star of David; the other sides bear a cross for Protestant services, and a crucifix for Catholic.[15] In another episode, a patient's parents argue over whether their son should be comforted by a Catholic priest or Baptist preacher, representing their respective faiths. Mulcahy assures the bickering parents that "our two faiths have more in common than you might be aware of," to which a Baptist preacher adds, "we've counseled mixed families before." Eventually, the arguing infects the other patients and even the two clerics, until Mulcahy reaches out to the minister, saying "we men of God have to stick together."[16]

November 11, 1975. Reviewed at UCLA, and off commercial DVD.

11. "September of '53: Together Again" (two-part pilot). Written by Larry Gelbart; directed by Burt Metcalfe (Part 1) and Nick Havinga (Part 2). Series executive produced by Burt Metcalfe. September 26, 1983. Reviewed at LOC; also available at PCM, and UCLA.

12. "Night Shift." Written by Everett Greenbaum and Elliott Reid; directed by Edward H. Feldman. October 24, 1983. Reviewed at LOC.

13. "Sunday Cruddy Sunday." Written by Dennis Koenig; directed by Nick Havinga. November 14, 1983. Reviewed at LOC.

14. "September of '53: Together Again."

15. "Thanksgiving of '53." Written by Ken Levine and David Isaacs; directed by Burt Metcalfe. November 21, 1983. Reviewed at LOC.

16. "Yours Truly, Max Klinger." Written by Ken Levine and David Isaacs; directed by Burt

At one point in the series, Mulcahy grows tired of living in a rectory with other clerics and moves into an apartment building which he later discovers is filled with prostitutes, loan sharks and gamblers. He decides to leave, but then finds that an acquaintance lives in the building: a prostitute who at the hospital became stuck in an elevator with Father Mulcahy, where he convinced her to reform her ways. She suggests he should stay to help the others in the building, as he did her. "Who knows," Mulcahy says, accepting the idea, "perhaps this could be my mission: helping the godless, teaching the lawless, yet still being able to catch a ballgame on weekends."[17] His residence increases Mulcahy's opportunities for ministry, as he helps the veteran's hospital patients by day and ministers to his seedy neighbors by night. As with all church-set programs of this era, *AfterMASH* emphasizes Mulcahy's commitment to remain relevant to the modern world. He has no counterpart with whom to argue about the direction of the church. Instead, his focus remains solely upon how most effectively to minister.

Similar to *M*A*S*H* in its inclusion of a minister as part of an ensemble of characters, the hour-long drama *Mariah* (ABC, 1987) focused on the staff of a modern penitentiary, and included Rev. Howard Bouchard, a chaplain who serves the spiritual needs of the prisoners alongside a psychiatrist, prison administrators and corrections officers. A Protestant chaplain serving under a Catholic Director of Religious Services, Reverend Bouchard's denominational affiliation is never clarified. Throughout, he wears a sports coat and tie instead of a clerical collar. He is also the second African-American cleric on a series, coming one year after the more successful comedy *Amen* introduced its Reverend Gregory. Reverend Bouchard is a caring, committed, staunch advocate for the inmates. He leads Bible classes and courses on religion (including Islam) and reads the Bible to despondent inmates. When one prisoner must be sedated, he scolds his superiors for risking a reactivation of his drug addiction.[18] In another episode, he himself goes behind bars to speak to an inmate who is threatening to commit suicide by slashing his own throat with glass. The minister gets the prisoner to think about how his suicide might affect his family, and assures him that "even in Mariah State [Prison], you can be free." The inmate puts down the glass as another prisoner, holding a rosary, looks on from behind bars. The minister later invites the saved inmate to serve as his clerk.[19]

The series also reflected upon significant issues arising at the time when the series was produced. In one episode, Reverend Bouchard ministers to inmates in the AIDS ward. He assures even the most self-loathing inmates that

Metcalfe. January 16, 1984. Reviewed at LOC.

17. "Fever Pitch." Written by Dennis Koenig; directed by Burt Metcalfe. February 27, 1984. Reviewed at LOC.

18. "Walls." Written by Robert J. Avrech; directed by Victor Lobl. Series executive produced by Gabriel Katzka and Gerald I. Isenberg. April 15, 1987. Reviewed at LOC.

19. "Equations." Written by Robert J. Avrech; directed by Kevin Hooks. April 1, 1987. Reviewed at PCM, and LOC.

they are loved, responding to one who calls himself filth by saying, "you're not filth; you're one of God's children." The episode finds the minister arguing with his wife, who does not want him to work in the AIDS ward for fear he will catch the disease and pass it on to their children. "These men are part of my congregation," Bouchard says, assuring his wife he is safe to work with the AIDS-infected prisoners. He later admits to his wife that he had once wondered whether AIDS was God's way of punishing people. He now realizes that is not for him to judge but to "stop it" and help "heal" and "love" the afflicted. He also notes that his work may occasionally put the family in danger but that his job is "to heal souls," and they will have to live with that.[20] Like his cleric compatriots of this era of TV programming, Bouchard is no combatant ideologue, so much as one dedicated to helping those in his care face modern crises.

Another cleric-focused program of this era was also the only one to spotlight the Jewish religion; this was the short-lived *Lanigan's Rabbi* (1977). Co-starring Bruce Solomon as Rabbi David Small and Art Carney as Chief of Police Paul Lanigan, the detective series focused on the efforts of a rabbi to help solve crime with his policeman buddy, Lanigan. Based upon the Harry Kemelman novel *Friday the Rabbi Slept Late*, the series occasionally was included in the *NBC Sunday Mystery Movie* lineup, known more for *McCloud*, *McMillan and Wife* and *Columbo*. Despite its unique focus on a rabbi, religion supplied little more to the series than a temple backdrop, a "cover" for the detective–rabbi, or a religious context for the inevitable Jewish jokes. Hence, the Rabbi discusses murder in front of a temple (which, he corrects an acquaintance, is not a "church"), or uses his temple connections to gain leads to solve cases. For example, to discover the identity of two suspects he sees, the Rabbi enlists the help of a hotel clerk he recognizes from a wedding at which he once officiated, claiming he is embarrassed to have forgotten the couple's names and asking the clerk to identify them.[21] The Jewish setting also supplies the basis for jokes here and there, the best of which occurs in the same episode, where Lanigan catches Rabbi Small spying while pretending to read a newspaper, which is upside-down; Lanigan remarks: "I'm a student of comparative religion. I know you read Hebrew right to left. Do you also read English upside-down?" Rabbi Small also quotes Jewish sages and the Talmud, citing scripture to suspects, witnesses and police officers. Similar to the forthcoming *Father Dowling Mysteries* series in its focus on a sleuthing cleric, *Lanigan's Rabbi* was unlike that later series in that it did not emphasize its religious setting, and was considerably less successful and more short-lived.

After these programs of the 1970s and early- to mid-1980s, wherein clerics striving to make a difference were part of an ensemble, programs *featuring*

---

20. "Dominion." Written by Robert J. Avrech; directed by Michael Switzer. April 8, 1987. Reviewed at LOC.

21. "Cadaver in the Clutter." Teleplay by Don M. Mankiewicz and Gordon Cotler; story by Robert Pirosh; directed by Joseph Pevney. Series executive produced by Leonard B. Stern. March 17, 1977. Reviewed at LOC.

ecclesiastics working to make the church relevant in the modern world would emerge and thrive in the next decade.[22] Nonetheless, two later programs that included an ecclesiastic as a member of an ensemble deserve mention. One was the short-lived comedy *Rachel Gunn, RN* (Fox, 1992). Focusing on the staff of a Nebraska hospital, the cast of characters included an overly joyful nun named Sister Joan, the only African-American nun appearing as a regular character on a TV series. Dressed in a fairly traditional habit and blouse, Sister Joan is most often on the periphery of episodes, providing occasional religious humor, although in one episode her efforts to raise money for the church and the needy are featured. She is able to get the other hospital workers to contribute donations, by saying: "people only give what they feel like giving . . . especially if they're not frightened by the guarantee of eternal damnation and the fiery abyss of hell, their flesh seething and boiling as they writhe under the weight of their everlasting sins." She says this pleasantly, smiling. As she turns and enters the elevator, all of her co-workers throw coins at her. "Thank you," she says cheerfully as she bends to pick up the change.[23] The program was canceled after about ten episodes.

A more successful program was the CBS drama *Hack* (2002–4). The series centers on Mike Olshansky, a Philadelphia police officer who loses his badge after stealing money recovered during a drug bust. He now drives a taxi cab and makes amends for his prior ethical failures by helping passengers who are facing crises. In this way the series focuses on themes of sin, redemption and atonement. At times he explicitly uses these terms in conversations with his best friend from high school, a priest nicknamed "Grizz" (short for Grzelak). Although appearing only in the first season of *Hack,* Father Grizz is the brooding cab driver's confidant and moral conscience. Often shown in church doing small chores (such as placing hymnals in pews) and occasionally doing more important priestly duties (such as administering last rites, officiating a funeral, or hearing confessions), the hefty priest just as often meets his friend in more secular settings, particularly a local bar. Here Father Grizz reveals his own moral challenges, such as not being able to control his drinking and gambling.

Another challenge Father Grizz faces is his attraction to a high-school sweetheart, Beth. She re-enters his life when she comes to church seeking religious counseling about divorcing her husband. "Marriage is a sacrament," the priest tells her, "not a club you can resign from when it's not fun anymore."[24] Nonetheless, in subsequent episodes Beth works at the church school, and

---

22. Although the title makes it seem to be relevant for this study, NBC's *Father Murphy* (1981–2) actually was a western featuring a drifter who posed as a priest. As it did not feature an actual cleric, the program is not pertinent to this study.

23. "A Fistful of Savings." Written by Ellen L. Fogle; directed by John Whitesell. Series executive produced by Katherine Green. July 12, 1992. Reviewed at LOC.

24. "Forgive, But Don't Forget." Written by David Ehram; directed by Bobby Roth. Series executive produced by David Koepp, Thomas Carter and Gavin Polone. January 31, 2003. Reviewed off broadcast television.

she and Father Grizz have some near-romantic moments together. The Bishop ultimately summons Grizz to discuss his allowing a woman seeking a divorce to work at the parish school, and to confront him about his feelings for the woman. This leads Father Grizz to question his calling. Beth notes that just because they have feelings for each other they need not act on them, and that regardless of what the Bishop thinks, "The church needs people like you, Grizz."[25] Ultimately, Grizz decides to remain a priest but transfer to a parish in New Orleans, to where he is relocated by the series' second season.

Grizz's departure coincides with the arrival of Mike's new neighbor — an ex-nun turned parole officer, named Liz. A sassy, outspoken activist who works with a battered women's shelter, Liz becomes a potential romantic interest for Mike. Upon meeting her, Mike mentions he is divorced, to which Liz responds, "Yeah, me too, in a manner of speaking. I was a nun, bride of Christ." When Mike expresses dismay, Liz continues, saying she was a nun "devotedly, for five years, until I realized that I could love God and myself, and maybe someone else too."[26] In a later episode, Liz says she has faith in Mike, leading him to say, "Faith is for nuns," and Liz to retort, "No, orthopedic shoes are for nuns; faith is for everyone." "Is that why you left the convent? Didn't like the uniforms?" Mike quips. "That," Liz wryly says, "and the no sex thing."[27] While Liz's former vocation clearly invites sensationalism, her cloistered past remains unmentioned in many episodes. Nonetheless, Grizz as a religious leader and Liz as a former one assist Mike as he helps his troubled passengers, from runaway teenagers and gamblers to crime victims and witnesses.

These programs highlight church leaders whose aim is to demonstrate how the church can be relevant to an increasingly secular society, without featuring clerics in conflict with each other. While the programs mentioned above did not regularly and principally focus on clerics, others did. Notably, most of these programs — *Sarge*, *Hell Town*, *Sister Kate*, *Have Faith*, *Father Dowling Mysteries*, and *Nothing Sacred* — continue the focus on the Catholic Church. Another program, *Good News*, would focus on a Protestant church. Nonetheless, all of these programs depict a church focused on remaining significant in contemporary society, without, as their predecessors had, spotlighting internal ideological struggles.

Sarge

An early entry in the cluster of series focusing on the church's effort to remain pertinent in the world is the NBC drama *Sarge* (1971–2). In it, a former San Diego

---

25. "All Others Pay Cash." Written by David Ehrman; directed by Phil Sgriccia. April 18, 2003. Reviewed off broadcast television.

26. "See No Evil." Written by Eugenie Ross-Lemming and Brad Buckner; directed by Robert Singer. September 27, 2003. Reviewed off broadcast television; also available at LOC.

27. "Hidden Agenda." Written by David Ehrman; directed by Phil Sgriccia. October 4, 2003. Reviewed off broadcast television.

police sergeant leaves the force, joins the priesthood and serves St. Aloysius Church, the parish where he once was a member. Out of habit, parishioners still call him by his police title — hence, the program's name. Although large and husky, Father Samuel Cavanaugh, or "Sarge" (played by George Kennedy), could be soft-spoken, perceptive and tender.[28] Among his church staff are Kenji, the Buddhist rectory cook who is also a martial arts expert, and Valerie, the parish secretary whom Father Cavanaugh took in off the street. The urban environment, a standard setting for Catholic-set programs, allows Sarge to capitalize on his police skills as he serves his parish while also working with the police.

The two-hour pilot, titled "The Cross and the Badge," tells how Sarge comes to be a priest.[29] At a celebration honoring the sergeant, a man explains that 25 years before, they had both been preparing to become priests, when the attack on Pearl Harbor led Cavanaugh to leave the seminary and enlist in the marines. This choice led Cavanaugh down a different career path and, when the war was over, he joined the police. After the party, Cavanaugh's wife is killed by a car bomb intended for him. He tells his superiors that he is too angry to carry a gun or badge and that he is contemplating a vocation as a priest. Cavanaugh's priest friend is concerned that the sergeant's decision is based too much on the recent events but arranges a meeting with the Bishop. The Bishop is worried about how long it has been since Cavanaugh attended seminary, saying he is not prepared to enter the ministry without further training. The Sarge insists he *wants* to return to seminary, to prove he is fit for ministry. He ends his plea by declaring to the Bishop, "I've got hutzpah, Bishop, ask anybody;" when a nearby priest offers to explain the term to his superior, the Bishop reassures him, saying, "I'm familiar with the term, Father, this is an ecumenical age." Ultimately, Cavanaugh enters the seminary. After two years there, the Bishop asks Cavanaugh to take a parish assignment. He explains that the priest of an inner city parish has just passed away and, while he has appointed a monsignor as the new pastor, he is concerned that the new appointee needs a "knowledgeable assistant." Because the parish is his old church, where everyone knew him as a police officer, Cavanaugh is concerned and suggests they may know him too well: "I lived with them," Cavanaugh confides, "I got drunk with them." The Bishop, amused, smiles at Cavanaugh's confession, but still grants him an early graduation and appoints him to serve the needy parish.

Harkening back on past generational conflicts in church-set programs, Cavanaugh finds that the Monsignor, Father Terrence, is a much younger man than he; in fact, Sarge is old enough to be Father's father. Stuffy and reserved but committed and articulate, the young priest is a contrast to the older, experienced ex-cop. While Sarge is more personable and adept at interacting

---

28. The character is named Father "Swanson" in the pilot, but "Cavanaugh" in the series; to avoid confusion, the latter is used throughout this discussion.
29. "The Badge or the Cross." Written by Don M. Mankiewicz; directed Richard A. Colla. Series executive produced by David Levy. February 22, 1971. Reviewed at LOC.

with parishioners, Father Terrence's strong suit is administration. Sarge assures him that in the marines he had men under him who were much older than he and he expected them to respect his authority; Sarge promises his younger superior that he will not need a reminder of who is in charge. Nonetheless, the two experience friction throughout the episode, sometimes mild, at other times explosive. This tension begins when Father Cavanaugh spots a young woman with a baby on the street, invites her to the parish and offers her room and board in exchange for secretarial service. The Monsignor is concerned that they know nothing of this woman, not even if she is married or the child is hers; Sarge notes they may get the chance to find out, and in the meantime will benefit from her help in the office, if the Monsignor will agree to the arrangement. Similarly, the youth of the parish ask Sarge to convince the Monsignor to allow them to hold a contemporary folk music service. He does so somewhat cautiously, telling Terrence it could be "beautiful or a mess" but that at least it would get the youth involved. Father Cavanaugh later hears the young people practicing rock music and warns them that that was not part of their agreement, and they grudgingly stick to playing folk songs. Sarge also helps other parishioners with problems such as gambling and estrangement from family, while his younger superior runs the parish office.

Ultimately, the plot centers on Sarge's efforts to help the police uncover who murdered his wife in the failed attempt to kill him, and why; it also highlights interactions with the young Monsignor. The trail leads Cavanaugh to a police superintendent who is worried about Sarge's interest in an old case and fears Cavanaugh might discover that he accepted a bribe from a criminal in order not to prosecute him. Cavanaugh puts the pieces together and realizes that the superintendent hired someone to plant the bomb in his car, causing his wife's death. As Father Cavanaugh leaves the parish to confront him, he bumps into Father Terrence. The Monsignor recognizes his colleague's distress and asks how he can help. Cavanaugh resists but Father Terrence persists, leading Sarge to ask what book he should look in (alluding to the Bible's inadequacy) for advice on what to do when a priest has the urge to kill. The Monsignor explains that priests are still men who feel "love, passion, lust, rage, even hatred," but that as priests they must learn to control these urges "by using the intellect that God gave us when He made us men." Sarge notes that is hard to do, to which the Monsignor responds, "I believe that every priest sometime or other in his life thinks he's been nailed to a cross; how he reacts to that tells us what kind of priest he is because if he can't handle it then maybe he shouldn't be a priest at all." Nonetheless, Father Cavanaugh goes off, wearing his clerical collar, to confront the man who killed his wife. When he does, the murderer pulls a gun on him, leading to a scuffle. The priest hits the dirty cop, and is about to do it again when he stops and yells "God forgive me!" He picks up the gun and, instead of pointing it at the criminal, throws it to him, explaining, "I'm a priest . . . that's what I am." Cavanaugh invites his former boss to reflect on who *he* is and whether he personally can kill another man. The superintendent walks off, ostensibly to be arrested or turn himself in later. Back at the church, the Monsignor greets the Sarge with words that relate both to his excursion and crisis of vocation, saying "Welcome home, Father."

While the continuing presence of the Monsignor might have added ongoing conflicts with a superior (similar to other church-set TV programs), this character was eliminated from the series, and Father Cavanaugh was left to serve the parish as its sole priest, thus emphasizing the trend of the era — programs focused on depicting the church as an institution striving to remain relevant, apart from internal struggles. As such, opportunities for the Irish-American priest to demonstrate his selfless heroism abound, TV here tapping into a long history of film depictions up to this time of upright Irish-American Catholics' "toughness" and "moral rectitude" — many of these in movies with religious settings.[30] Indeed, the series also taps into a trend in Catholic-set crime movies, wherein "priests were to become major heroic figures," working side-by-side with law enforcement and "other agents of morality" to fight crimes against the "American way," appearing as a "Super-padre" who wields his religion and morality as undefeatable weapons.[31] The fact that *Sarge*'s Father Cavanaugh is both priest and (former) police officer allows him to straddle the two worlds seamlessly, in a single embodiment, and reconcile tensions between religious and civil law.

Some episodes featured situations arising from Father Cavanaugh's church duties, while others took place almost entirely in police headquarters or on the "beat," away from the parish. Indeed, in one episode the Bishop makes a remark about the priest's divided loyalties, when Father Cavanaugh investigates the intentions of a possibly drugged donor who leaves thousands of dollars in the church's collection bin and is then shot and killed outside. The Bishop visits the parish (remarking it is no problem to do so when that kind of money is involved) and instructs Cavanaugh to determine if it was a "well-meant gift" and, if so, what to do with the money. The Bishop observes, "I shouldn't think that would be too difficult for the only priest in this diocese who seems to divide his time between the rectory and the police station," and that he should have no trouble uncovering relevant facts, given his "peculiar talents." By episode's end Cavanaugh discovers that the man had a guilty conscience for having been involved years before in making a pornographic film, and an overdose of medication led him to make the large donation. Since the underground porn film involved a well-known actress and an up-and-coming politician, he was killed to make sure he did not reveal those details in public. Ultimately, Sarge hands the money over to the police lieutenant, who asks what he should do with it since all involved have confessed and evidence is not necessary; Sarge suggests he

---

30. Colleen McDannell (ed.) (2008), *Catholics in the Movies*. New York: Oxford University Press, p. 230. Notably, this depiction of Irish Americans in film would change in coming years, when they would be portrayed as "corrupt and racist" (p. 232).

31. Les Keyser and Barbara Keyser (1984), *Hollywood and the Catholic Church: The Image of Roman Catholicism in American Movies*. Chicago: Loyola Press, p. 62.

donate the money to the church, whereupon the policeman hands the stack of money back to the priest — another example of creative fundraising on the part of television's church leaders.[32]

In most other episodes, the church setting provides a jumping-off point for investigative activities outside the parish. For example, Father Cavanaugh counsels an engaged couple, only to discover that the man is hiding a secret — that he believes he killed a woman years before. The priest uses his police contacts to dig up evidence that at first seems to support this conclusion, leading the would-be wife to accuse him of having an "everlasting suspicious cop mind" and forcing her fiancé to confess to something he did not do. Over time, Cavanaugh uncovers evidence clearing the young man and identifying the real killer. In the end the couple is married, thanks to the priest's skills as a detective.[33] In another episode, Father Cavanaugh is visiting patients in a hospital when he bumps into a parishioner whom he learns is dying. He also discovers that this parishioner is seeking revenge on a man who years before humiliated him in front of his son. With the parishioner holding a gun on the man who disgraced him, Father Cavanaugh insists he be allowed to give the intended victim last rites; he then asks his friend if it is worthwhile to kill a man who has just been absolved of his sins, asking "Who'd be better off?" The sick man puts down his gun. Thus Cavanaugh manages to resolve the conflict.[34]

In another episode where the church provides little more than a backdrop, Father Cavanaugh gives last rites and presides over the funeral of a policeman killed in the line of duty, only to find an overly aggressive reporter harassing the cop's widow at the cemetery. Cavanaugh stops him from bothering the woman and suggests the reporter should focus on more positive stories, like an athletic program he and the police run for troubled youth. The resulting news story portrays the facility as enabling juvenile delinquents to meet and plan crimes. When the reporter is almost gunned down and one of the boys in the program is named as a suspect, the priest uses his connections and skills to uncover the fact that the reporter staged the attempt on his own life in an effort to gain ratings.[35] Once again, most of the story happens away from the church and draws more upon the Sarge's skills as a detective rather than as a cleric, trivializing the latter. Other episodes likewise treat his ecclesiastic training as inconsequential compared to his more sensational detective's experience, as the Sarge's unique background takes him places where he might not otherwise be able to go while also constructing him as the aforementioned tough, moral

---

32. "Psst! Wanna Buy a Dirty Picture?" Written by Howard Dimsdale; directed by Richard Donner. October 5, 1971. Reviewed at LOC.

33. "Ring Out, Ring In." Written by Edward DeBlasio; directed by Daniel Haller. September 28, 1971. Reviewed at LOC.

34. "A Terminal Case of Vengeance." Written by Joel Oliansky; directed by John M. Badham. September 21, 1971. Reviewed at LOC.

35. "John Michael O'Flaherty Presents the Eleven O'Clock War." Written by Robert Collins; directed by Seymour Robbie. November 2, 1971. Reviewed at LOC.

super-patriot. For example, the Bishop asks Cavanaugh to serve as an army chaplain and hear confessions of marines while the regular Catholic chaplain recovers from surgery. While on the base he meets a young marine sleeping in the chapel, whom he assumes is there to confess. When the man asks why he should confess, that he has done nothing wrong, Father Cavanaugh quips that his first customer of the day is a saint, to which the marine replies, "No sir, just a Baptist." Denominational differences aside, the priest becomes aware that the young soldier is being abused by a drill sergeant who is embarrassed that the man is a hillbilly, like him, and is displacing his self-hatred onto the soldier. When the young man disappears, Cavanaugh confronts the drill sergeant in the officers' club. He assures the drill sergeant, who offers to buy him a drink, that priests do drink, but only with friends, and he is no friend. The two wind up in a physical scuffle, for which the priest later apologizes. In the end, the priest discovers that the drill sergeant is holding the marine hostage and is staging an accidental death for the young man, when Father Cavanaugh steps in and thwarts the plan, saving the boy's life.[36] Few priestly skills are involved. In another episode, Cavanaugh, as both police chaplain and a former colleague, hears the unofficial confession of a detective who is having problems controlling stress on the job. Sarge uses his position to help the detective solve the case of a serial killer without allowing him to lose control and kill the criminal. The story takes place almost entirely outside of the church, Cavanaugh even telling his Bishop he is taking a few days off to help with the matter.[37]

One storyline plays upon Catholic church doctrine, as Father Cavanaugh goes to prison to visit a man he once arrested for assault, meeting him as a priest in the prison's rather stark chapel. The inmate is being released and his ex-wife has asked Sarge to convince him not to make trouble for her and her new husband. Trouble, however, is just what the man has in mind, as he returns to their former home and tries to act as if he and his ex-wife are still married, much to the chagrin of the woman's new husband. The episode is interesting in that the released inmate's refusal to accept his divorce highlights Cavanaugh's role as a leader of a church that does not recognize divorce. In fact, the former inmate confronts the priest with this fact, insisting that according to the church they are still married and Cavanaugh should not stand in the way of his efforts to assume his position in their household. "Oh no," the priest protests, "don't you give me that argument. You haven't been inside of a church in seven years, and you're the one who filed for divorce." Father Cavanaugh suggests the woman get an annulment. Ultimately, she decides to leave both of the men when Cavanaugh uncovers the fact that her new husband has tried to frame the old one for attempting to murder him, so he will be justified in killing the ex-husband

---

36. "The Combatants." Written by Walter Black; directed by Walter Doniger. November 30, 1971. Reviewed at LOC.

37. "A Push Over the Edge." Teleplay by David Levinson; story by Stanford Whitmore; directed by John M. Badham. October 26, 1971. Reviewed at LOC.

in self-defense.[38] His dual roles as former detective and religious counselor help him reveal the immorality of the men and advise the woman how to redeem herself from the situation (in orthodox fashion, no less).

On the whole, *Sarge* depicts a cleric who dutifully performs his priestly responsibilities — administering last rites, officiating funerals, visiting the sick in hospitals, marrying the betrothed and collecting donations on behalf of the church — while nonetheless de-emphasizing these duties in favor of the more exciting ones of a detective who solves murder mysteries, uncovers corruption and saves lives. Clearly, he is concerned with being effective in the modern world, more so than arguing with other ecclesiastics over the direction of the church. In fact, he seems neither decidedly liberal nor conservative, perhaps because the situations he faces are most often matters needing detective skills rather than ecclesiastic ones. While occasionally given to mild violence in pursuit of criminals or protecting himself, Father Cavanaugh seems a solemn, even-tempered man who uses wisdom and real-life experience to serve the somewhat sensational needs of his parishioners and community. This is in stark contrast to the next cleric to emerge on television who would serve the needs of an inner-city parish with skills garnered from real life. Not a former detective but an ex-con, and not exhibiting a careful balance between intellect and brute force but decidedly in favor of the latter, *Hell Town*'s Father Noah Hardstep would push the envelop far beyond Father Cavanaugh's depiction.

Hell Town

Of all the church-set programs to air on American broadcast television, *Hell Town* (1985) was the most sensational. Starring Robert Blake, best known for playing the tough, streetwise cop in the police drama *Baretta* (1975–8), *Hell Town* may best be described as Baretta-turned-cleric. Still playing a hardened do-gooder who confronts trouble, gets into fights and flirts with women, Blake is credited with having developed the idea for *Hell Town*, a series about a two-fisted priest and a cohort of streetwise nuns who do their best to meet the needs of the people of their East Los Angeles parish. Blake's character is a former convict turned priest called Father Noah "Hardstep" Rivers, so named because he began his life as an unwanted child left on a stoop in a rainstorm. Father Hardstep is surrounded by equally colorful characters.

Among his colleagues at the church are an order of nuns, including: Mother Maggie, the formidable, strong leader of the sisters who run the church's orphanage; Sister Indigo, a streetwise reformed prostitute; Sister Angel Cakes, a wet-behind-the-ears nun who recently arrived from DeMoines, Iowa, and holds a master's degree in psychology; and Sister Daisy, an innocent young nun who in one episode must confront the moral issues arising from being raped

---

38. "A Bad Case of Monogamy." Written by Robert van Scoyk; directed by Joel Oliansky. November 23, 1971. Reviewed at LOC.

and discovering she is pregnant. Rounding out Hardstep's circle of friends are a number of secular characters: Sam, an attorney who helps manage the legal affairs of Hardstep and his parish; One Ball, Hardstep's pool-playing sidekick; Crazy Horse, a rooftop dweller who is Hardstep's street informant; and Stump, an oversized simpleton whose brute size contrasts with his big heart and child-like acumen.

That *Hell Town*'s depiction of a priest would be colorful is apparent from the series' opening sequence, which begins with Father Hardstep declaring "Heavenly Father, let us go among 'em." The images that follow include Hardstep on the streets, in a pool hall, praying on his knees, preaching and drinking a beer in a bar while watching a stripper. The theme song itself is gritty and reminiscent of the theme for Baretta; as he did for the cop drama, Sammy Davis, Jr. sings the lyrics: "You can't keep us down, we're walking tall and proud, in Hell Town; Now don't come and strut your stuff, 'cause nobody's bad enough, and we're all hanging tough, in Hell Town; You can't keep us down." The opening makes it clear that this program would be concerned with this priest's struggle to be relevant to people's needs in the modern world. Given *Hell Town*'s urban setting, these needs include confronting gang violence, pornographers' exploitation of young women, and city politicians' indifference to the needs of inner-city kids.

Father Noah Hardstep is a committed religious leader who sees himself as God's champion fighting on behalf of the disadvantaged in Hell Town. His religious nature is established by his frequent prayers, sermons and Bible quotations. Father Hardstep performs traditional clerical duties for Hell Town's residents, from hearing confessions and performing marriages to giving last rites and leading funeral services. The pageantry of the church is also established by his wearing liturgical robes and clerical collars, blessing himself with holy water, tracing the sign of the cross and reciting traditional church prayers (such as the "Our Father") and psalms (such as the 23rd). His religious rhetoric is almost always geared towards the hardships faced by those in the inner city, such as in a sermon from one episode:

In Hell Town, we must take God with us every day and every night. It takes strength and courage just to live in Hell Town. It takes strength and courage to live six, eight, ten in a room through the heat and cold. It takes strength and courage to face your hungry children and not run away or not get a gun to feed them. That's why you are special and the people across town, they will never know your courage. The meek shall inherit the earth and you are truly God's children. God bless and keep each of you, and God bless Hell Town.

He occasionally misquotes scripture or misidentifies a text's chapter and verse, but Hardstep is at his most eloquent when encouraging or defending his parishioners. A rough-around-the-edges priest, he nonetheless is concerned with serving society's downtrodden, in his parish or on the streets.

Even so, Hardstep clearly is not a traditional man of the cloth, and is presented in as sensational a manner as possible. While Noah might sermonize about the virtues of the meek, his disposition often leads him to violence rather than turning the other cheek. For example, in "Hell Town Goes Bananas," two winos steal money from a bag lady who intended to donate her savings to the church as thanks for a miracle. A furious Father Hardstep directs One Ball that when they find the thieves, he should "drive them into me," and Noah lifts a clenched fist; when One Ball reminds him that the Lord says "vengeance is mine," Noah responds, "You remind me that when I've got my hands on 'em."[39] In "The People Versus Willy the Goat," Hardstep threatens an animal control agent sent to the church to recover a goat. Since the goat has helped draw a child out of withdrawal, this rouses Hardstep's displeasure, and he tells the agent, "Now we can tangle or we can not tangle, that's up to you, but when it's over you will get up off the ground and off this private property . . ."[40] Now and again he engages in fist fights, as when he helps rescue a kidnapped woman and then prays, "Oh Lord, forgive me for wackin' that guy around, and forgive me for enjoying this," as he kisses the woman he has just helped.

This illustrates another way in which Hardstep is nontraditional: his unrestrained expression of his sexual desires. While *Hell Town* was not the first program to explore the sexuality of celibate church leaders (recall the episode of *In the Beginning* that considered Sister Aggie's desires), and would not be the last, Father Hardstep's indulgences most often are gratuitous. He frequents a bar that features scantily clad women dancing for the male customers; Hardstep's smile reveals more than unconditional love. On one occasion, the bar's owner notices this and says, "Noah, you've still got a way of eyeing ladies," to which the priest responds, "Oh Brandy, the flesh is weak . . . especially today." Similarly in the pilot episode, Hardstep sees a dancer and offers an unusual prayer: "Heavenly Father, when I took my vows you promised me this feeling would go away. Well, it ain't. I'm gonna give you six more months. Then I'm going over the wall." More explicitly, Noah reveals his desires when he meets a woman helping illegal immigrants as part of the Sanctuary movement. This occurs in "The Last Kiss," which finds Hardstep on a beach in Mexico, passionately holding and kissing a woman, and wondering in a voice-over how he got there. In flashbacks, the episode traces their relationship and the efforts of the woman, Shelley, to help immigrants elude the authorities. At one point, Noah prays: "I'm feeling feelings I haven't felt in years. I don't know what to do with 'em. She's everything that I could ever love. I can't turn my back on your work — St. Dominic's, the orphanage, and the children. Father, I love Hell Town but I love her too and I don't know what to do. Please, get me out of this one. Show me the way." At

---

39. "Hell Town Goes Bananas" (Parts 1 and 2). Written by George F. McGough; directed by Don Medford. Series executive produced by Lyman P. Docker. October 2, 1985. Reviewed at LOC.

40. "Love and Four Corners." Written by Patt Shea and Harriett Weiss; directed by Joseph Manduke. November 20, 1985. Reviewed at LOC.

the episode's end, as the two are saying goodbye, Shelley notes with gratitude that God "gave us this little bit of time together and that has to be enough. Oh Noah, we had nothing really, but we had it all, didn't we?" Noah replies, "We sure did, pal. And we always will."[41] While never going so far as to show the couple being sexually intimate, the behavior that the episode does show is suggestive, inappropriate and scandalous.

Compared to earlier Catholic-set programs, in which ecclesiastic social service was rendered with more innocence, the characters of *Hell Town* are decidedly, even deliberately, excessive and crude. The clear virtues of TV's previous priests and nuns here give way to a gratuitously immoderate caricature, just as one-dimensional as their forebears, but now with a shocking portrayal replacing the sentimental. Despite his more reverential and pious moments, of which there are a few, the depiction of Hardstep most often is vulgar and iconoclastic. The grittiness of the setting is a welcome contrast to the glossiness of some earlier shows, and affords Hell Town's religious leaders opportunities to minister to people previously underserved by TV's clerics — gang members, winos, the homeless, battered women and rape victims. Yet, despite forging into daring new territory, the overtly sensational approach of the series made its portrayals crass.

The sensational images and themes of the series were apparent right from its pilot. In the opening of the two-hour premiere, a lone woman struts down an alley late at night. Up on a rooftop watching over the woman are Father Hardstep and Sister Indigo, the latter wearing a black leather skirt and blue blouse. Hardstep says to the sexually alluring sister, "I'll bet that when you took your final vows the world lost one helluva street hustler, didn't they?" Sister Indigo replies, "Yeah, well the street's loss is Saint Dominic's gain." Meanwhile, below in the alley a man appears and sells drugs to the woman. Father Hardstep offers a short "prayer": "Heavenly Father, let's go among 'em." With that, he climbs down a fire escape and attacks the drug dealer, throwing him to the ground and punching him. When the dealer gives in and tells the priest to just arrest him, Hardstep replies, "You hunk of garbage, I ain't no cop. I'm the priest down here in Hell Town and this is my turf. You ever come around here selling your garbage again, I'll tear your arms out." He takes the dealer's drug money and tells Sister Indigo to give it to Mother Maggie, saying it is a gift from a parishioner. Hardstep heads to a bar where the female employees dance about in short skirts as he plays pool and drinks a beer. Hence in its very first minute or so, the series depicts a priest who commits violence and expresses sexual interest, and a streetwise nun who uses her experience to help the priest protect the innocent from evildoers. With this, the premise of *Hell Town* is set: the series would focus in a sensationalized manner on inner-city ecclesiastics committed to serving society's downtrodden in as radical a manner as necessary.

As the pilot progresses, Hardstep helps a young girl who is being abused

---

41. "Hell Town Goes Bananas" (Parts 1 and 2).

by her father. When Crazy Horse sends word that he has heard the girl yelling, the priest breaks into an apartment, assaults the father, finds the girl locked in a closet and hides her away in the sewers to keep her safe from both the father and police, who are searching for the "kidnapped" child. Two moments are particularly noteworthy in terms of the representation of church leaders involved in a crisis. One comes when Hardstep prays for both the child *and* her father. Another involves the Mother Superior at St. Dominic's and a lieutenant who is searching for the little girl. The nun defends the church's right to defy unjust authorities with civil disobedience. The lieutenant instructs Mother Maggie that she should have more respect for the law, to which the nun replies: "Lieutenant, at one time the lessons of God and the rules of the court walked hand in hand. But through the years I've seen certain lawyers and certain politicians widen the gap between that bond. Now in certain cases, it's possible for a case of civil disobedience to be God's will." No longer working with police (as in *Going My Way* and *Sarge*), the ecclesiastics here are defiant of civic authority — and this would not be the last time. Eventually, the angry father searches for his daughter at St. Dominic's church during a worship service. Hardstep, in hiding with the girl, and knowing the father has brought a gun, creates a distraction to lure the armed man away from the congregation, where he successfully wrestles the gun away. The episode ends with Father Hardstep leading the congregation in prayer.

Throughout, the pilot labors to establish Hardstep's religious devotion and commitment to social justice, as well as his radical streetwise personality. In this light, Hardstep prays, blesses himself with holy water, traces the sign of the cross and shows a steadfast dedication to helping the needy. When a woman comes to the rectory and seeks help delivering her baby, Hardstep shows intercultural awareness by instructing the nuns that because the woman is American Indian, she needs her child to be born near water; he calms the woman by pouring some between two pans. Scenes in which Hardstep leaves or returns to the parish highlight the presence of the orphans and homeless who inhabit the church grounds and whom the priest protects. All of this would be unproblematic were it not for more sensational moments. Hardstep flirts with women, threatens men and authorities and freely engages in physical violence. He prays for wisdom to help those around him and for God's help winning a baseball bet, before he traces the sign of the cross and guzzles a beer. When a police officer tells Hardstep he does not like the way the priest uses his collar, Hardstep responds that he does not like the way the cop uses his badge, adding, "I guess we won't know who's right till they plant us and we meet the man upstairs." When Father Hardstep learns that one of the nuns went alone at night to pick up medicine for one of the orphans, he scolds her and tells her to take someone with her next time, to which she replies, "Father, I fear no evil, for the Lord walketh with me." The priest's response is typical: "Well, sometimes the Lord is busy. Take a bat wit'ya."

The boldness of the series could involve the subject of entire episodes. One noteworthy installment, "The One Called Daisy," is quite daring, for it deals in theological terms with abortion, a heated issue in American society.[42] The episode opens with Sister Daisy picking up medicine for a friend at a pharmacy late at night. As she leaves, a man rapes her at knifepoint. Afterwards, Daisy is concerned only that the medicine gets to the person who needs it. She goes to a hospital, where doctors give her medicine to prevent pregnancy and disease. Later, the nuns at St. Dominic's attend to her, and all pray to God in thanks for bringing Daisy back to them. All Daisy can do is say how sorry she is for what has happened to her.

The early part of the episode involves some frank dialogue, revealing the ecclesiastics' hardened experience and their grappling with Christian ideals. Addressing Daisy's hesitance to share with her news of the rape, Sister Indigo responds, "Do you think I was *born* in a convent? I have been around a couple of times. There's not much left that can shock me." More gritty is Father Hardstep's response to Daisy's confession that she is "so full of fear and hate," he responds, saying:

> I got a confession, Daisy. I hate too. A lot. It's hard to be the shepherd and not hate the wolf. That's what I am, I'm a shepherd here in Hell Town and the wolves are everywhere. Hard to remember that they're God's children. I'm supposed to love them because even a wolf has a soul, but I don't. I hate 'em. I hate the pimps and the drug dealers and the abusers and the rapists. I hate all those wolves that come to Hell Town to prey on my flock. So you see, we both have to ask the Father to help us not to hate the wolf. Oh, we have to put him away, we want to put the wolf away, so he can't eat the sheep, but we don't want to hate 'em cause the Father teaches us that's wrong. Hate just eats us up inside. So let's both of us get on our knees and ask the Father to be more like him. Heavenly Father, I pray that you're with me if I ever find this particular wolf.

Ultimately, they do catch the rapist and discover that he has also raped the daughter of one of St. Dominic's parishioners. Once the rapist is out on bail, Father Hardstep warns him that there are people out to punish him for what he has done. Rather than face his accusers, the rapist kills himself, and Father Hardstep prays over the body.

A bold plot twist is then revealed — Daisy is pregnant. The rest of the story focuses on her decision whether to have the child or an abortion. The opposing sides of the argument are voiced by Father Hardstep, who counsels Daisy to have the child, and a doctor at a clinic, who encourages her to consider an abortion. Daisy, much younger than these two, is confused and torn. Hardstep begins the dialogue with Daisy:

---

42. "The One Called Daisy." Written by Gerry Day; directed by Ernest Pintoff. November 13, 1985. Reviewed at LOC.

Hardstep: Daisy, it wasn't really that little baby's fault, was it?

Daisy: Is it really a baby? The people at the clinic, they said . . .

Hardstep: I don't care what the people at the clinic say. It is. It's a life, and to "terminate" is just a fancy word for killin', Daisy, for killin'.

Hardstep then shares with Daisy that six men raped him in prison. He relates this to Daisy's situation: "They say you gotta go to hell to find God. They sent me to hell and I found God! You see, Daisy, that's the miracle. I found God in hell, so I gotta believe that He knows what He's doin'. I don't understand it all, nobody does, but that's what faith is, isn't it?" Hardstep tells Daisy he believes God wants her to have the baby.

Arguing the opposing side is Daisy's doctor — a woman who tells her she can offer information about when something is and is not a fetus. At this moment, Father Hardstep shows up. A dialogue occurs between the priest and doctor, including a religious indictment of scientific progress on one side and a defense of clinical doctors as noble public servants on the other:

Hardstep: How about all the babies that don't get born every year, do you have compassion for them?

Doctor: Babies that are born or not are up to the women who are pregnant.

Hardstep: Alright, fine, we're never gonna agree on that, but we can both agree that we want what's best for Daisy.

Doctor: What's best for Daisy is not to go through nine months of pregnancy by a man she hates.

Hardstep: And what's your solution gonna do for her? Scrapin' out a womb is easy, but scrapin' out a memory for a lifetime!

Doctor: If you would've let me have her in the beginning it would be a lot easier on her now. But I'll fix that.

Hardstep: Oh you'll fix that! You scientists are always gonna fix things! Like you were gonna fix the world with DDT and almost destroyed us, and nuclear energy was gonna be the answer to all of our problems, and now we're buried in it. How can you be so sure of yourself when you make such big terrible mistakes?

Doctor: I am sure of what I'm doing. I have wanted to do this ever since I was a kid. I worked my tail off for my master's and doctorate. I could be making $300 an hour, but I'm not. I am here because I want to work with women like Daisy, and I am as sure of my opinion as you are of yours.

The polemics show them both believing their own tradition to be in the moral right and claiming to have Daisy's well-being as their primary concern.

Yet the argument is not confined to the doctor and Father Hardstep. It continues between Hardstep and Daisy in an exchange that is again noteworthy for its religious rhetoric:

Father Hardstep: Look Daisy, I'm not gonna throw God or the Bible or your vows at you, but I honestly believe from the bottom of my heart, Daisy, God as my judge, that I'm here to help you, and to help that little unborn child.

Daisy: Is it a soul, Father?

Father Hardstep: What if it is, Daisy? Are you ready to take the chance? If you are, I'll blow outa here right now.

Daisy: He was a monster, a murderer. What will I be bringing into this world?

Father Hardstep: Oh, you mean we're supposed to kill all the orphans at St. Dominic's because we don't know if their parents are murderers or not? Should I kill myself because I don't know what my parents were? Aw, Daisy, isn't a soul just as pure, no matter the parents?

Daisy: I've dedicated my whole life to the service of God and for the first time I don't even know what he wants from me.

Father Hardstep: Fair enough. We could sit here and argue what God wants and doesn't want till the cows come home, it doesn't make any difference. What matters is what's in your heart. There are Sisters in Ethiopia who are risking their lives to keep thousands of babies every day, just to keep 'em alive. If one of those sisters gets sick, a whole bunch of babies die. Aw heck, Daisy, all you gotta do is stay fat for seven or eight months to keep this baby alive.

Daisy: Father, they chose to go there.

Father Hardstep: And you chose to be a nun. Is it too much to ask of yourself that you stay uncomfortable for seven or eight months? You know that waiting list to adopt this baby is miles long, Daisy.

Although Father Hardstep's simplistic notion that the sacrifices of pregnancy (particularly one resulting from rape) are limited to being "fat" and "uncomfortable," Daisy's response is to tell the priest that she considers this a matter between God and herself. She thanks him for his help, and asks that he and the doctor leave the decision to her. The nun says goodbye and walks away.

Months later, Daisy calls Father Hardstep to tell him she is working at a soup kitchen and has decided she will have the child, after which she plans to return to St. Dominic's. Sister Daisy then shares her despair with Noah — that she wants to return to the parish and remain a nun, but also to keep her child. They discuss how those who have faith can do anything. Noah comes up with a plan. He arranges for a local couple to adopt the baby, so Daisy can stay a nun and still see her child. Months later, a baby is left at the church's steps. Sister Daisy picks up the child, exclaiming, "I can't imagine anyone giving up their baby," to which Hardstep coyly smiles, replying "me neither." Mother Maggie, reading between the lines, looks at Noah and says, "Clever, Hardstep, very clever," to which an innocent looking Hardstep responds, "Mother Maggie, you got a suspicious nature." Father Hardstep looks at Sister Daisy holding the baby — and winks.

The episode is careful to balance different responses to the young woman's situation. It avoids bias towards one perspective, presenting the cleric and doctor as both devoted to their point of view and to helping the woman facing a crisis. Here, the Catholic priest upholds orthodoxy on the issue and makes the case for the church's viewpoint; in this way the program errs on the side of conservatism. Other treatments of priests counseling a woman considering an abortion would emerge on later church-set TV programs (*Trinity* and *Nothing Sacred*), one following the orthodox perspective, the other taking a more progressive approach. The series' use of this hot-button issue to afford it a sense of relevance is noteworthy, yet mitigated by two factors: first, the need to sensationalize the story by focusing on a raped nun; and second, the outlandish ending, where the priest schemes to allow the nun to raise her own child, ensuring a happy ending which mollifies the impact of her decision to have the child but give it up for adoption.

Other episodes deal with similarly dramatic situations. In one *Romeo and Juliet/West Side Story*-inspired episode, two street gangs clash while a member of one gang falls in love with the sister of a member of the opposing gang. The imagery includes one gang massing for violence in front of graffiti paintings of Jesus and Mary. To stop the violence, Father Hardstep becomes involved in a scuffle and is later seen before Mass with a black eye and bandages. One might expect that a series focusing on rape and gang violence would be consistently serious and dramatic. This, however, was not the case. From episode to episode the tone of the series changed significantly, sometimes involving controversial topics and serious drama, while in others reducing itself to slapstick comedy. For example, the series' bumbling winos at times engage in overdone physical comedy, staggering around accompanied by Laurel and Hardy style music. This inconsistency of tone may be one reason for the program's downfall, together with its immoderacy. A *New York Times* critic concluded that while the program should be recognized for "exploring the decidedly less glamorous terrain of some of society's rejects — the junkies and pushers, the homeless and the mentally disturbed," it nonetheless fails in that, despite Blake's "determination and enthusiasm, he has reduced everything to the dimensions of a comic strip" whose main character is a "silly caricature."[43] One critic wryly concluded the show might be said to have created a new television genre, called "populist-existentialist-religio-dramatic sitcom."[44] For their part, church critics were not pleased with the series either, one saying it trivializes "the reality of the poor, and of those who work with the poor,"[45] another saying it "exploits and vulgarizes" the experience of those who suffer and the church

43. John J. O'Connor (1985), "TV reviews: Robert Blake as priest in *Hell Town* on NBC." *New York Times* March 6, C22.

44. Paul Buhle (1985), "The Gospel according to Robert Blake." *The Village Voice*, September 17, 33–5.

45. Mary Jo Leddy (1985), "Enough!" *Catholic New Times* (Toronto), 9, October 13, 7.

leaders who would help them.[46] In the end, *Hell Town* ran for only one season, ending in December 1985. For its excesses in depicting religious leaders, it is remembered as a landmark in American popular television. Clearly sensational in approach and relegated to a one-season run, the program nonetheless focused on the church's struggle to remain relevant, to help solve problems of the contemporary world.

Sister Kate

Just as firm as Father Noah Hardstep but less extreme was a later church character to appear on television — Sister Kate. An NBC program named for its featured ecclesiastic, *Sister Kate* (1989–90) starred Stephanie Beacham as a dry-witted nun whose stoic exterior masks her caring heart. Sister Kate serves as caretaker of an orphanage where seven semi-delinquent youngsters regularly test her authority and patience. The children have scared off her predecessors, all of whom were priests, but the orphans soon discover that the cynical and stern, yet wise and dedicated Sister Kate is not as easy to intimidate. Meeting the children of Redemption House in the pilot episode, Sister Kate concisely reveals her disposition (and backstory) in her introductory remarks to the orphans:

> Twenty-four hours ago I was supervising an archaeological dig on the banks of the Tigris River, sifting through the remnants of ancient skeletons — which is my preferred way of dealing with people. But then the church, in its infinite wisdom, decided to send me here — to sift through your bones instead . . . From what I've heard, you people have the reputation for being recalcitrant, unrepentant, nasty and somewhat deranged. (Smiling.)
>
> Well, so do I. Which means we should all get along just fine.

This middle-aged, crusty nun presents quite a contrast to the young, perky Sister Bertrille, who gleefully sang and played guitar for her kindergarten class. Sister Kate makes this clear in a discussion with the youngest two orphans, who are African-American, declaring she will not tolerate stereotypes — especially about nuns:

> Violet: Are you really a nun?
> Sister Kate: Yes child.
> Neville: So where's your guitar?
> Sister Kate: I don't know. Where are your tap shoes? You see Neville, we must learn not to think in terms of stereotypes. Just because a person is black doesn't mean to say he can tap dance, and just because a person

---

46. Michael Gallagher (1985), "*Hell Town* no tribute to inner-city Catholics." *Catholic New Times* (Toronto), 9, October 13, 7.

happens to be a nun, that doesn't mean she sings or plays guitar. (Pause.) Or, incidentally, likes children.[47]

No Sister Bertrille indeed.

Around Sister Kate is an assortment of orphans. The youngest is Violet, a pretty, pleasant little girl desperate to be adopted. She is African-American, as is Neville, a mischievous Rastafarian-styled little boy who fakes a Jamaican accent to hide his true origins in Jamaica, New York. The next oldest are Eugene, an aspiring juvenile delinquent who reads gun and ammunition magazines and enjoys getting into trouble, and Hilary, a wheelchair-bound girl who is rather bitter, given her slim prospects for adoption. The older children include April, a blonde and busty but ditsy 16-year-old, and Freddy, a quick-witted, tough working-class girl. Finally there is Todd, a simple-minded but pleasant young man whose good looks make him the target of would-be foster mothers' flirtations. Later in the series a cute but mischievous little boy named Buster joins the clan and becomes the youngest orphan under Sister Kate's care, the only one too young for school, and hence prone to irritate the nun while the other children are away.

The pilot makes it clear that the series' humor would be more adult and edgy than that of earlier church-set series. Seizing the chance to bribe Mr. Underwood, the director of the orphanage who has fallen asleep on the couch, Eugene snaps Polaroid pictures while the two oldest girls, clad in nightgowns, pose in compromising positions with the man. That edgy comedy runs through the initial episode and peaks near the end, when Sister Kate finds April with a wealthy boy who has lured her to a shed at his parents' country club. The boy's intentions become clear as he speaks of girls he has invited there to kiss, and then releases the spring on a portable bed, which quickly falls open. As April becomes aware of her compromised position, the door opens with a bolt of lightning and Sister Kate enters in her habit, holding a golf club. "What are you doing here?" the young man inquires, to which the nun matter-of-factly replies, "I've come to hit some balls." The young man, looking surprised and worried, rushes out.

The remainder of this scene highlights Sister Kate's dry wit, reserved affection and insightful guidance. As April sobs, Sister Kate shows characteristic self-interest, tenderly saying "There, there, don't cry," a nice sentiment, until she adds, "it gets on Sister Katherine's nerves." She suggests that April should not be so concerned with what one young boy ("who's probably an Episcopalian") thinks of orphans, inviting her to imagine the stereotypes Sister Kate endures as a nun, and detailing these. When April asks what all that has to do with her, Sister Kate responds, "Nothing, dear, but I feel better." Afterwards, she shows

---

47. "Pilot." Written by Frank Dungan, Jeff Stein and Tony Sheehan; directed by Noam Pitlik. Series executive produced by Frank Dungan, Jeff Stein and Tony Sheehan. September 16, 1989. Reviewed off broadcast television; also available at UCLA.

tenderness and wisdom when offering theological insight to her young charge: "April, I don't know if God actually has a plan for everything or if he just wings it. But I do know he tends to even things out. He may make a young man rich but also an insensitive jerk, and he may make someone else an orphan but give her a beautiful smile and a resilient heart . . ." Tender enough, yet lest we forget Sister Kate's cynicism, it is followed by a contrasting moment: April thanks her, says she feels as if now she has a real mom, and hugs Sister Kate, as the straight-faced nun stands emotionless. When the girl leaves, Sister Kate looks up at the heavens and sarcastically remarks, "Thank you!" In this and other episodes, *Sister Kate* depicts a representative of the church who is concerned with remaining relevant to the problems people face in the modern world. Notably, her manner breaks stereotypes of the cheery, inoffensive comic nuns audiences met on earlier TV programs.

Even so, some parallels exist between *Sister Kate* and *The Flying Nun*. One concerns the interest in money making for the church. Whereas *The Flying Nun* featured Sister Bertrille's zany schemes to sell goods and services, in *Sister Kate* the fiscal focus emerged mainly in an episode titled "Bingo."[48] Here, Father Delaney stops by the orphanage to discuss a problem he faces and how Sister Kate may help. The local church is being fumigated and the diocese needs a building to use in the interim. "You want to hold Mass here?" Sister Kate says with pride and devotion. "Oh no, no, no, we've canceled all that," Father Delaney dismissively explains, "but we have to have a place where we can hold bingo!" Concerns over church finances come before those of its ritual life. Reluctant at first, Sister Kate is swayed when the priest offers to cut the orphanage in on the night's profits, promising her they will raise enough money to send the children to summer camp. Hence, the church uses the orphanage to raise money from bingo, and the orphanage profits as well. Sister Bertrille would be proud.

As in *The Flying Nun*, Sister Kate must deal with a young girl who prematurely and naively decides to be a nun. This happens when Todd begins to see a girl named Sharon, realizes that she knows a lot of guys and suspects she may be promiscuous. He seeks Sister Kate to ask if she can speak with the girl to encourage her to have more self-esteem. Sharon confesses to the nun that she sometimes feels lost. Sister Kate delicately assures the girl she has a lot more to offer the world ". . . than what you're presently giving it." The nun confides that she once felt similarly lost until she realized what she was waiting for, and that when she decided to become a nun she knew that was the right choice for her. Sharon misconstrues Sister Kate's intention. When Todd enters and asks how their talk is going, Sharon declares everything is wonderful — and blissfully announces she has decided to become a nun. She exits, leaving Sister Kate and Todd stunned and silent.

Later, the nun tries explaining the nature of calling to the young girl. Through

---

48. "Bingo." Written by Brenda Hampton-Cain and William C. Kenny; directed by Michael Zinberg. July 23, 1990. Reviewed off broadcast television.

unusual circumstances, the orphans are able to attend a drive-in movie in a limousine. There, in the back seat, Sister Kate has a heart-to-heart discussion with Sharon. "I know your intentions are good," the nun says, "but the decision to become a nun is not one to be made lightly. There's a good deal of sacrifice involved. Isn't that right Maurice," she remarks to the limo driver, as she ironically sips champagne from a crystal flute. Sharon proudly announces she has already started sacrificing by limiting her use of make-up and donating her spandex to the homeless. Tenderly, Sister Kate responds, "That's very commendable, dear, however the sisterhood is an internal calling. It comes from the heart, not the heat of the moment." She convinces the girl that her interest in the sisterhood seems motivated by boy trouble more than a sincere calling (similar to the advice Father O'Malley gave to a man considering the priesthood due to his problems with a fiancée). When Todd returns to the limousine, Sister Kate excuses herself, and Sharon reveals she has decided not to become a nun. Gesturing at the limo and champagne, she remarks, "I guess I'm just not cut out for all of this."[49] Thus the episode maintains its comic focus, while also commenting on the solemnity of the decision to take vows and become a nun.

Another similarity with *The Flying Nun* concerns the focus on caring for youngsters, although Sister Kate's hardened demeanor sets her apart from the pleasant nuns of the Convent San Tanco. Whereas Sister Bertrille was more flighty and hip, Sister Katherine embodies what MaryAnn Janosik, in her discussion of representations of nuns in film, calls the "Earth Mother Madonna": one who has a "no-nonsense personality" and a "traditional, maternal image" portraying "strictness and caring, distance and understanding."[50] Channeling the spirit of nuns played by Ingrid Bergman (*The Bells of St. Mary's*), Rosalind Russell (*The Trouble with Angels*) and Maggie Smith (*Sister Act*), Beacham's Sister Kate is a similar character. Moments of care for the children are tempered by less affectionate ones, such as when she refers to them as "you little heathens,"[51] or raises her hand to strike one who challenges her, saying, "I am not going to let you provoke me into breaking any of God's laws . . . or federal statutes."[52] She even feigns excitement at the prospect of staging an arson to close the orphanage.[53] In one episode, Sister Kate receives a letter from the diocese telling her she must return to her old assignment, conducting biblical archaeology in the Middle East. "Hey, have you been praying again?" one of the children quips to the nun, who assures the children she has no intention of leaving. Later, the children accidentally videotape Sister Kate on the phone

---

49. "Todd's Cheap Date." Written by Frank Dungan and Jeff Stein; directed by Jeff Melman. July 30, 1990. Reviewed at LOC.

50. MaryAnn Janosik (1997), "Madonnas in our midst: representations of women religious in Hollywood film." *U.S. Catholic Historian*, 15(3), 83.

51. "Todd's Cheap Date."

52. "Eugene's Secret." Written by Frank Dungan, Jeff Stein and Tony Sheehan; directed by Jeff Melman. September 24, 1989. Reviewed at UCLA.

53. "Underwood Underfoot." Written by Tony Sheehan; directed by Jeff Melman. September 1, 1990. Reviewed at LOC.

speaking to Mr. Underwood, telling him, "I have never failed in anything in my life and I'm not going to start now" and that she intends to tell the Bishop that she does not intend to leave the orphanage "until each of those annoying little wretches is gone." The orphans eventually confront her, accusing her of being more interested in her track record than helping them. She explains that she sincerely hopes to find them all proper homes, doing so by way of a videotaped message. It begins with her sitting at her desk, addressing the orphans by grumbling, "Hello, wretches," and admitting with some difficulty that she is sorry. She eventually shares the following admission:

> When I first came here, I admit that my aim was to get you scrubbed, sufficiently civilized and adopted, and that still is my aim. I want you out of this dreary institution and into proper homes, and maybe that is because I hate to fail. But if I succeed, I'll be missing something. I'll be losing your warmth, and the laughter, and yes, the love of the only real family I've ever known.

Changing tone, clearly unaccustomed to showing emotion, she adds, "There, I've said it." And then, taking her cue from the *Mission: Impossible* TV series, Sister Kate adds, "This tape will self destruct in five seconds." And it does.[54]

Notably, Sister Kate helps the children cope with issues Sister Bertrille never encountered, such as stealing, cheating, addiction and becoming sexually active. One example occurs when Sister Kate discovers Freddy is smoking and tries to help the teenager quit. Her efforts to convince Freddy to stop fail until she decides the girl may smoke all she wants, but that whenever she does the rest of the children will be forced to do household chores. "It's a little technique we nuns taught the Marine Corps," Sister Kate explains. "It's called: you light up, they clean up," to which Todd replies, "Of yeah, I remember seeing that in *Full Metal Habit*." Guilt-ridden and ready to concede, Freddy comes to the nun, tells her she wins, and pulls cigarettes out of every imaginable part of her body and clothing, placing them on Sister Kate's desk. Freddy tells Kate she has kicked everything else and will kick this habit too. Puzzled, Sister Kate asks what the 16-year-old means. Freddy explains that her mother was a "junkie" and that she was born addicted to drugs, and that over the years she overcame addictions to "pills, coke, grass and booze," and now she will overcome this one too — her last addiction. "I am sorry," the nun replies with sincere concern, "I really had no idea."[55]

Stoic to the end, Sister Kate helps the orphans deal with the challenges in their lives. In the end, her sarcasm matches the children's rebelliousness and

---

54. "Sweet Sixteen." Written by Frank Dugan and Jeff Stein; directed by Michael Zinberg. July 16, 1990. Reviewed off broadcast television.
55. "Freddy's Bad Habit." Written by Frank Dungan and Jeff Stein; directed by Jeff Melman. September 21, 1989. Reviewed at UCLA.

they achieve a symbiosis, all of the confrontations and verbal sparring masking mutual affection. Her kinship with the children may derive from her own past: she once confides that after her dad died she was raised by a stepfather who abused both her and her mother, until Kate whacked him with a rifle and warned him never to hit them again.[56]

The series attracted lukewarm ratings and lasted only one year, yet went into syndication for a period after its initial run. It is noteworthy for its focus on the efforts of a lone nun to remain relevant in the lives of orphans as she helped them face modern problems. Set not in a parish or convent but in a diocesan orphanage, the program's setting makes it unique among television programs focusing on ecclesiastics.

Have Faith

Parish life was the focus of a short-lived ABC program called *Have Faith* (1989), a sitcom about four priests who served a Chicago church, St. Catherine's. Notably, this was the first program on which the authority figure was a young liberal, and the challenges he faced included how to respond to the behavior of an older, traditional colleague.

The head of the parish is Monsignor "Mac" MacKenzie, a wacky young cleric who plays basketball in his office and plays outlandish practical jokes on the Bishop, such as stealing his cherished knight's armor. Two of the other priests, Fathers Gabe and Vincent, share Mac's sense of humor, joking around and saying grace with the words "Rub-a-dub, thanks for the grub . . . Yeah God!" The stick-in-the-mud is Father Edgar, an older conservative who bristles at his fellow clerics' antics and whose "traditional" methods cause concern among them. This is the central plot of the premiere episode in which Father Edgar, who is somewhat uninvolved with the goings-on at the parish, is excited to be given a job teaching history at the local Catholic school. His fellow clerics are shocked when they receive word that he hit a rowdy student on the knuckles with a ruler. Father Edgar is miffed when his actions draw fire, saying to Monsignor MacKenzie, "It's the way I've always solved these kinds of problems." To this Monsignor MacKenzie responds, "Edgar, it's not 1958. We don't punish children like that anymore." Mac removes Father Edgar from his teaching post and convinces the parents of the child not to sue if Edgar agrees to apologize. "No doubt," Edgar wryly notes, "you persuaded them to feel sorry for me, your doddering old priest who's lost touch with the world." Mac humorously responds, "Are you tapping my phone?" Their conflict, and Mac's attempts to help Edgar update his methods, ultimately lead to this exchange:

Father Edgar: It may come as a surprise to you, but I love this church.
Monsignor Mac: So do I. Maybe that's why I want this doddering old

---

56. "Eugene's Secret."

priest to get involved with the people it serves. They need you, Edgar. I need you.

Father Edgar proves his value in the next scene, delicately suggesting to a parishioner who claims to be possessed by a demon that sometimes lonesome people imagine others' presence. His insightful diagnosis, and tender way of suggesting it, demonstrate the contributions a seasoned priest may make to the parish. Mac later says to Edgar, "Maybe we'll have to try to meet somewhere in the middle," a comment that acknowledges a mutual respect between younger and older generations of clerics, despite differing methods.[57]

The parishioner who claims to be possessed touches on a trend in the series to highlight the miraculous, and nostalgically show how local priests can make a difference in people's lives. This tendency is somewhat unique in church-set series. In another episode focusing on the miraculous (called "The Window") a woman brings her bathroom window to the priests so they can see what she sees — that it miraculously glows every night by God's power — and thereby "vindicate" her claim. To offer pastoral care, Father Gabe stay ups and watches the window with her. When morning comes and the window has shown no illumination, Father Gabe wonders if the glow could be coming from headlights outside her window or some other natural cause. "Maybe it's a heavenly beacon of goodness, an everlasting hope from Almighty God," the parishioner counters, to which the priest jests, "That's right. Hit below the belt." Another day goes by and the two continue their vigil waiting for the window to glow. The woman thanks Gabe for being patient with her, whereupon Gabe offers the following nostalgic remark:

> Father Gabe: It's not important whether your window glows or not. What's really important is that you have faith in it.
> Woman: Oh my. I like that.
> Father Gabe: I've been practicing saying it all day.

Finally, while Mac — who has also had a crisis of faith that episode — wonders aloud whether the church has anything to offer people nowadays, an emergency light short-circuits, causing the church to go dark while it lights up. A beam of light falls on the bathroom window, beautifully illuminating it. All look on in awe at the glowing window and the "miraculous" coincidence that caused it to light, as the church secretary sarcastically responds to Mac, saying, "Yeah, I see what you mean." The parishioner's faith in the miracle is vindicated as the faith of the parish priests also is renewed.[58]

---

57. "The Teacher." Written by Nat Mauldin; directed by Noam Pitlik. Series executive produced by Nat Mauldin, Robert M. Myman and John Ritter. April 18, 1989. Reviewed at PCM and LOC.

58. "The Window." Written by Nat Mauldin; directed by Noam Pitlik. May 2, 1989. Reviewed

Somewhat unique among programs of its time, *Have Faith* centers on the traditional activities of parish priests. Some episodes focus on sermon preparation and the hearing of confessions, others on visiting the sick and administering last rites. The series weaves its priests' traditional duties into comic situations. A sermon preparation episode finds Father Gabe nervously preparing his first homily and working to make everything about the Mass perfect. He auditions altar boys and cantors to find just the right ones. All is going well, until he meets the lector for that Sunday and discovers he stutters. Gabe tries to find a way to conduct the Mass without the lector, while also not hurting the enthusiastic reader's feelings. Mac understands Gabe's concerns, and shares how at his own first sermon the lector spoke like Porky Pig but did a fine job until he said "Wevelations." He advises Gabe it is just as important to show "compassion and charity" to others. In the end, a more enlightened Gabe happily shares the pulpit with his stuttering lector.[59]

The inexperienced Father Gabe must also overcome his jitters about hearing confessions. To prepare, he shows Monsignor MacKenzie a stack of index cards with the names of sins written on the front and helpful comments to make for each sin written on the back. After proudly showing Mac the "Gs" (Guile, Garishness, Gluttony, Greed and Goaltending), the Monsignor agrees to give him a chance, but advises him not to rely on the cards. Mac also tries to share a story about his first time hearing confessions, but at some point stops himself (with comic effect) as he realizes he is bound to secrecy and cannot share the story with the novice after all. This same constriction nearly results in Father Gabe's undoing. He hears a man confess to arson, revealing he likes to watch buildings burn. Gabe, who has only heard but not seen the man, later realizes that one of the electricians working at his church is the confessor. He is frustrated that he cannot warn his fellow clerics. At one point, he asks Father Edgar what would happen if he revealed something said in the confessional, to which Edgar replies, ". . . you mean besides burning in hell for all eternity?" Gabe stays awake all night in the church to protect it from the arsonist, until a fire starts on a desk and Gabe is nearly driven to reveal the truth. He stops just short of doing so when the electrician himself breaks down, confesses it was him, and implores all for their forgiveness. Father Gabe embraces the crying man. Gabe asks if he is in trouble for almost revealing the man's confession, to which Monsignor Mac responds:

> You never breached his confidence, Gabe. In fact, you probably would have jumped in front of a truck to defend it. I'll tell you what you did do: you walked up to a sinner and took his hand, and that's what being a good priest is all about. You didn't need index cards, textbooks . . . That kind of wisdom comes from your gut.

---

at LOC.
    59. "Bingo." Written by Tony Sheehan; directed by Noam Pitlik. May 16, 1989. Reviewed at LOC.

In this way, *Have Faith* again uniquely highlights clerical duties while also maintaining a comic focus.

In the same episode, Mac himself administers pastoral care. A nursing home resident summons him, claiming he is near death and wants a priest to administer last rites. Racing to the home, Mac rushes through the ritual, asking the old man if he is sorry for having offended God in the sins of his past life and anointing him in the name of the Holy Trinity. Upon completion of the ritual, the man hops up, says he feels much better and asks why Regis Philbin is not on TV. In the days that follow, the old man summons Mac to the home time and again; he claims he felt "the big one" coming and had visions of Saint Peter, but seems more interested in playing chess or receiving the donuts Mac always brings when visiting. Mac recognizes the man is abusing the priest's obligation to come when called for last rites and suggests that if the old man is lonely he can simply call for a visit and Mac will come. On a subsequent call for last rites, Mac sends Edgar, quipping that a visit from the crusty old priest may stop the unnecessary calls. He realizes that this time the man was not crying wolf when Father Edgar returns to the parish with a full bag of uneaten donuts. Visiting the home, Mac tells the deceased man's roommate that he wishes he had come when called, only to be told by the roommate that the old man had a good "racket" going to produce an "instant priest," and calling Mac a chump. Realizing the man's mild hostility masks a need for companionship, Mac asks is he is okay, giving him the donuts intended for the roommate and sitting down to play chess with him. The man's manner changes slightly, as he is pleased to spend time with the priest.[60]

In addition to such sentimental moments, the series also manages to highlight more stereotypical portrayals of the church, already well established by previous church-set programs. Most prominent among these is the church's devotion to fundraising. In addition to the occasional mention of a bake sale, or concerns about how a rambunctious student's lawsuit might affect the church finances ("Lawyers! There go the bingo receipts!" one priest exclaims), *Have Faith* is yet another series in which an entire episode is devoted to bingo. Father Edgar tells Monsignor Mac that an unusually large number of people are in church for a Wednesday night; Mac assumes they are there for Mass, musing that the assembly represents a new trend of people less concerned with wealth and material things and more interested in the spiritual. "G-49!" Father Vincent yells as Mac enters the church to find that the assembly is playing bingo. When Mac inquires why Monday night bingo is being held on Wednesday, Father Vincent (the parish accountant) notes it was "so lucrative" that he had to do it twice a week. Concerned with his colleague's emphasis on fundraising, Mac discontinues bingo. In true sitcom fashion, the congregants' reaction is exaggerated and they riot outside the church, throwing eggs at the priests. Ultimately, mysterious

---

60. "Holy Smoke." Written by Nat Mauldin; directed by Noam Pitlik. April 25, 1989. Reviewed at LOC.

signs appear advertising the reinstatement of bingo night. Although no one is sure who has posted the signs, people gather on the announced night to play. Mac addresses them, explaining why he chose to cancel bingo:

> I just decided that bingo was becoming too big a part of our parish. It was overwhelming our real purpose here. Above all else, our church should be a place where you can come to pray, to give thanks, to be with your God.

The people at first quip that they thank God when they win, and pray for their numbers to be called, but then tell Mac that the real reason they crave bingo is their need for fellowship. Realizing they are sincere, Mac allows the weekly bingo gathering to continue. When he discovers his secretary posted the bingo signs because she knew the people needed friendship, the Monsignor gives her a raise.[61] So ends another nostalgic episode.

In another, the priests come to terms with the commercialization of religion. Focusing on Edgar's merciful patronage of a poor traveling religious paraphernalia salesman, the episode is rife with kitschy, tasteless religious items for sale: a Burning Bush wall thermometer; a Ten Commandments bun basket; a Peter and Paul spice rack; Last Supper napkin rings; a Battle of Jericho fly swatter; a Sermon on the Mount lint remover; a glow-in-the-dark Madonna. Though the salesman also tries to sell more useful or inventive products (such as Velcro hymnals that stick to the pews), Father Edgar ultimately protests the commercialization of religious items. Witnessing the onslaught of commercial items with "trite religious connotation," Father Gabe remarks, "This is getting too commercial, even for me!" Ultimately Father Edgar sends the salesman away, refusing to buy any more banal items and suggesting to the salesman that perhaps it is time to consider retirement. In this way the commercial television series takes a somewhat ironic stand against commercialization of religion.

Similar to other church-set programs, this episode also deals with the nature of a priest's calling and vocation, in yet another episode where an unsuitable candidate seeks a position in church leadership and must be persuaded not to. This happens when Rick Shepherd, Mac's roommate from the seminary who left the priesthood, comes to visit. Rick tells Mac tales of his secular life, which involves bar hopping, meeting women and traveling as an insurance salesman. All seems fine until Rick helps a woman light a candle for her dead husband. When she thanks him for his kindness and leaves, Rick walks into the empty, dark sanctuary, looks at the altar and begins to cry. He is overcome with regret for having left the priesthood. The following morning everyone is surprised when Rick comes to breakfast wearing a priest's collar. He explains that he plans to go to the chancery to tell them of his intent to return to service as a priest. That evening he tells Mac of his pride at having people greet him as "Father," how

---

61. "Bingo."

that salutation makes him feel good. Rick hands Mac a letter of intent, saying that although the Bishop suggests he should spend some time in a monastery before resuming priestly duties he may be placed directly in a parish if the Monsignor endorses his letter. Mac hesitates, questioning whether his friend should base his decision to return to service as a priest on merely the trappings of the job. They begin to argue. Mac reveals that he has always believed Rick is not cut out to be a priest and that others at the seminary knew this as well. "You never had the patience," Mac explains. "You never had the conviction, you were always expecting to get out whatever you put in." "What's wrong with that?" Rick queries. "Nothing," responds the Monsignor, "nothing, unless you wear that collar." Surprised, Rick complains that his friend should have told him this years before. He confides that he is jealous when visiting "perfect" families while selling insurance and that he would like a family. He admits his identity crisis, removes the collar and wonders what path he should follow. At the church door, Rick concedes to Mac, "You were right, you know. I never really was sure about it." He departs, whereupon the Monsignor opens the door and yells a confession to his friend: "Sometimes I'm not that sure myself!"[62]

This episode is a poignant example of a trend in church-set television programs to examine the vocational satisfaction and doubts of people in ordained ministry. Nonetheless, it also foregrounds one critique of this program's representation of people serving the church. Mac and Rick wrestle on the floor, imitate classic sitcom characters, steal the Bishop's armor, and stage mock arguments to play with those around them. Meanwhile, the other priests (save Father Edgar) are as goofy as their leader. In this way, the series engages in personality worship wherein the priests are valued as much for their wackiness as their devotion. Nonetheless, it tempers this over-the-top character adoration with touching moments, showing the impact of faith, dedication and pastoral care. That the superior, Monsignor Mac, is the young progressive, served by the older, traditional Father Edgar, occasions the first reversal of the usual schema begun years before on church-set television series. Choosing to highlight the effectiveness of the madcap priests, instead of the internal conflicts between Edgar and Mac (the subject of only one episode), the program continues the trend of church-set series to focus on the church's struggle for relevance in the modern world.

Father Dowling Mysteries

Yet another Catholic-set program of this era was a detective show, *Father Dowling Mysteries*. Based upon characters from Ralph McInery's Father Dowling novels, this hour-long mystery series aired from 1989 to 1991 — the first season on NBC, later seasons on ABC. With Tom Bosley in the title role, and Tracey Nelson as Sister Stephanie (or "Steve," for short), the program

---

62. "The Window."

chronicles the ecclesiastic duo's pursuit of Father Dowling's hobby — amateur sleuthing. Following the example of his role model, Sherlock Holmes, Frank Dowling involves himself in solving the many murders, thefts and other capers which seem to be drawn to his modest Chicago parish, St. Michael's Church. Playing Watson to his Holmes, the streetwise Sister Stephanie tags along, snooping around and otherwise helping Father Dowling solve these mysteries. Other regular characters working with the parish are housekeeper Marie, who serves up pot roasts and advice to the sleuthing twosome in the church rectory, and bishop's aid Father Phil Prestwick, who constantly pokes his nose around the parish at the most inopportune times, making himself something of a pest.

Often the opening images of individual episodes are rather sensational, particularly given that the series centers on a priest, a nun and their church; these include: a sequence involving a gunshot-wounded man hiding in the pews of St. Michael's; images of a woman with an investigator's identification card and a gun, changing from secular clothes into a nun's habit; close-ups of a call girl's body as she puts on fishnet stockings, lipstick, eye shadow, jewelry and a provocative dress; and a dream sequence in which a bride and groom stand at the altar in St. Michael's in the presence of Father Dowling and Sister Steve, whereupon the groom and sister suddenly turn into rough-looking men who rip off the bride's gown down to her underwear, push her onto a bed, and hover over her ready to attack. Balanced against these images are more traditional ones, of Dowling or Steve involved in choir practice, preparing the altar, hearing confessions or praying in pews. Indeed, the sensationalism arises in part from the rapid juxtaposition of these contrasting images.

Between Father Dowling and Sister Steve there is a hint of the older traditionalist, younger modernist relationship. Their rapport, however, is one in which each appreciates the other's strengths and uses these to serve the church — and solve crimes. While Father Dowling is traditional, reserved and several decades Steve's senior, he nonetheless relies upon, even enjoys the sister's company and progressive outlook. As for Sister Steve, she began her relationship with the priest when he caught her shoplifting as a 10-year-old girl. He took her under his wing, and she eventually became a nun. Nonetheless, her wrong-side-of-the-tracks skills and knowledge come in handy, as she is able to pick locks, engage in street talk with thugs and prostitutes, handle a car like a stunt driver and do odd jobs such as bartender and waitress (on roller skates) when she must remove her habit and go undercover. Just as interesting as what she wears and does while undercover is what she says in her effort to maintain her cover while also remaining truthful. The result: the nun becomes expert at making statements with double meanings. For example, while posing as a prostitute, she says to a man on whom she is spying "bet I could get you to paradise" and "the place I work out of is real special; just walking in the door, you're half way to heaven." When in the same episode a thug asks who her boss is she replies "Big Frank," and explains that he has "been responsible for a lot of funerals."[63] When she poses as a princess and is hounded by the press for statements on her taste in fashion, the undercover nun replies "I don't think you can go wrong with basic black."[64] Sister Steve's hipster skills are helpful in serving the parish as well: for example, she uses gambling scenarios to teach the parish's streetwise kids remedial math; and she races bikes with juvenile convicts assigned to the parish for community service so they will not become truant. She always speaks highly of religious life, telling others she could not be happier with her vocation. Her devotion also is reflected in her actions, as she regularly shows genuine concern for others.

Similarly, Father Dowling is shown performing priest's duties and serving the church. He and Steve visit houses around St. Michael's to introduce neighbors to the parish's many services, such as day care. He leads worship services, listens to parishioners in the confessional, and prepares sermons (which go unheard by the television viewers). When a man is shot and killed, Dowling gives him absolution and touches the man's forehead. Like Steve, he also says things while undercover to conceal his true identity. Occasionally, he uses the privileges of the collar to snoop around where he otherwise could not. Wearing his clerical collar, for example, he convinces a doorman to let him look around a suspect's apartment, the doorman commenting if he cannot trust a priest, who can he trust. When Dowling and Steve discover mob activity taking place at a winery, the priest distracts the owner by pretending to be purchasing bottles of sacramental wine, allowing Sister Stephanie to spy on the warehouse.[65] Speaking with parishioners or victims, he is sensitive and comforting, and even tries to convince convicts to leave their criminal ways. Nonetheless, Father Dowling's sleuthing duties sometimes take precedence over those of his parish; once he even leaves a wedding ceremony at which he is about to preside so he can race to a crime scene.[66] Alas, the preponderance of Father Dowling's and Sister Stephanie's activities are investigatory and take place outside of the parish. In fact, as the two run off from the rectory to explore a lead, Marie sarcastically comments, "Of course, why would I think even for a moment it might be church business?!"[67]

Of all the characters in the series, it is Father Phil Prestwick whose constant focus is on the church, albeit to a fault. The nerdy, nosy bishop's assistant is often more interested in self-advancement and serving the church hierarchy than he is in becoming involved in the lives of parishioners at the local level. When he

---

63. "The Mafia Priest Mystery" (Parts 1 and 2). Written by Robert Hamilton; directed by Charles S. Dubin. Series executive produced by Fred Silverman and Dean Hargrove. February 17 and 24, 1989. Reviewed at LOC.

64. "The Royal Mystery." Written by Gerry Conway; directed by Christopher Hibler. September 20, 1990. Reviewed at PCM.

65. "The Missing Body Mystery" (Parts 1 and 2). Written by Rob Gilmer; directed by Christopher Hibler. January 20, 1989. Reviewed at LOC.

66. "The Mafia Priest Mystery" (Parts 1 and 2).

67. "The What Do You Call a Call Girl Mystery." Written by Robert Hamilton; directed by Charles S. Dubin. January 27, 1989. Reviewed at LOC; also available at UCLA.

is first introduced in the series, the Bishop has requested that Father Prestwick spend time at Father Dowling's parish so the younger priest may be prepared to lead a parish of his own one day. Knowing the Bishop is displeased with the trouble and publicity Dowling's and Steve's outside activities bring, the sleuthing duo surmise that the parish Prestwick may one day take over is St. Michael's. The Bishop makes this explicit on a visit to the church, saying his plan is to send Father Dowling to serve a parish in Anchorage, Alaska. Father Prestwick's fixation on church finances, attendance and inventory, however, leads Dowling to erupt in anger at his younger counterpart, scolding him for not showing any interest in getting to know the members of the congregation: "All you're concerned about is the business of the church," he yells, continuing, "well, the business of the church is its congregation, and the sooner you learn that, the better you'll be able to serve them!" By the episode's end, a mix-up has Prestwick himself falling out of favor with the Bishop and being sent off to Alaska.[68] He returns later in the series, proclaiming (without seeming to understand the implications) that the Bishop in Alaska was "so impressed" with him that he sent him back to serve his original diocese. As the Bishop's private secretary, he coordinates diocesan events — a job constantly leading him to intrude on St. Michael's, where he most often annoys everyone with his insensitive remarks and meddling ways.

"The Visiting Priest Mystery" serves as a good introduction to the overall character of the series. It opens in a stockyard, where a shadowy figure is paying a hit man to shoot someone the next day. Later at St. Michael's, Sister Steve finds Marie in the kitchen preparing a meal for a visiting priest who has apparently charmed her; she explains he is passing through town on his way to a new assignment. Steve finds Father Dowling speaking with the priest, Father Damon, a man wearing a black suit and clerical collar. Lo and behold, it is the hit man himself. Dowling, at first unaware of his guest's true identity, offers to allow Father Damon to conduct that evening's Mass. After dinner, Sister Steve and Father Dowling share their suspicions that the visitor is not who he claims to be. Their suspicions peak during Mass, when as Steve and Damon are distributing communion at the altar one of their parishioners looks startled and afraid when he sees Damon. This older man follows Damon into an office after the service, says he recognizes him and intends to turn him in. The fake priest chokes the old man, who falls to the floor, ripping off Damon's crucifix. When Father Dowling walks in to find the man on the floor, Damon explains he must be having a stroke. Later, Steve, Dowling and Damon are with the man in the hospital, and Dowling and Steve bless him. When he awakes, he sees the fake priest, looks petrified and dies. The two real ecclesiastics see Damon speaking with a nurse later; when Steve asks her what they spoke about, the nurse says he wanted to know if the man said anything before he died.

At the church, the phony priest looks for the broken necklace and finds it just as Sister Stephanie enters the room. To avert suspicion, he says it is not

68. "The Missing Body Mystery" (Parts 1 and 2).

his and that it must have been the old man's. But Dowling later notices that the necklace is broken and looks like it was yanked. He decides to visit the late parishioner's granddaughter to return the necklace; she confirms that it is not her grandfather's. She also tells Dowling that her granddad had worked for a mobster before he found religion. Meanwhile, Sister Steve snaps a photo of the impostor and takes the picture to a hotel after finding bars of soap with that hotel's insignia in Damon's room. One by one she asks the hotel staff if they recognize the man. One does, and tells Steve where he is staying. Steve tries to use a hairpin to pick the lock, but when a housekeeper sees the nun at the door, she asks if she has lost her key and lets her in. (Throughout the series, the writers are careful about how Sister Steve gets past locked doors; often she claims to have found them unlocked, as she mischievously smiles and puts a pin back in her hair.) While Steve snoops inside the fake priest's room, Damon returns and the nun hides on the ledge outside the window — a dozen floors up. She peeks in as he undresses and spies a scar around his neck where the man pulled the necklace.

Father Dowling and Sister Steve later follow Damon, who is now wearing secular attire. When he goes into a pornographic movie house, Steve — wearing her habit — goes right up to the ticket booth and asks for two tickets. Father Dowling, wearing his clerical collar, notes they cannot possibly go in there, but Steve convinces him that the impostor must have come there for a reason. "This better be worth it," Dowling says, to which a smiling Sister Stephanie retorts, "I read a couple of good reviews." When they walk inside, Dowling sees what is on the screen and immediately covers the sister's eyes. They hide behind a curtain and observe their suspect receiving a gun from a man sitting next to him. The streetwise Sister observes it must be "cold," a gun with the serial number removed, and must be intended for a "hit." Putting this together with what the parishioner's granddaughter told him, Dowling figures the hit will be the mobster and goes to warn him.

At the retired mobster's mansion, the crime boss thinks Dowling is collecting donations. Dowling explains he is there for another reason, but will happily accept a check. He remarks that he believes the gangster's life is in danger and, while not approving of his criminal past, does not wish to see him killed. Dowling spots the hit man coming up the walkway and anxiously warns the boss to take cover, until Damon walks in to reveal the two men not only know each other but that the mobster has hired the hit man. The boss explains to Dowling that a man who betrayed him and is now in the witness protection program has a daughter who is to be married at St. Michael's. He has hired the hit man to pose as a priest and shoot the traitor during the service. Damon then leaves to head for St. Michael's. With Sister Steve's help, Dowling manages to escape from the mobsters, and Dowling tells her they must hurry to get to the church. Meanwhile at St. Michael's, Father Damon lies to Father Prestwick, saying Dowling asked him to ask Prestwick to conduct the ceremony. The scene cuts back and forth between the priest and nun, racing through the streets of Chicago in the parish wagon, and the church, where agents are guarding the front door while others escort the informant inside. When the organ begins to play the bride's entrance, the robed hit man, standing at the altar, reaches for his gun. When no bride appears, the organist begins again. This time the doors open and a veiled bride enters with her informant father, the two of them arm in arm. As they get closer to the altar, the hit man pulls the gun from under his robe. Just then, the bride throws off her veil. It is Dowling's friend Sergeant Clancy, who draws her own gun and fires at the hit man on the altar, shooting him in the shoulder. He falls, blood seeping through his robe. "Nice shooting, Clancy!" Father Dowling compliments his friend, who responds, "Nice timing, Father," referring to his apparently opportune arrival at the church.[69]

This episode illustrates a number of trends in the series: Sister Stephanie's street smarts and dedication to helping Dowling, even to the point of putting her life on the line; Dowling's powers of deduction; the stunt car driving opportunities that thrill the nun and frighten the Father; the clerical humor throughout, such as having Dowling and Steve enter a house of porn; Steve's and Dowling's occasional work on behalf of the church, such as pursuing donations from a mobster; sensational imagery, such as the bridal-gown-wearing detective shooting the liturgical robe-wearing hit man during a wedding ceremony, the hit man's bloody body falling onto the altar; and quite a number of episodes that involve Dowling and Steve interacting with Mafia families, the series capitalizing on its Chicago setting — a notorious mob city. This last point is illustrated by a two-part episode, titled "The Mafia Priest Mystery," in which a young, gentle priest is sent to train at St. Michael's. His Mafia family sets him up to take the blame for a murder he did not commit, and Dowling and Steve must work to prove his innocence.[70] Still another episode finds a mobster trying to protect his daughter from a plot to kidnap her and hold her for ransom. His daughter happens to be a postulant, who reconsiders becoming a nun because she fears her father's lifestyle makes her unworthy. She seeks the counsel of Sister Stephanie, whom she knows is from a similarly colorful background. Steve, Dowling and the postulant, Vicki, discuss the nature of calling:

> Vicki: From the time I was a little girl I wanted to be a nun. But my father was a crook, a very bad man. How could I be a nun?
>
> Father Dowling: That feeling you had was God calling you. You see, we don't go after Him, He comes after us . . .
>
> Sister Stephanie: God doesn't care who our fathers are or what kind of bad stuff they've done. I mean, I should know, my family was no picnic, believe me. It's kind of like I got an invitation. I don't know why, but I'm glad, I'm really glad. So now He's invited you. You gonna turn Him down?

---

69. "The Visiting Priest Mystery." Written by David Hoffman and Leslie Daryl Zerg; directed by Christopher Hibler. January 4, 1990. Reviewed at PCM.
70. "The Mafia Priest Mystery" (Parts 1 and 2).

Vicki says no, she will not turn down God's call. She asks Stephanie to "pray for me, Sister," to which Steve responds "and you pray for me, Sister." And the two hug.[71]

The correlation of religion, ethnic heritage and crime in the Father Dowling series channels a similar juxtaposition in a number of Italian Mafia-focused films, most notably Francis Ford Coppola's *Godfather* series. The traditions of the Catholic Church intersect with those of Italian-Americans, the church setting providing an expedient visual context within which to relate the mobsters' activities to their ethnic heritage.[72] The convenience of this correlation is regularly capitalized upon in the Father Dowling TV series, particularly given its setting in the archetypal mob town of Chicago. Using the pageantry of church ceremony to hide criminal activity, the Mafiosos corrupt ritual. Against this backdrop, Father Dowling and Sister Steve are able to fight not only for justice (embodying the aforementioned prototype of the American "Super padre"), but also against the defilement of sacred rites, as in the wedding discussed above, and the Jubilee Mass discussed below; this might seem admirable, were it not for the fact that the series seems so eager to set criminal activity within ritual settings, exploiting the juxtaposition for sensational purposes.

Indeed, "The Undercover Nun Mystery" involves not only the mob and sensational imagery but also a glance at Sister Stephanie's life as a postulant, as she returns to Holy Mother Convent to celebrate the Silver Jubilee of Mother Superior Margaret. This episode is also noteworthy for comparison with Sister Bertrille and Mother Superior Placido of *The Flying Nun* as here another young, progressive nun is paired with a stern, older, traditional Mother Superior. Speaking to Father Dowling about her mischievous ways at the convent and the penance she was given, Steve recalls, "When I was a postulant I must have scrubbed about 500 miles of linoleum." Dowling is also a confidant of the Reverend Mother's, who compliments him on his patience with Steve, adding, "she believes rules were made to be broken; she is a real test of patience." Early in the episode, Steve visits the Reverend Mother in her office. Sister Stephanie kneels by Mother Margaret's side next to her desk, and the Mother Superior welcomes the younger nun, tracing the sign of the cross on her forehead and offering Steve her blessing. At first pleasant but distant, the Reverend Mother quickly loses patience with Steve when the young nun pursues a matter too far, sternly declaring, "the subject is closed!" To regain her poise, the Reverend Mother then speaks more tenderly to Steve: "You have a problem with obedience, Sister, but it's my fault. I have failed you." This leads Steve to object, saying, "No, no, you did your best. It's me. I'm stubborn." Although the differences between the two do lead to tension, the pair nonetheless seems to appreciate how the other challenges her and helps her grow.

---

71. "The Substitute Sister Mystery." Teleplay by Gerry Conway; story by Gerry Conway and Brian Clemens; directed by Charles S. Dubin. January 10, 1991. Reviewed at LOC.
72. McDannell 2008, pp. 184–5.

Later in the episode, Steve notices that a visiting nun has a gun strapped in an ankle holster under her habit and surmises that the visitor is an undercover policewoman. Steve privately lets her know she is aware of her identity and warns her to keep her habit pulled over her ankles. When the fake nun is stabbed to death in her sleep, Steve and Dowling are on the case. In the end, Dowling and Steve realize that the Mother Superior's celebration is involved in a plot to smuggle an on-the-run crime boss out of the country. They deduce he is posing as one of several monks from Sardinia who are there to present the Reverend Mother with the one-millionth bottle of wine produced by the Brothers of St. Sebastian. His monk's disguise, Dowling realizes, will allow him to flee the country after the Jubilee Mass. As they speed to the convent to catch the gangster, the Jubilee Mass proceeds. The episode intercuts shots of their race to the ceremony (Sister Stephanie again at the wheel of the parish station wagon) with images of the ritual itself: a choir of nuns chanting responsively with a priest; the Reverend Mother kneeling before a statue of the Virgin Mary and lighting a candle; postulants proceeding in and offering roses to Mother Margaret; nuns singing "Ave Maria" as the Reverend Mother receives communion. The solemnity of the ritual is contrasted with the duo's race to the convent and what transpires when they arrive: When Dowling yells at the monks as they depart the head-shaven mob boss, realizing he is caught, pulls a gun from under his robe, aims it at Dowling and yells, "You're a dead man, Father!" Suddenly nuns all about the gardens draw guns from under their habits. They are undercover police officers, including Sergeant Clancy. In the end, the mystery is solved and the criminals are caught.

The final scene is between Sister Stephanie and Mother Margaret as they say goodbye outside of the convent. When Steve asks the Reverend Mother if there is anything she can do for her, Mother Margaret says, "Pray for me," leading Steve to note, "I do every day." "I might have known," says the Mother Superior as the two hug. Mother Margaret then confides: "I have many spiritual daughters who scrupulously follow the rules, but none whose heart is as charitable and loving as yours." Sister Stephanie thanks her, and the Reverend Mother marks the sign of the cross on Steve's forehead while offering her a blessing. She asks the younger nun to come visit her. Steve walks away and blows the Reverend Mother a kiss.[73] In the end, the episode is noteworthy for several things: for its solemn images of a Jubilee Mass, as much as for its interruption of this ritual with intercut images of the station wagon racing through Chicago's streets; for its depiction of the sometimes strained, ultimately warm and appreciative relationship between a younger, modern nun and her older, traditional Mother Superior; as another example of episodes focusing on Dowling's investigations into mob activity; and as an illustration of the series' use of sensational imagery.

---

73. "The Undercover Nun Mystery." Teleplay by Joyce Burditt; story by Dean Hargrove and Joyce Burditt; directed by James Frawley. November 1, 1990. Reviewed off broadcast television.

Several episodes focusing on the sexuality of the two principal characters also strive to maintain a balance between the sensational and reverential. In one, an old flame of Sister Steve's, Jack, turns up at the rectory. He is now divorced and Sister Steve reveals to Father Dowling that she once was going to marry the visitor. Not surprisingly, the man is involved in a murder, having witnessed a man shoot another. When Steve discovers that the killer knows Jack is at St. Michael's, she takes her friend to their old school grounds to hide him away. There they reminisce about their childhood together, prompting an exchange between the two where she recalls how she once had to choose between her calling to be a nun and her love for this man. They touch, get close and — with Sister Stephanie in her habit — exchange several kisses. Steve later confides these events and her feelings for Jack to Father Dowling while they sit in the church. She is concerned because she confesses she liked their closeness and wants more. "Sister," Dowling says tenderly, "we're taught that our faith really doesn't mean very much unless we're forced to test it." She notes that if that was a test she "flunked" it. She cries, not knowing what to do, and Dowling comforts her by telling her, "God is always there for you." Later, she tells Jack that her one-time decision was the hardest she ever had to make, and concludes she must stay a nun, saying, "the truth is, I have no choice." By the episode's end the killer is caught, another caper is solved, and Jack comes to St. Michael's to find Sister Stephanie praying at the altar. She notes "This is where I belong," and he kisses her on the cheek.[74] While other church-set programs (such as *In the Beginning*) explored the sexuality of nuns, sometimes sensationally (as in *Hell Town*), this is the first to show the startling image of a nun kissing a man. Even so, the sensationalism of that image is balanced with her solemn soul-searching, moral reasoning, and ultimate reaffirmation of her calling.

A similar crisis of calling and morality faces Father Dowling in "The Prodigal Son Mystery," when a young man comes to him in the confessional claiming to be his son. The man becomes upset that he broke a promise to his dead mother by revealing this secret. He mentions her name and runs out of the church. When Sister Steve later finds the priest ruminating in a pew, he reveals that the year before he entered seminary he fell in love and decided not to pursue ordination and instead to ask his girlfriend — whose name the man had mentioned — to marry him. She accepted his proposal and they spent a week away together. When they returned home, however, she reconsidered, saying Dowling had a "true vocation as a priest" and did not wish to come between him and his calling. Dowling says once he entered the seminary he realized she was right about him being suited for the priesthood. He avoided seeing her after that, and so would not know if their weekend together resulted in pregnancy, and ultimately a child — a possibility Dowling now accepts as fact. He realizes she never contacted him so he could continue to serve God in the priesthood without question. Over

---

74. "The Man Who Came to Dinner Mystery." Written by Diana Kopald Marcus; directed by Alan Cooke. February 10, 1989. Reviewed at LOC.

the course of the episode, Father Dowling is guilt ridden about being a priest with a son, and further that, unbeknown to him, he abandoned that son and the boy's mother. Sister Steve comforts the priest, saying, "You were forgiven for your affair a long time ago and since you didn't know that you had a son, you haven't committed any sin." "I know," Father Dowling replies, "but it feels like a sin." At that moment Father Prestwick enters. He has been grumbling about not being respected by the others. In a moment of unusual tenderness between the two, Father Dowling asks Father Prestwick to hear his confession. After the rite (unseen), Prestwick tells him to go in peace and makes the sign of the cross towards Dowling.[75] The episode ends, having explored issues of a priest's calling and celibacy together in one carefully balanced episode. Sensational and unusual, yet handled with tact and delicacy, the story is emblematic of the series' style.

Occasionally, the series would delve into spiritual matters in an imaginative way, as in an episode in which Sister Stephanie sells her soul to the devil in exchange for that of her brother. In "The Devil and the Deep Blue Sea Mystery," the devil is made manifest in the form of a mobster, but it does not take Father Dowling long to realize the man's true identity — that he is Satan himself. The climax finds Dowling transported to the underworld, where he pleads to a jury of gruesome murderers, assembled by Satan, to free Stephanie's soul. Noting "greater love hath no man than that he lay down his life for his brother," and that hers was "the ultimate act of love, the ultimate act of selfless charity, and one that should be rewarded, not punished," Dowling asks the panel if they would be in the place they are had someone selflessly been there to help them. His speech moves the jury and in the end Sister Stephanie's soul is returned to her. Thus, evil incarnate is defeated by Father Dowling's heartfelt, Bible-quoting oratory.[76] While this episode featured a spiritual struggle, most of the battles facing the nun and priest were decidedly more secular.

Overall, the series can be accused of capitalizing on its Catholic setting to present a sensational contrast to the provocative images and underworld activities depicted. Father Dowling and Sister Steve are more often outside the parish snooping around to solve a crime than they are serving the parish and its congregation. Nonetheless, the show maintains a reverential tone. Even the sensational storylines in *Father Dowling Mysteries* are less shocking than those of *Hell Town*, due to the careful balance the series provides with more solemn moments. Amid their investigations, criminal encounters and narrow escapes, Father Dowling and Sister Stephanie remain true to their beliefs. Unfortunately, the only character dedicated to the broader institutional church, Father Prestwick, is depicted as an immature, self-serving dimwit. Even so, the

---

75. "The Prodigal Son Mystery." Teleplay by Jack Burbitt; story by Dean Hargrove and Joyce Burditt; directed by James Frawley. January 31, 1991. Reviewed at LOC.
76. "The Devil and the Deep Blue Sea Mystery." Written by Dean Hargrave and Joyce Burditt; directed by Christopher Hibler. October 4, 1990. Reviewed at PCM.

older, more traditional priest and younger, progressive nun at the heart of Dowling Mysteries are clearly less concerned with any differences between them than they are with having an impact on the world around them — even if this is as often in the form of solving crimes as it is helping parishioners with problems.

Good News

Just over a decade after the highly successful *Amen* became the first church-set program to feature an African-American cast, *Good News* (1997–8) followed suit and enjoyed a short run on the emerging UPN network. Developed for MTM Productions in part by famed executive producer and writer Ed Weinberger (who also worked on *Amen*, *The Cosby Show* and *Taxi*), the series focused on the challenges facing the new acting pastor of a church in California — a handsome, single man-of-the-cloth who oversaw the congregation and its gospel choir. Assisting the young pastor was the church's feisty widowed cook and a cohort of youthful church members. The program in part highlighted the church's role in helping congregants face challenges in their modern lives — challenges ranging from gangs and sexually transmitted diseases, to issues involving homosexuality and racism. The program also prominently featured Gospel music performances by the series' church choir and various noteworthy guest stars.

The first episode introduces the two primary characters of the series — Reverend Randolph and Mrs. Dixon, the church's volunteer cook — as well as the series' focus on African-American issues and somewhat edgy storylines. Pastor David Randolph arrives at the Church of Life parish full of enthusiasm, only to be greeted by an unhappy assembly of church workers. They explain that the church's previous leader had suddenly declared he needed time off from his clerical duties and, much to the chagrin of his congregation, announced Pastor Randolph would serve as "acting pastor" instead of the congregation's own associate pastor. As a result, the displeased church staff greets the new "acting" pastor by announcing that they are quitting and intend to start a new congregation under their associate pastor, whom they note is a "righteous man of God if ever there was one, and a darn good fundraiser too." After they leave, Pastor Randolph is left with Vera, a rather flirtatious young church member who obviously is smitten with the handsome young pastor. Alone with her, the new pastor expresses his dismay:

> Pastor Randolph: I can't believe it. Is that all this job is about? Petty jealousies, popularity contests and money?
> Vera: Well, of course. You're our minister.
> Pastor Randolph: Vera, I became a minister so that when a troubled person comes through my door I will be ready, with God's help, to aid and comfort them.

From this moment it becomes clear that *Good News* will focus in part on Pastor Randolph's challenge to maintain his idealism when faced with the everyday practicalities of running a parish.

Later, a troubled young man named Eldridge speaks with the new pastor. He confides that he is gay and wants to bring his boyfriend to church with him. Randolph assures Eldridge he will do all he can to make the young man and his friend feel welcome. The young man then reveals that what he really needs help with is telling his secret to his mother — who turns out to be Mrs. Dixon. The next day, Mrs. Dixon comes to the pastor's office to find her son and the clergyman waiting for her. After Eldridge stutters a bit, the pastor advises him to "speak the truth, and the truth will set you free." Finally the young man announces that he is gay. Mrs. Dixon responds with amused annoyance, exclaiming "That's it!? That's what you drug me down here for? Boy, I knew that even before you did. I knew it when you was nine-years-old." As Mrs. Dixon makes herself ready to leave, the boy adds that he wants to bring his boyfriend to church. The mom approves and invites them both to pot roast afterwards. Eldridge adds there is more, surprising both Mrs. Dixon and Pastor Randolph with one last fact: his boyfriend is white.

Mrs. Dixon and Pastor Randolph sit down, in silence.

In a comic twist, the mother — who was fine with her son being gay — yells at her son for dating outside of their race: "What's the matter with you, boy? There aren't enough nice black men out there?" Thinking the pastor had more involvement than he let on, Mrs. Dixon blames Randolph for the problem and tells the boy he needs therapy. Pastor Randolph reminds Mrs. Dixon that "this is a house of God and everyone, regardless of color or creed, who comes here in good faith, I will not turn away." The cook warns the pastor that if her son's white boyfriend attends the service she will leave, assuring the pastor that the entire congregation will follow her. When Sunday arrives, the pastor begins the service by having Eldridge, a choir member, introduce his friend as a new member of the congregation. As Mrs. Dixon rises in anger, ready to leave, the pastor tells the congregants to turn to the people beside them and tell those people how good it is to have them in church. Mrs. Dixon and her son's boyfriend do so, the cook somewhat reluctantly. Pastor Randolph instructs the congrega-tion to tell those around them, "I love you like I love myself." Somewhat more comfortably, Mrs. Dixon and the boyfriend do so, while Gospel music plays in the background. Finally the pastor, yelling passionately, instructs everyone to hug their neighbor "in Jesus' name." Mrs. Dixon and the young man hug for a long time and she kisses him. Eldridge leaves the choir and hugs his mom, before all three of them hug each other. Finally, Eldridge shakes the pastor's hand.[77] Mission accomplished: the Dixon family will stay together, the congregation will

_____

77. "Pilot." Written by Ed Weinberger; directed by Ed Weinberger. Series executive produced by Ed Weinberger, Samm-Art Williams, Robi Reed-Holmes and Reuben Cannon. August 25, 1997. Reviewed at LOC.

not walk out, and the pastor has successfully fulfilled his charge to "aid and comfort" those who need it.

Notably, in subsequent episodes neither Eldridge nor his white boyfriend appear. The pilot's storyline was fine to establish the series' edginess and generate interest, but may have been too controversial to continue. As the series progresses, however, a handful of other characters are added to the cast: Little T, a high-spirited young church member, and his girlfriend, Cassie; Mona, the youth director, whose privileged background places her out of step with other congregants; and the church's new secretary, Venita. In fact, storylines centering around these last two characters exemplify one trend in the series — its focus on social issues, such as condom usage and the prevalence of street gangs, and the church's role in addressing them.

Venita is introduced in an episode about "safe sex," where the doctor of a local health center asks Pastor Randolph to distribute condoms in the church. Meeting with Randolph after a church service, the doctor makes his request after saying how impressed he is that in his sermon the minister proclaimed we "must not be indifferent to the problems of society." The pastor rejects the appeal, saying he believes "abstinence outside of marriage is the answer." Conceding that this is the best response, and how abstinence is 100 percent effective in stopping unwanted pregnancies and the spread of sexually transmitted diseases, the doctor nonetheless presses the cleric: "Do you realize how difficult it is for a young person with raging hormones to suppress his sexual urges?" After a long, silent stare from the pastor, Randolph replies, "Yes, yes, yes I do." The doctor discusses how many young people must deal with teenage pregnancy and STDs, including AIDS, and offers to send Randolph more information. The pastor agrees to read whatever information the doctor sends.

Newly hired as church secretary, and with a clear attraction to Pastor Randolph, Venita invites the minister to dinner, explaining that her parents used to belong to the church and she believes they will return if they met the impressive new pastor. When Mrs. Dixon hears about the new hire she is pleased, mentioning that when they were members her parents used to pay off an annual $25,000 note on behalf of the church, and that the church needs this money. She volunteers to cook for the gathering and invites them to dine at the parsonage. The event turns out to be a comic disaster when the pastor opens a box of condoms sent by the doctor just before the guests arrive, its contents spilling all over the place. Randolph and Little T frantically try to stuff the items everywhere to hide them from the wealthy former parishioners, who might get the wrong idea if they discover thousands of prophylactics scattered about the pastor's house. Throughout the evening, stray condoms turn up everywhere. Randolph and Little T desperately try to keep the guests from noticing them. By the evening's end they are partially successful, as the only one to discover the condoms is Venita, who quits her job and tells Pastor Randolph, "You preach one thing and practice another . . . and it looks like you get a lot of practice."

Venita and her parents come to church that Sunday to hear Pastor Randolph's sermon. The pastor, however, announces that instead of a sermon he wishes to share a story with the congregation and explains about the condoms and how he tried to hide them because their presence would be embarrassing — that "*condom* is supposed to be a dirty word." He continues:

> We're all embarrassed when we have to talk about teen pregnancies, AIDS and other sexually transmitted diseases. Now I'm not here to tell you, church, that I got the answers to all these problems. But what I am here to tell you is that we can not, and we will not hide from these problems one more day because these problems will not go away, and that we as a church must at least begin to face these problems. So maybe with God's help and a little bit of help from the good doctors as well, we together can face these problems, to make it a better world for our children and our children's children, and our children's children's children.

The congregation is excited and clapping, the choir begins to sing, and Mrs. Dixon (with a little attitude) hands Venita's father the collection basket, whereupon he reluctantly writes a check. Venita apologizes for the misunderstanding and asks for her job back. In the end, the episode is significant not only because it once again involves the ongoing focus of church-set programs on finances, but also highlights the church's relevance in responding to contemporary social problems.

Another example of this arises in an episode featuring Mona, the youth minister, who attempts to organize a dance at the church. When Mrs. Dixon catches wind of the upcoming event she voices her displeasure with the idea to Pastor Randolph, saying the "loud music" will "attract a bad element," to which Pastor Randolph retorts that that is just fine with him — that "it is the bad element that needs to be saved." Mrs. Dixon mockingly calls Randolph "Reverend Soul Train," and warns that she smells trouble. Mrs. Dixon's warning is well-founded. Unknowingly, Mona has invited members of rival gangs to the same dance. Unsuccessful in their attempts to get one or both gangs to skip the dance, the congregants ultimately find themselves playing host to both. Members of the gangs arrive wearing their gang colors, and confront each other as Mona naively tries to start the dance. Announcing that the hip-hop band could not make it that evening, she introduces their replacement: "The Hop Alongs," a country-western band with dancers. The dancers grab the gang members, getting them to do-si-do together. The gangsters enjoy themselves so much they eventually smile and hug each other. Mrs. Dixon enters with thugs to protect the church only to find matters well in hand. She and the pastor dance together and in the end bid fond farewell to the peaceful gang members. While the episode implausibly oversimplifies the problems of gang violence, it nonetheless exemplifies *Good News*' attempt to incorporate the church's response to contemporary issues, especially those facing African-American communities in urban settings.

Significantly, the appearance and focus of *Good News* had much to do with trends in television programming at the time and the practices of fledgling networks in development. When Fox challenged the absolute rule of the "big three" networks (ABC, CBS and NBC) in 1987, a pattern emerged whereby new networks would initially program for minorities to draw an audience and establish themselves, and then later "broaden" their programming, often abandoning "ethnic" shows.[78] Fox did this in 1994, canceling shows like *Rock*, *South Central* and *The Sinbad Show*, in favor of programs with "whiter appeal" such as *Beverly Hills 90210*, *Melrose Place* and *Party of Five*.[79] UPN and WB networks, which both began broadcasting in 1995, likewise initially appealed to minority markets with ethnic programming.[80] *Good News* (1997–8), a UPN program, was part of this programming strategy, sharing its place on UPN's Monday lineup with other programs featuring black casts, such as *In the House*, *Malcolm & Eddie* and *Sparks*. It was also part of a season which saw an overall increase in the number of major network programs featuring African-American casts.[81] This helps contextualize the series' particular focus on black characters and issues.

For example, one episode that not only features the church's role in helping families face crises but also demonstrates the series' focus on African-American culture and concerns is "Amazing Grace."[82] Two boys are left parentless when their father, a parishioner, dies. He leaves instructions for the boys to be raised by their uncle. The pastor locates Uncle Jerry and is surprised that he is a very light-skinned man who has changed his last name to McCallister. "I'm the Jerry McCallister you've been expecting," the man explains, "I'm just not the shade of black you were expecting." The man tells the pastor that he and his brother had a fight a long time ago and had not since spoken with each other. The uncle tells Reverend Randolph that he will not raise the boys. The pastor then perceives that "Mr. McCallister" is "passing" for white and accuses him of not wanting to take the boys because doing so would reveal to his friends and co-workers his racial identity. The pastor also correctly figures that this is the basis of the trouble between the brothers. "My brother never forgave me for passing," Jim McCallister says. "No, that's not true," corrects Reverend Randolph, "I think he did. He trusted you to raise his two kids. That sounds like forgiveness to me." The pastor observes that the uncle can still "pass" if he raises the boys as a foster parent, never telling them or anyone that he is their uncle.

78. Christopher John Farley (1996), "TV's black flight." *Time*, June, available at http://www.time.com/time/magazine/article/0,9171,984646,00.html (accessed May 25, 2007).

79. Kristal Brent Zook, interview with Brooke Gladstone, "Gentrifying the airwaves." *On the Media* radio program, WNYC — New York Public Radio, transcript of January 27, 2006, available at http://www.onthemedia.org/transcripts/2006/01/27/04 (accessed May 25, 2007).

80. It should be noted that while WB later focused more on the youth market, UPN maintained a focus on ethnic, urban programming.

81. "The 1997 TV season: what's black and what's back." *Ebony*, October, 84.

82. "Amazing Grace." Written by Michael Elias; directed by Michael Elias. March 2, 1998. Reviewed at LOC.

After meeting Jerry, Mrs. Dixon confides in the pastor that she thinks he had plastic surgery to change his nose, and says she is upset with the idea of his raising the boys without disclosing that he is their uncle, calling the situation a lie. "Yes, Mrs. Dixon, I know," replies Reverend Randolph, "but it's a white lie." The boys meet their potential "foster" parent and share their skepticism about living with a white man who is a complete stranger. Randolph realizes that his solution requires too much lying and wonders what they should do with the boys. At the memorial service, Reverend Randolph tells the story of the prodigal son, saying, "for even though the son rejected his family, when he returned home, he was welcomed, for even as our Lord told us, 'If thy brother trespasses against thee, rebuke him; and if he repents, forgive him." Not explaining the allegory and how it applies to Jerry's "passing," the pastor then introduces Jerry "McCallister" to the congregation as an old friend of Doug's and asks if he has anything he wants to say. Jerry finally reveals that he is Doug's brother and has been lying about his racial identity for 20 years, but that he can no longer lie. He announces that he will raise the boys if they will let him, upon which the boys hug their uncle and the congregation cries, "Praise the Lord!" Again, although oversimplifying complex issues, the episode shows the church involved in helping families solve problems. It also exemplifies the series' inclusion of issues relevant to the African-American community.

This focus on African-American issues and culture reoccurs throughout the series. A two-part episode, for example, reflects upon American society's uneven treatment of black entertainers, even including a sermon on the subject.[83] A homeless man visits the parish and before long the pastor realizes that he is "Red Beans," one half of an old-time vaudeville comedy act called "Red Beans and Rice." The pastor invites him to participate in an upcoming talent show. Not sure that the congregation will appreciate an older black man's act, Red Beans recalls how black people complained about how *Amos 'n' Andy* involved stupid black characters, contributing to the program's cancelation. The pastor assures the man that his congregation will accept and appreciate his act, to which Red Beans replies that the pastor has a lot of faith in his congregation. The minister says he also has faith in *him*. During the talent show, after Little T raps about God and the power of the church, Red Beans does his act and later a musical number with the cast, both appreciated by the congregation.

At the episode's end, Reverend Randolph gives a sermon about laughter and racism — how "laughter is truly one of God's greatest gifts" — and recalls memories of his father falling off the couch while watching *Amos 'n' Andy*. The pastor then criticizes CBS for keeping episodes of *Amos 'n' Andy* locked away "as if they're our people's dirtiest secrets." Reverend Randolph mentions W. C. Fields, Jack Benny, Phil Silvers and Lucille Ball as examples of comedians who

---

83. "Back in the Day" (Parts 1 and 2). Written by Richard Dubin; directed by Tony Singletary (Part 1) and Ed Weinberger (Part 2). February 16 and 23, 1998. Reviewed at LOC.

played "a drunk," "a miser," "a slick con man" and "an unliberated, scatter-brained housewife":

> But see, those beautiful comedians were white, and they were never judged as spokespeople for a race. So my hope is that one day in this beautiful country, our wonderful black actors and our black actresses would not be judged for their image, but for their God-given gift to entertain. Church, we must not give in to what people think we should be, but we should love ourselves and all people for what they are.

As the pastor speaks these words, Red Beans sits in the congregation shedding tears of happiness and appreciation.

Not all episodes focused on issues of particular interest to racial minorities, such as "passing" and how they are represented in the media. Quite a number, for example, focus on marital issues facing congregants, while also involving the church setting. Hence, Reverend Randolph helps a used-car salesman reconcile with God and his wife when he reveals he sponsored a 24-hour gospel marathon to benefit the church in order to occupy his chorister wife while he had an affair.[84] Another episode, "Love, Honor and Obey," finds Randolph counseling a man who cites scripture to justify his desire to keep his wife subservient and deny her wish to pursue a career.[85] This episode is noteworthy for the sermon with which it ends — a finishing touch offered on a number of episodes of *Good News*. In this instance, the pastor addresses the congregation (including the married couple) with the following:

> The Bible is a powerful book, but sometimes we forget that there is a danger in the power. Too often when I hear people quote from the Bible, they are not using it to serve our God or to praise our Father, but they're using it to serve their own selfish purposes. So saints, let us remember to use the Bible as a tool that draws us closer to our Father, not as a weapon to win an argument against those who may not share the same views.

The pastor's "teaching" sermons on subjects like this, and those discussed above, allowed the series to advocate positions on a range of matters. Some of these positions were progressive; for example, though a contemporaneous survey of black ministers found that three-quarters did not support distribution of condoms, *Good News* not only promoted the idea but even had its preacher sermonize about it.[86]

---

84. "Show Me the Money" (Parts 1 and 2). Written by Robert Howe; directed by Kim Friedman (Part 1) and Ed Weinberger (Part 2). November 3 and 10, 1997. Reviewed at LOC.

85. "Love, Honor and Obey." Written by David Chambers and Darice Rollins; directed by Anna Maria Horsford. January 12, 1998. Reviewed at LOC.

86. Robert M. Franklin (1977), *Another Day's Journey: Black Churches Confronting the American Crisis*. Minnesota: Augsburg Fortress, p. 80.

The regularity of the short sermons is unique in the history of half-hour sitcoms set in the church. Beyond this, *Good News* also regularly featured depictions of the life of worship of the church. Likewise the frequent musical numbers highlighted gospel music. Only *The Flying Nun* regularly featured music before this; however, the music therein was in the style of musical theater, with lyrics about non-religious matters. The music in *Good News* was true church, gospel music, with lyrics about God or Christ or the Spirit, and arose in moments where singing would really happen, as the gospel choir performed during worship services. Occasionally rituals of the church were spotlighted, such as the baptism of an abandoned boy Mrs. Dixon adopts.[87] And the routine quotations from the Bible or references to Biblical characters grounded the series in the church setting. In these ways, *Good News* stands alone as a half-hour sitcom that regularly portrayed the sights and sounds of worship.

For all its overly simplified storylines and zany sitcom scenarios, *Good News* nonetheless highlighted the music, rituals, values and religious rhetoric one would find in many local parishes, and it did so in ways that set it apart from other half-hour sitcoms set in the church. While *Good News* occasionally focused on issues facing families, its main focus was on showing how the church could help all its members — particularly the church's youth — face an array of modern-day problems.

Nothing Sacred

Perhaps the most ambitious program to examine the lives and vocations of church leaders was *Nothing Sacred* (1997–8), an hour-long drama airing on ABC which focused on the daily activities of the clerics and lay leaders of St. Thomas Church, an urban Catholic parish. While not neglecting the personal lives of the featured ecclesiastics, the program examined a number of issues facing the modern church: abortion; teenage drug use; women serving as preachers and clerics; gay priests; the church's response to people living with HIV/AIDS; concerns about the dwindling numbers of women in the sisterhood and men in the priesthood; critiques of the church from the perspectives of feminist and black theology; and offering sanctuary to undocumented immigrants. *Nothing Sacred* addressed such issues amid more traditional activities of the church leaders, from running a soup kitchen and advocating for the homeless to visiting the sick, saying Masses, preaching sermons and hearing confessions. Although conflicts between conservatives and liberals in the church occasionally arose in earlier episodes, and became a focus of the last few, the overall focus was on the church's commitment to ministering to those in the modern world, to be relevant in their lives.

The featured cleric on the program is Father Francis Xavier Reyneaux, or

---

87. "The Baby on the Door Step." Written by Samm-Art Williams and David Chambers; directed by Stan Daniels. September 15, 1997. Reviewed at LOC.

"Ray" for short, played by 37-year-old Kevin Anderson. More comfortable wearing jeans and a sweater than the traditional cleric, Father Ray leads the parish team with a delicate balance of devotion, passion and self-doubt. His doubts often are answered by his wise, older mentor Father Leo, the former pastor of St. Thomas Church whose quick wit and insight mask his struggle with being a recovered alcoholic. Rounding out the trio of clerics serving the parish is the wet-behind-the-ears, idealistic young Father Eric, who is devoted to the church but not always appreciative of Father Ray's nontraditional approach to ministry and preaching. Finally, there is Sister Maureen Brody, or Sister "Mo" — a feisty feminist whose passion for serving others is matched by her frustration with the church's patriarchy. Other church leaders would join the parish late in the season, but these four characters form the core of the program's ecclesiastic team. Among the lay leaders at the church are: Rachel, the church's high-school-aged secretary; Sidney Walters, the church's accountant and resident atheist; and J. A. Ortiz, the youth minister and handyman.

The tone and focus of the program is established from its opening sequence, which juxtaposes images of the church (stained glass, a preacher in liturgical robes, a priest hearing confession, the church's exterior) with those of the inner city (kids playing basketball, people fighting or tiredly standing on city streets, flowers behind a chain-link fence). Contrasting choir and percussion music blend nicely, as the theme of sacred and secular is further established by two separate hands slowly writing a single word each: one writes "Sacred" in calligraphic script on a piece of paper, while the other spray paints "Nothing" on a wall. Finally, Father Ray is shown on his knees in his room at night, praying before a window which reveals the city outside . . . and he smiles. The church and the city it serves live side by side it seems, as those dedicated to serving God contentedly minister to the city.

The series was the creation of a Jesuit priest, Father Bill Cain, who worked together with executive producer David Mason on developing the show. Concerned that revealing his identity as a priest could be considered a marketing strategy, Cain used the pseudonym Paul Leland for the program's credits.[88] Cain himself ministered at an inner-city parish in Manhattan, and said he created the program to allow audiences to see what happens to a priest when "he's embroiled in the mess of life" — that "to live a life of faith is to be immersed in doubt."[89] The priest's doubts, and the "messes" he encountered — from parishioners considering divorce, an abortion or leaving the church, and municipal opposition to church programs to his and his fellow ecclesiastics' questions of calling or church policies — led some to call this program groundbreaking and realistic, and others to call it propaganda and encourage boycotts (as we will see). That the church leaders at the heart of the program are mostly liberal was bound to

---

88. James Sterngold (1997), "A Jesuit takes the heat for a gritty TV series about a doubting priest." *New York Times*, October 25, sec. B, 7.

89. Ibid.

cause debate. For his part, Cain says his aim was "to depict genuine people struggling to be faithful to the church."[90] This struggle would involve not only customary challenges facing the church — such as financial concerns, and serving the poor — but also more politically charged challenges regarding pregnancy, divorce, sexuality and the role of women in the Catholic Church.

One ongoing storyline of the series which certainly highlights the traditional mission of the church concerns its operation of a soup kitchen. Indeed, the homeless are welcomed at St. Thomas Church in a number of ways. Ray greets them in the morning on the steps of the church, offering them hot coffee before taking his daily run. The members of the parish leadership are clearly friendly with many of the homeless, greeting them by name, knowing their habits and on occasion offering them a little money in compensation for during small chores around the church, such as cleaning the grounds. In "Song of Songs," the meal program is a particular focus since an inspector is coming to evaluate the operation.[91] The episode depicts various congregants helping to run the kitchen, and grounds their food service in the Biblical tradition, as Jesus' feeding of the five thousand is mentioned throughout. In fact, St. Thomas Church's ability to feed all of the homeless on that critical inspection day is itself presented as something of a miracle, as the church staff, lacking adequate food supplies, accidentally use food being stored at the church for a wedding that evening. The inventive church leaders later find innovative ways to help the bride and groom make do, such as frosting Twinkies and presenting them as delicacies, and telling the wedding guests that a chicken dish is pheasant. To the program's credit, the soup kitchen is not simply the subject of a single episode but is woven throughout the series, which regularly shows the clerics both discussing and running the program, thus emphasizing the church's mission to the needy.

The church's devotion to serving the poor is also heard in the passionate defense of this ministry by the church leaders, as they argue with those who oppose it. When a well-to-do man complains to Father Ray about his church allowing the homeless to sleep on the steps and "relieve" themselves on the street, Ray asks whether the dog the man is walking "holds it in."[92] When one of the confirmands helping to prepare a meal for the homeless suggests that those who do not work should not eat, Sister Maureen responds, "If somebody's hungry, you feed 'em. It's that simple." Sister Mo later prays with the confirmands just before welcoming the homeless, suggesting that in the homeless they meet God.[93] Similarly, when late in the season a power-seeking priest is assigned to

---

90. John Dart (1997), "The 'sacred' debate television: as ABC renews its drama about a liberal priest, Catholics remain divided over the show's intent." *Los Angeles Times*, December 4, sec. F, 50.

91. "Song of Songs." Written by Paul Leland; directed by John Coles. September 25, 1997. Reviewed off broadcast television.

92. "Proofs for the Existence of God." Written by Paul Leland; directed by Richard Pearce. September 11, 1997. Reviewed of broadcast television.

93. "Song of Songs."

St. Thomas Church to help reform its progressive ways, his attempt to end the soup kitchen program is met with opposition from the other priests, Father Ray noting that the soup kitchen is as important as the Masses because "it's where we meet Christ."[94] Most pointedly, Father Ray defends the meal program at public hearings called by civic officials to hear the church's response to claims that the kitchen brings "vagrants" and "undesirables" to the community. Father Ray notes that they are "guests" of the church, not vagrants; that the "undesirables" are the "yuppie scum" who are overtaking "what has become one of the few stable racially mixed neighborhoods in the city"; that he too wants to help improve the neighborhood, but in a way that includes the homeless because "everything has let these people down . . . everything: government, housing, politics, education. But the church will not! By God, it will not!"[95] Compassionate and progressive, Father Ray and his colleagues are presented as dedicated to the church's mission and to social transformation in the inner city.

All this might not have caused controversy were it not for the show's inclusion of politically heated storylines. One such story that runs throughout the series merits particular attention, not only for how it is framed but also for comparison with other programs; it concerns a young woman who contemplates having an abortion.[96] Rachel, the teenaged church secretary, first comes to Father Ray about the matter in the confessional. Unlike in *Hell Town*, where the morality of abortion is debated by Father Hardstep and a doctor, in *Nothing Sacred* such deliberation immediately is left to the young woman. Father Ray tells Rachel, "You're an adult with your own conscience. I can't tell you what to do, I can only tell you what the church teaches . . . if you want, what I think." With some prodding, Rachel gets Father Ray to say exactly what his personal thoughts are about abortion. Although the audience never hears these opinions (the scene ends when he agrees to speak his mind), one may surmise that they are not in keeping with orthodox views of the church: he notes afterward that he is sure he will get in trouble for what he said. When Rachel returns to the confessional, she finds Father Leo there. He asks her, "Why do you keep coming here? There are plenty of places that will tell you what you want to hear. Do you want someone to punish you? 'Cause I won't. Neither will Father Ray." Rachel asks if God will send her to hell, and Leo dismissively notes that Catholics were once told they would be sent there for eating meat on Fridays. When Rachel inquires whether he believes in hell or not, Father Leo responds, "Yes, I believe in hell. I believe it's a place of fear, isolation, loneliness, desperation. Yes, I believe in hell. Will God send you there? What worse hell can you be in than the one you're in right now?"

---

94. "Kindred Spirits." Teleplay by Marlene Meyer; story by Marlane Meyer and Gary Rieck; directed by Robert Young. March 7, 1998. Reviewed off broadcast television.

95. "Proofs for the Existence of God."

96. "Proofs for the Existence of God"; and "Parents and Children." Teleplay by Jan Oxenberg; story by Jan Oxenberg and Paul Leland; directed by Claudia Weill. October 9, 1997. Reviewed off broadcast television.

Father Ray continues to tell Rachel that he can only tell her what the church teaches about abortion, but that ultimately the decision is up to her and her own conscience. Leo, however, is not aware of Ray's advice and tells Rachel that they will support her whether she decides to keep the child or give it up for adoption. When she tells Leo what advice Ray has been giving, Leo becomes edgy. He confronts Father Ray, noting that Rachel's constant return to the confessional indicates that she wants someone to talk her out of having an abortion. Ray responds that it is Rachel who will have to live with the results of her decision. The focus is on her needs, not debating theology. Both priests later talk with Rachel alone, Leo expressing concern with how Rachel might handle an abortion and not wanting to see her in pain, Ray finally telling her that he owes her a clear explanation of what he personally thinks about her situation and that "the world can only be a better place with a child of yours in it . . . 'cause of who you are, 'cause of your goodness, your grace, and your intelligence." Rachel tells him she has decided to have the child. After all this, Father Ray discovers a business card from a clinic and goes there to meet Rachel outside, where she reveals that she has gone through with the abortion. "So I guess that's it for me and God, right?" she asks, to which Father Ray responds, "No, Rachel. On the contrary." In later episodes, Father Leo asks Rachel's forgiveness for having judged her, and Sister Maureen helps her realize that she is still welcome in the church. Overall the story is presented in terms of these church leaders' response to the needs of a person in crisis, and less so on ideological debates about the issue.

"House of Rage" finds members of the parish staff involved in responding to another crisis, and is noteworthy for taking an unorthodox approach to a matter facing many modern Catholics. It concerns a couple whom Father Ray married, who are now having serious marital problems and are considering divorce. Among these troubles is the husband's occasional violence. To complicate matters, the couple have a son who drinks to escape the family's difficulties. Father Ray tries to counsel the couple. He and Father Leo at one point discuss the perspective of clergy who see couples they married eventually divorce. Leo remarks this is a burden older clergy must face as the social acceptance of divorce has made it more common than when he first began ministry. *Nothing Sacred* handles the issue with its usual frankness and poignancy. When the wife discusses with Sister Maureen the nun's idea of establishing a home for battered women, the wife says she does not think the church should support such a place because it would break up families. Sister Maureen responds with her usual candor, saying, "Some families need to break up." After the wife attempts suicide, she and Father Ray discuss her failing marriage in confession. At the episode's end, Father Ray sits quietly at a table with his two friends and performs a reverse wedding ceremony. Reciting the wedding vows, he asks each if they agree to them. When their answers are "no," he asks what they want, one of the two suggesting an annulment. They ask Ray to pray for them, and he does. The two then tell each other they release the other in love and kindness, the man adding, "I'm so sorry."[97] Thus, the series dealt seriously with a reality facing the church and many of its modern parishioners.

One of the innovations *Nothing Sacred* introduced to the history of church-set programs concerns the use of inclusive language — a controversial practice for many churches. Throughout the series Sister Mo criticizes the exclusive reference to God as "He" or "Father," beginning with the first episode, when the parish staff sit around discussing God in strictly masculine terms. Others in the congregation share her position, for during Mass they seem accustomed to making additions to the Creed, such as inserting "and Mother" after references to God as "Father," and adding "and women" after phrases like "for all men." This places St. Thomas Church at the center of contemporaneous discussions regarding the use of inclusive language in the church. Nonetheless, while many churches have begun using inclusive language in their lectionaries and hymnals, this often is done subtly enough not to be noticed by many congregants. The enthusiastic, self-conscious practice of inclusive language by the congregation of the television series would put it at the forefront of the movement and make it particularly liberal. Further, the reference to God as Mother, while commonplace in feminist metaphorical theology, is not often as fully embraced as it is at the parish of *Nothing Sacred*. In fact, when a conservative priest attends Mass and asks that the congregants not use inclusive language, they defiantly do so anyway. Certainly, the series' depiction of this matter taps into an issue facing the modern-day church, while also establishing this congregation as a rather progressive one.

More broadly, *Nothing Sacred* also examines issues regarding women in the church. This subject is sprinkled throughout the series: early on Ray meets an old friend who had been one of the first women admitted to a Catholic seminary; female preachers from other countries and/or church denominations appear here and there; late in the series a new character, Dr. Justine Madsen Judd, joins the parish staff to serve as Director of Religious Education and supervisor of preaching. Not surprisingly, many of the issues regarding the role of women in the church revolve around Sister Maureen. While Sister Mo clearly enjoys serving the church, she also is increasingly frustrated with the limited role afforded her by the Catholic Church. In "Calling," Sister Maureen is invited to preach at a neighborhood Episcopal church by that parish's minister, Reverend Elizabeth.[98] The female cleric offers Sister Maureen this opportunity after Sister Mo sits in the sanctuary and listens to the Reverend practice her upcoming sermon. Uncertain as to whether she should accept the offer, since women cannot preach in the Catholic Church, and not clear about how she feels preaching in the church of another denomination, Sister Mo nonetheless

---

97. "House of Rage." Written by Marlane Meyer; directed by Joan Tewkesbury. December 11, 1997. Reviewed off broadcast television.

98. "Calling." Written by Jason Cahill; directed by Robert M. Young. November 6, 1997. Reviewed off broadcast television; also available at LOC.

prepares for the opportunity — just in case. She practices in St. Thomas Church's sanctuary, receiving advice about projection from the church's youth minister. Ultimately Sister Maureen declines, telling Reverend Elizabeth that she would prefer to wait until she can preach in her own church. When they discuss the likely lengthiness of her wait, Reverend Elizabeth responds, "Let's pray it isn't." Indeed, the matter comes up again in *"Hodie Christus Natus Est"* (Today Christ is Born), when Sister Maureen misunderstands Father Ray's offer to "speak" at midnight Mass on Christmas Eve, thinking she has been invited to give a homily.[99] Father Eric, himself eager for any opportunity to preach, takes the opportunity to challenge Sister Maureen's eagerness to preach, saying, "Need I remind you that no woman . . . only an ordained person can give the homily." To this, the nun retorts, "And may I remind you that without a woman there would be no midnight Mass." Father Leo notes with some irony, "Who better to preach on the virgin birth than a woman?" Nonetheless, the older priest himself pressures Father Ray to allow *him* to preach that evening. By the episode's end, Fathers Ray, Leo and Eric are all arrested on assault charges for their attempt to help undocumented immigrants, fleeing persecution for preaching the Gospel in El Salvador, evade the police. Sitting in their cell before leading an impromptu Mass for their fellow inmates, Father Ray begins to laugh, realizing that the only person left at St. Thomas Church to lead the midnight Mass is Sister Maureen. Back at the parish, Sister Maureen explains why the parish's ordained ministers are not available to lead Mass, and suggests they all worship at other churches that evening. The congregation protests and insists that Sister Mo lead the service. Careful to note that she is not a priest and what follows will be a "prayer service," not a Mass, she complies with their wishes and leads the service. Thus, in another way, the series breaks new ground.

No discussion of *Nothing Sacred* is complete without a consideration of "HIV Priest: Film at 11." The episode did not air due to network concerns about it being too controversial. The story concerns a gay Catholic cleric, Father Jesse, who confides in his friend-since-seminary Father Ray that he has AIDS. Father Ray hears that his friend has not been showing up at his parish for several days. Ray finds the priest moving into an apartment and asks why he is avoiding his parish. When Father Jesse responds that Ray would not understand, Ray says he is not concerned that Jesse is gay, something he apparently has known for a while. Jesse then shares that he is not only HIV-positive but also has full-blown AIDS. He fears how those in the church will respond, and is considering leaving ordained ministry. Hereafter, the program focuses not only on the drama of a priest living with AIDS but also more broadly on a consideration of the nature of religious calling. Father Ray tells Father Jesse he should not leave the priesthood because he broke his vows and has become sick, and that he is a good priest.

99. *"Hodie Christus Natus Est"* (Today Christ is Born). Teleplay by Michael Breault; story by Bill Cain and Michael Breault; directed by David Manson. December 18, 1997. Reviewed off broadcast television; also available at LOC, Paley Center for Media and UCLA.

Ray adds, "I'm sick of crossing faces off the ordination picture, alright? Too many guys have left. But not you. Stay. Stay." Later, Father Jesse says, "I can't afford a vocation, Ray. I need a job," explaining that staying alive and managing his illness is a full-time occupation and he believes he cannot rely on the church to support him once his illness becomes known. Father Ray expresses anger at his friend's abandoning his vocation for fear of people's reaction to his situation, saying, "Is that all you're worried about? That you've changed, that you're not worthy? Wake up, Jesse. God! It isn't about worthiness. You can't deserve this, you can't earn this. It's a calling. You know that. It's about love . . ."

By the program's end Father Jesse finds himself at a weekly poker game attended by a handful of priests and their monsignor. Jesse has previously told Ray how offensive he finds the Monsignor's weekly toast: "Gentlemen, to the last six celibate, heterosexual priests in the world." This time, Father Jesse confronts his superior, declaring that the toast is bigoted — and untrue. He reveals to his fellow priests his situation, upon which each of them reveals something with which he struggles, from battling cancer to having a drinking problem to seeing a psychoanalyst. Finally the Monsignor speaks at length, stating how important the vow of chastity is, but then recalls how disappointed he was when a beloved friend of his, "a good priest," just disappeared "when all of this first started," apparently speaking of the AIDS epidemic. Ultimately the Monsignor tells Father Jesse, "you don't have to leave on my account." In a touching moment at the program's end, Fathers Ray and Jesse find themselves alone with the leftover bread from the gathering, which hints at the sacrament of Holy Communion and the presence of God it signifies. Upon hearing Jesse share how afraid he is, Ray observes, "This is how it started. All of it. Who we are, what we do." When Jesse humorously questions if he is referring to the card game, Ray continues: "No. With a man in his early thirties who knew he was gonna die . . . took bread and he broke and he gave it to his friend and said . . ." Jesse, teary eyed, then looks at his friend and says: ". . . remember me."[100]

Writing in defense of the series in general and this episode in particular, noted Catholic author and sociologist Reverend Andrew M. Greeley charged that, "The decision to suppress the episode is based, it seems to me, on a curious kind of anti-Catholicism, the conviction (widespread in the upper news media and academia) that Catholics are really unsophisticated and indeed unthinking peasants or 'hard hats' who would react in shocked horror to the suggestion that a priest might have AIDS." Continuing his argument, Greeley notes that, "The emphasis in the story is not on AIDS or on homosexuality. Rather the script . . . is about forgiveness and new beginnings" and that, despite the series' "modern, even hip" ambiance, its main character, Father Ray, "is very much a traditional priest — compassionate, sensitive, concerned, involved. He is never more

---

100. "HIV Priest." Teleplay by Richard Kramer; story by Paul Leland and Richard Kramer; directed by James Hayman. Unaired. Reviewed at PCM; also available at UCLA.

priestly than in his reconciliation of Jesse to the priesthood."[101] Regardless of one's opinions about homosexuality, gay priests or HIV/AIDS, it is noteworthy that the producers of the series wished to deal with such issues, relevant as they are to the church and the world today.

Nonetheless, critics of the series remarked that by emphasizing the clerics' empathy for people in crisis in stories like those discussed above, it was setting an unfair standard against which to judge those taking more orthodox views. The conservative Catholic League for Religious and Civil Rights, for example, charged the program with striving to "convince viewers that those Catholics who challenge the church's teachings on women and sexuality are more compassionate . . . than those who uphold church teachings."[102] Organizations such as this one called for boycotts of the show's advertisers. Other Catholics, including some in upper ranks of the hierarchy, defended the program and appealed to advertisers to continue their sponsorship of the program.[103] In an ad published in several newspapers defending the show, prominent Catholics were quoted, including Greeley, who said, "It illuminates the compassion of priests and the humanity of the church with rare clarity."[104] Clearly, the show's approach set off a debate about the impact of representations of the church on television. To be sure, this debate included not only the fictional church leaders' response to issues such as those discussed above, but also the show's regular presentation of the clerics' own doubts and struggles.[105]

In this light, the priests and nun of Nothing Sacred question and reaffirm their vocation throughout the series. The ecclesiastics deal regularly with challenges imposed by their vocation and their ongoing need to recommit themselves to ministry. Father Ray ponders about vocation while speaking at a group counseling session. Commenting on one man's search for meaningful work, Ray soon contemplates his own career, wondering aloud if he should have become a priest. Later, the priest meets an old high school acquaintance. Refusing to reveal his vocation to his friend, Ray characterizes his work as "social work mostly." After discussing the challenges they both have and their need to face them, the friend drives Ray to his "home," where it becomes clear that Ray is a priest. Ray then reaffirms his commitment to his vocation, telling his friend anytime he needs help, to look for him at the church: "Anytime. I'm always here."[106] Undergoing a similar crisis of identity, Father Leo abruptly leaves the parish at the end of this episode, walking off with packed bags and disappearing until three episodes later, when he confides that he needed to get away and now realizes that he

101. Andrew M. Greeley (1998), "A Nothing Sacred episode you haven't seen." New York Times, March 1, sec. 2, 36.

102. Dart (1997), 50.

103. Ibid.

104. Sterngold (1997), 7.

105. Dart (1997), 50.

106. "Roman Catholic Holiday." Teleplay by Marlane Meyer; story by Marlane Meyer and Paul Leland; directed by Sarah Pia Anderson. October 16, 1997. Reviewed off broadcast television.

belongs at the church. Similarly, another episode finds Father Eric concerned with how the staff's efforts to hide El Salvadoran refugees from authorities is disrupting the church's regular ministries, finally removing his collar and declaring, "If this is what it means to be a priest, I don't want to be one." He later returns after one of the refugees tells him the story of her family's demise at the hands of her own government, which killed them because she had preached the Gospel. Sister Maureen questions her vocation when the last nun of an order dies, leading Sister Mo to confront her own life choices and their implications. Maureen speaks with an apparition of her younger self about the choices she made as a young woman, defiantly telling her adolescent self that she can undo any decision made by her younger counterpart. When the series ends, she is in fact on a leave of absence from the parish, exploring a secular career as the city's director of community relations.[107]

As with that of questioning one's vocation, other themes from earlier church-set programs, from sexuality, to clerical attire and church finances, likewise challenge *Nothing Sacred*'s clerics. Hence, Ray bumps into an old female lover (from before he was ordained) who is now married with children; when their former attraction reignites, the priest almost sleeps with her, going so far as to meet her in a hotel room, before coming to his senses. Father Ray's preference of secular wear (jeans and a sweater) to clerical garb embitters a newly widowered parishioner. Realizing the man sees this matter as related to broader issues of modernization in the church, Ray responds, "The church had to change, Joe. It couldn't keep doing things the old way." Ultimately, Ray wears the collar when meeting the widower so that he can effectively offer pastoral care. In a touching conclusion, Ray sings along with the tradition-minded widower when during the funeral service he spontaneously begins singing an almost forgotten Latin hymn from the old Mass.[108] As with earlier TV clerics, the leaders of St. Thomas Church are every bit as fiscally challenged as previous church leaders on television series: scaffolding in the sanctuary signifies ongoing repairs; statues about the church are broken; problems with the boiler plague the parish. Rather than scheme to raise money, however, they gripe about parishioners' misplaced priorities when counting the week's meager offering, Sister Mo wryly saying, "Give unto Caesar what is Caesar's, give to the church your spare change."[109] In these ways, the series picked up on established themes from the history of church-set programs, spinning them in its own way.

Rather than present clerics' humanity sensationally or as a comic end in itself, as did most other programs, *Nothing Sacred* began with the premise that clerics are ordinary people and moved beyond that to show what church leaders, faults and all, can accomplish. All this the program did while featuring

---

107. "A Nun's Story." Teleplay by Jan Oxenberg and Richard Kramer; story by Jan Oxenberg; directed by Jan Egleson. January 24, 1998. Reviewed off broadcast television.
108. "Mixed Blessings." Teleplay by Matt Fulony; story by Matt Fulony and Paul Leland; directed by Eugene Corr. October 2, 1997. Reviewed of broadcast television.
109. "Mixed Blessings."

the daily activities of parish leaders: visiting the sick; offering Mass and preaching; ministering to the poor and homeless; praying. In the end *Nothing Sacred* thoughtfully presented church leaders as dedicated but imperfect, wholly human and trying their best to serve the church they loved, sometimes controversially but always struggling to keep it relevant in the modern world. As such, *Nothing Sacred* is a noteworthy church-set program which, despite critical acclaim and vigorous defense by some church leaders, ultimately succumbed to low ratings and the efforts of some in the church to have it canceled.[110]

Discussion

The cluster of programs examined in this chapter focused on church leaders striving to remain relevant in the modern world. The ecclesiastics of this era of television programs — centered in the 1980s and 1990s — were not as concerned with ideological differences and learning to work with those with differing attitudes, so much as with remaining effective and having an impact on the lives of people facing contemporary problems. The programs in this grouping continued to focus on Catholic church leaders, with five of the six shows discussed in depth (*Hell Town*, *Sister Kate*, *Have Faith*, *Father Dowling Mysteries* and *Nothing Sacred*) focusing on Catholic ecclesiastics, in addition to two others (*M*A*S*H* and *Hack*) discussed in brief. Some questions arise: Does the focus on Catholic clerics and their ministries two or more decades after Vatican II reflect a shift in focus occurring among actual Catholic leaders of the 1980s and 1990s, from internal struggles to an effort to remain externally relevant? What of the particular issues and concerns raised on these programs; are these in keeping with issues and concerns faced by the Catholic Church in this era? And was the manner of response depicted on television commensurate with that of the Catholic Church? What of the one Protestant, African-American-focused program in this cluster — *Good News*? Do the representations on this program ring true to the experiences of black churches of the era? These questions will guide the discussion of programs considered in this chapter.

The transition from programs that focused on internal ideological struggles to external efforts to remain relevant in the modern world can be seen in a number of ways. For one, the ecclesiastics on these programs either work alone and are not paired with an ideological opposite (*M*A*S*H* and *AfterMASH*, *Lanigan's Rabbi*, *Sister Kate*, *Hack*, *Good News*) or work as members of a service-oriented team who are predominantly politically likeminded (*Hell Town*, *Have Faith*, *Father Dowling Mysteries*, *Nothing Sacred*). The vocations of many of the unpaired

---

110. Cynthia Seal (1997), "Is nothing sacred? Hollywood's treatment of Catholicism." *San Francisco Faith*, November, available at http://www.sffaith.com/ed/articles/1997/1197cs. htm (accessed June 6, 2006). Other discussions of the program appeared in: Andy Meisler (1997), "Battling demons (and ratings) at the pulpit." *New York Times*, Television, October 26–November 1; Ted Johnson (1997), "Holy role," *TV Guide*, October 18, 41–5.

ecclesiastics emphasize their service orientation, from army and hospital chaplain (*M*A*S*H* and *AfterMASH*), to orphanage leader (*Sister Kate*) and parole officer (*Hack*). The range of issues dealt with likewise attest to the church leaders' focus on remaining relevant to a variety of social concerns, from gang violence, contraception and sexually transmitted diseases to abortion, racism and women's equality. When conflicts do arise for clerics about these issues, they are typically with secular professionals or the laity, or representatives of the church hierarchy and not, as in the previous cluster of programs, with another local ecclesiastic with whom they served. For example: Father Noah Hardstep's debates are with doctors and law enforcement professionals; Father Ray's disputes are with parishioners, city officials and police officers and the Bishop's office; Father Dowling's problems are with the Bishop and the Bishop's traveling secretary; Reverend Randolph's difficult encounters are with parishioners and people outside of the church, such as gang leaders.

For all this, there are areas of continuity with the preceding era of programs, such as in the continued focus on Catholicism, and their urban setting. *Hack* is set in Philadelphia, *Hell Town* and *Good News* in Los Angeles, *Sarge* in San Diego, *Have Faith* and *Father Dowling Mysteries* in Chicago, and *Nothing Sacred* in an unidentified city (perhaps an "every city"). This continued focus on urban parishes for the Catholic-set programs certainly reflects the Catholic emphasis on urban ministry over the course of the twentieth century, as well as the historic association of the Catholic Church with the city in film and television. Even so, it does this at the expense of considering the growing experience of Catholic parishes in the suburbs — an emerging reality in the Catholic church. Having successfully helped Americanize European immigrants coming to the inner cities, the Catholic Church moved with its congregants to the suburbs as they became more educated and successful.[111] None of the Catholic-set programs airing on popular American television (including *Trinity*, discussed in the next chapter) were set anywhere but in urban locales. Even so, given what Ellis calls Catholicism's historically "overwhelmingly urban" character, and the fact that even as the Catholic Church followed Protestant churches into the suburbs, they nonetheless "remained behind [in urban settings] longer and in greater numbers than Protestants"; hence, this continuing focus of television programs is in some ways justified.[112]

The urban setting also allowed such programs to focus on church leaders' response to many of the social issues that were particularly visible in urban environs. Dolan notes that the decades immediately following Vatican II set up a situation wherein a concern with social issues would be a taken-for-granted reality after this period: "City parishes took on a new look in the 1960s and

111. John Tracy Ellis (1969), *American Catholicism*, 2nd edn, rev. The Chicago History of American Civilization series, edited by Daniel J. Boorstin. Chicago: University of Chicago Press, pp. 170–1.

112. Ellis (1969), *American Catholicism*, pp. 166, 170.

1970s. Breaking out of narrow parochial concerns, they began to redefine their mission. As one priest put it, they were 'groping for relevance'."[113] By the end of the 1970s, he writes, the concerns of the 1960s were taken for granted; a concern for social justice pervaded the country and the church, and "city pastors became politicized."[114] Having grown through a period where issues of "civil rights, women's rights, and peace swept across the landscape," the church found itself interacting with culture in these and other areas, and "the demands for social justice increased." The result, he continues, was that "Catholics responded in an unprecedented manner," and the movement towards a "social Gospel" or public religion "gained momentum" during the 1970s and 1980s.[115] The ways in which television's clerics became political advocates and social activists (now taking for granted the debates that preceded this period) agree with this account of the era.

Historians concur that, in the years following Vatican II, the propensity of Catholic clerics to raise their voices in regard to high-profile national issues received prominent national attention, particularly in relation to the peace movement and criticism of government policies regarding the war in Vietnam.[116] Whereas many Catholics aspired to be "superpatriots" — that is immigrants (or descendants of immigrants) who wanted to prove their allegiance to America — growing concern with US policies in Asia led many others to become prominent leaders of the peace movement.[117] Given this, Father Mulcahy's prominence as a Catholic cleric and advocate of peace in the 1972–83 TV series M*A*S*H was well-timed. Although set in Korea in the 1950s, M*A*S*H, given the period of its airing, served as a metaphor for the war in Vietnam. In this context, the outspoken doctors and soft-spoken cleric served as advocates for the peace movement. Although not as "radical" as the surgeons with whom he served or some of his real-life counterparts protesting the Vietnamese conflict, Father Mulcahy frequently spoke of his longing for an end to the war and prayed for peace. Not only did Father Mulcahy strive to remain relevant in his service to his M*A*S*H unit, but his prominence as the most visible cleric on a television series over the course of the 1970s and early 1980s led the way for increasingly politically and socially active TV clerics to come — much as lay Catholic leaders in the peace movement did for later leaders in "public Catholicism."[118]

Among the public debates in which Catholic leaders became most visible in coming decades was that over abortion. After abortion was legalized with

---

113. Jay P. Dolan (1985), *The American Catholic Experience: A History from Colonial Times to the Present*. New York: Doubleday & Company, p. 449.

114. Dolan (1985), *The American Catholic Experience*, pp. 423–4.

115. Jay P. Dolan, (2002), *In Search of an American Catholicism: A History of Religion and Culture in Tension*. New York: Oxford University Press, p. 199.

116. Chester Gillis (1999), *Roman Catholicism in America*. Columbia Contemporary American Religion Series. New York: Columbia University Press, p. 104; Dolan (2002), *In Search of an American Catholicism*, pp. 198–9.

117. Dolan (1985), *The American Catholic Experience*, p. 450; Gillis (1999), 104.

118. Dolan (2002), *In Search of an American Catholicism*, p. 198.

Roe v. Wade in 1973, the official Catholic Church response was to uphold the position already articulated during Vatican II, that abortion was unethical and should be opposed. A movement led by Catholic bishops developed over the 1970s to increase public support for the outlawing of abortion, but this did not stop Catholic laity from debating the issue in a rather public way over the course of the coming decades, including in high-profile exchanges between well-known Catholic politicians who supported keeping abortion legal (such as New York Governor Mario Cuomo and Vice-Presidential candidate Geraldine Ferraro) and members of the church hierarchy who criticized their position.[119] Given this visibility, it is not surprising that two of the Catholic-set network dramas dealt with abortion, either in a particular episode (*Hell Town*) or as a story arch spanning several episodes (*Nothing Sacred*). *Hell Town*'s depiction of the debate, placing Father Hardstep in opposition to a member of the medical community, took a traditional Catholic position, the cleric arguing against abortion. Of course, the sensational nature of the episode (wherein a nun is raped and must decide whether or not to have an abortion and whether or not she may remain a nun) provided a rather extreme context within which to frame this debate, as did Hardstep's impassioned but rough-around-the edges rhetoric. Further, the *dues ex machina* ending, wherein the nun was able to have the child and give it up for adoption, only to have a baby (which the audience knows is hers) "mysteriously" left on the church's doorstep months later, allowed the plot to skirt the moral dilemma it raised.

This contrasts with the depiction of the issue a decade later in *Nothing Sacred*, when Father Ray refused to tell a young woman considering an abortion what she should do, preferring to leave the decision up to the young woman and her conscience. Ray offered to articulate both the church's position and his own thoughts on the subject, but refused to make a moral pronouncement or seek to pressure the young woman into complying with official church teachings. In the end, she chose to have an abortion, and the clerics at her parish responded by providing not judgment but pastoral support. Given that polls at the time showed that American Catholics were about evenly divided between "pro-life" and "pro-choice," and that most upheld a woman's right to choose despite their personal disapproval of abortions,[120] the hesitance of Father Ray to be absolutist reflected something of the tenor of American Catholicism of the era. In this way, *Nothing Sacred* also echoed what one historian wrote, that "while many priests regularly preach against abortion, others mention it rarely and do not stress the church's teaching because people have heard it, and the priests do not want the church to be perceived as a one-issue institution, particularly an issue with which many Catholics disagree."[121] In this light, it is interesting that abortion was

---

119. Ibid., pp. 202–3.
120. Steinfels, Peter (2003), *A People Adrift: The Crisis of the Roman Catholic Church in America*. New York: Simon & Schuster, pp. 95–6.
121. Gillis (1999), pp. 184–5.

dealt with only in Catholic-set programs (including *Trinity*, where a priest helps convince his sister not to have an abortion), and was not addressed in any of the Protestant-set programs.

On the other hand, it is just as noteworthy that the only programs to include episodes focused on birth control and contraception were Protestant-set programs. *Good News* devoted one episode to the idea that church leaders needed to face the issue of teenagers having sex and support programs that not only make young people aware of the risks involved in sexual activity but also provide contraception for those who do become sexually active. This and *7th Heaven*, a Protestant program discussed in the coming chapter (where a pastor's son is found to have condoms and be sexually active), are the only two programs that considered the issue. While it is true that debates about contraception and teenage (premarital) sex were not unknown to Protestant churches, the issue was a high-profile matter in the Catholic Church, making its absence as a topic of consideration on popular TV programs significant. Even on the cutting edge *Nothing Sacred*, the only reference to contraception came in the first episode when Father Ray scolded the church from the pulpit for having reduced religion to a number of hot-button issues, mentioning by name contraception, homosexuality, promiscuity and abortion, and noting that the Gospels are concerned with much broader concerns. Issues of contraception and birth control received considerable attention when the Vatican issued the encyclical *Humanae Vitae* in the 1960s as a reiteration of the Catholic Church's official stand on these issues, banning all forms of artificial birth control. Nonetheless, while the official policy of Rome initially received considerable attention and these teachings remain in effect today, many Catholics do not agree with the Vatican on these issues and do not adhere to its dictates.[122] They remain Catholic, even though they simply do not take seriously Rome's position on matters of sexuality.[123] In fact, Catholic attitudes towards sexual matters (such as premarital sex) in the era of these television programs were often more liberal than those of Protestants.[124] As such, while the issue of contraception is associated with official teachings of the Catholic Church, it is nonetheless a nonissue for many, though not all, American Catholics and hence its absence as a topic of consideration on Catholic-set programs may reflect this.

One area of the Catholic Church's growing ministry that is touched upon in some of the television programs is ministry to a new wave of Hispanic immigrants coming from not Europe but Mexico, Puerto Rico and Cuba.[125] For these immigrants, Catholicism was a "deeply ingrained" part of their culture and their increasing numbers over the course of the twentieth century challenged the

---

122. Andrew M. Greeley (1990), *The Catholic Myth: The Behavior and Beliefs of American Catholics*. New York: Simon & Schuster, pp. 95–6; Gillis (1999), pp. 106–8.
123. Greeley (1990), *The Catholic Myth*, p. 96.
124. Ibid., p. 97.
125. Dolan (2002), *In Search of an American Catholicism*, pp. 215–19.

church to respond to their needs and welcome their contributions.[126] Although the number of Catholic Hispanics is declining as some become Protestant, the vast majority (upwards of 70 percent) have been Catholic, particularly in the period under consideration.[127] While *Going My Way* included immigrants from Spain, and *The Flying Nun* was set in Puerto Rico, more recent programs included Hispanic immigrants from the Americas. Both *Hell Town* and *Nothing Sacred* involved Hispanic characters. Given *Hell Town*'s setting in East Los Angeles, this was particularly fitting and natural, but *Nothing Sacred* also included Hispanic characters, foremost among these being Juan Alberto (played by Jose Zuniga), the church's youth minister. (Indeed, the first episode of *Nothing Sacred* ends with the baptism of Anna Maria Tiffany Beverly Gonzalez.) Both programs also devoted plots to the Sanctuary Movement, an effort begun in the 1980s to help refugees from Central American countries, fleeing religious and political persecution, find asylum in the United States, even as "illegal immigrants." The movement was led by church leaders as an underground network that smuggled refugees through Mexico into the United States and then helped them evade government officials empowered to deport them. Focusing episodes on the Sanctuary Movement highlighted the church's effort to remain relevant in modern-day struggles. While a smaller wave of later twentieth-century immigrants to the Catholic Church came from Asian countries,[128] little focus has been placed on such characters in church-set programs; indeed, this absence is part of a broader, well-documented underrepresentation of Asian-Americans on American television in general.[129]

Another small population of immigrants who largely joined the Roman Catholic Church upon arrival in the United States was Haitian.[130] These immigrants, together with "upwardly mobile African-Americans seeking parochial educational alternatives to urban public school systems," accounted for a rise in the membership of black people in the Roman Catholic Church, from under a million in 1985 to about two million by 1990.[131] Even with this surge, however, the African-American presence in the Catholic Church has been limited, as

---

126. Gillis (1999), p. 21.

127. Greeley (1990), *The Catholic Myth*, p. 121.

128. Gillis (1999), pp. 21–2; Dolan (2002), *In Search of an American Catholicism*, pp. 220–1.

129. See for example the following: Donal Brown (2006), "Asian Americans go missing when it comes to TV." *New American Media*, August 28, available at http://news.newamericamedia.org/news/view_article.html?article_id=2187822d260441c375f65241320819d0 (accessed September 17, 2006); Erin Quill (undated), "Why there are 'no' Asians on television" (Four Part Series), Asian American Village at IMDiversity, available at http://www.imdiversity.com/villages/asian/arts_culture_media/quill_asian_TVa_0805.asp (for subsequent installments of the series, replace TVa with TVb, TVc, and TVd) (accessed September 17, 2006); Darrell Y. Hamamoto (1994), *Monitored Peril: Asian Americans and the Politics of TV Representation*. Minneapolis: University of Minnesota Press.

130. Gillis (1999), p. 85.

131. C. Eric Lincoln and Lawrence H. Mamiya (1990), *The Black Church in the African American Experience*. Durham: Duke University Press, pp. 159, 342.

"only about 5 percent of American blacks are Catholic, and they comprise less than 3 percent of the [Catholic] church."[132] Along these lines, *Father Dowling Mysteries'* inclusion of black churchgoers is largely reserved for a mystery set in a Baptist church.[133] Further, one episode of *Nothing Sacred* depicts a young African-American confirmand who is pressured by his upwardly mobile mother to become Catholic; however, he does not feel at home in his mother's parish (he questions why all of the statuary is of white people) and, with Pastor Ray's support, decides to join a local Baptist church where he feels more at home with the predominantly black congregation and its style of worship.[134] Indeed, the vast majority of African-American churchgoers (80 percent) belong to one of the major black denominations in the United States.[135] Given this, the relative scarcity of black faces among congregants in television's Catholic parishes was realistic, as was the abundance of such faces in single episodes where the main characters visited African-American characters at predominantly black churches. Most representative of the experience of African-American churchgoers among these programs was *Good News*.

In its portrayal of the black church, *Good News* surely touched on areas of importance to such churches. Certainly the emphasis on music, in particular contemporary gospel music, was distinctive of *Good News*, and reflected the same emphasis in modern black churches. As black church sociologists C. Eric Lincoln and Lawrence H. Mamiya write, "music, or more precisely, *singing* is second only to preaching as the magnet of attraction and the primary vehicle of spiritual transport for the worshipping congregation."[136] That most black churches in the United States have at least two choirs, the average being closer to three, attests to the centrality of the choir in the black worship experience.[137] Hence, the regular appearance of the gospel choir in *Good News* reflected one of the most central aspects of the black church worship experience. Also depicted were other facets of black church experience. The focus on contraception, sexually transmitted diseases and teen pregnancy, for instance, tied in with challenges that faced the African-American community, and reflected ongoing efforts by black churches to provide organized programs in response to such issues.[138] Likewise, efforts at community organizing and outreach to youth reflected what Lincoln and Mamiya write would be a particular emphasis of black churches in the 1990s. This outreach included "strategies for dealing with black children, teenagers and young adults and their families" with "a mix of traditional programs like youth choirs, evangelism and revivals with progressive programs";

132. Gillis (1999), p. 85.

133. "The Joyful Noise Mystery." Teleplay by Gerry Conway; story by Dean Hargrove and Joyce Burditt; directed by Bob Bralver. May 2, 1991. Reviewed at LOC.

134. "Signs and Wonders." Written by Lee Blessing and Jeanne Blake; directed by Robert Allen Ackerman. January 7, 1998. Reviewed off broadcast television.

135. Lincoln and Mamiya (1990), p. xii.

136. Ibid., p. 346.

137. Ibid., pp. 377–8.

138. Ibid., pp. 339–40.

they continue, noting that "historically, among black churches there has seldom been a discrete bifurcation of the social and religious dimensions" and that the involvement of black churches in "progressive programs to ameliorate the problems of black youth and families is a continuation of this long tradition."[139] Even so, the depiction of a successful intervention by the church in gang violence was unlikely because, even though bringing unchurched urban youth into the church necessitates dealing with gang membership, gangs socialize members and recruits to avoid "mainstream activities and institutions," particularly the black church.[140] Nonetheless, the emphasis on gospel music and social issues, and the limited portrayal of blacks in Catholic-set programs, rings true to the overall experience of African-Americans in churches of the era.

Beyond African-Americans, another group that received increased representation on popular American TV programs set in the church (as they did on television as a whole) was gay men. (To date, lesbians have appeared on only one church-set program: the most recent one, *The Book of Daniel*.) Two of the programs considered in this chapter included an episode-specific gay character and issues concerning inclusion of gay people in the church. Those programs that did include gay characters and issues were among the more recent. *Good News*' pilot specifically dealt with acceptance of gay people in general, and as congregants in particular. *Nothing Sacred* went further and acknowledged the existence of gay clergy, albeit in an episode that went unaired and yet received much media attention. Both were programs of the mid-1990s, so their inclusion of gay characters and issues was part of a growing trend on American TV programs.[141] The gay rights movement, begun in the late 1960s, had resulted in more visibility of gay people and more discussion of issues of sexuality, including the church's response to these matters. Churches of all denominations began to struggle with their response to this increased visibility and the role gays sought in the life of the church in general (including blessings of their unions) and the ordained ministry in particular. While various Protestant denominations of this era developed criteria under which gay clergy could or could not be ordained (most often insisting on celibacy), the issue became more of a problem for the Catholic Church. In contrast to most Protestant denominations, which allow married men and women to be ordained, the Catholic acceptance of only unmarried, celibate males to become priests has led to what many acknowledge is a quiet gay subculture in American seminaries, where estimates of the number of homosexual men enrolled range from 10 percent to over 50 percent.[142]

---

139. Ibid., pp. 341–2.
140. Ibid., p. 322.
141. See the growing number of books on this phenomenon: Stephen Tropiano (2002), *The Prime Time Closet: A History of Gays and Lesbians on TV*. New York: Applause Books; Larry Gross (2002), *Up From Invisibility*. New York: Columbia University Press; Walters, Suzanna Danuta (2003), *All the Rage: The Story of Gay Visibility in America*. Chicago: University of Chicago Press; Ron Becker (2006), *Gay TV and Straight America*. New Jersey: Rutgers University Press.
142. Steinfels (2003), p. 323.

During the time of these television programs, the existence of gay priests in the Catholic Church was an oft-assumed but little publicly discussed truism, and so television's relative silence on the matter may have followed that of the church itself. Discussions of the sexuality of priests developed more in the coming decade, as priest child abuse scandals made headlines, and more recently as Pope Benedict XVI pronounced that men with "deep seated" homosexual tendencies would not be permitted in Catholic seminaries.[143] Nonetheless, in the mid-1990s this hot-button issue may have been too controversial for episodic television programs to depict, as only the unaired episode of *Nothing Sacred* dared touch upon the subject. Even more controversial but less acknowledged than the existence of gay clergy may be the reality of priests dying of AIDS, which a study reported by the Associated Press in 2000 indicates may be more common than many realize.[144]

Another concern in the Catholic Church has been the dwindling number of men entering the priesthood — a topic which is extensively discussed by church historians.[145] After rising significantly in the years after World War II, the number of Catholic priests in the United States leveled off and in the post-Vatican II years; it peaked at 58,909 in 1975, and declined to 42,839 in 2005.[146] The decrease is due in part to the ordained leaving the priesthood — some because of the challenges of celibacy — and in part due to fewer candidates entering seminaries;[147] the number of seminarians dropped from 8,325 in 1965 to 3,308 in 2005, while similarly the number of ordinations dropped from 994 to 454 in the same years.[148] Meanwhile, as the number of Catholics in the United States has increased, so too has the number of parishes without a resident priest, which rose from 549 in 1965 to 3,251 in 2005.[149] The resulting situation concerns many Catholics, who worry about the lack of trained religious leaders and the morale of those priests who remain.[150] Of the television series in this era, it is only *Nothing Sacred* that most regularly and seriously included consideration of these issues. Father Ray commented upon being tired of crossing out faces from his ordination picture, lamenting the number of his seminary classmates who have left the priesthood. He also questioned his own calling, from when he encountered an old girlfriend and had to renew his commitment to celibacy, to

---

143. Ian Fisher and Laurie Goodstein (2005), "In strong terms, Rome is to ban gays as priests." *New York Times*, November 23.

144. Associated Press (2000), "Priests hit hard by hidden AIDS epidemic." Cable News Network report, January 31, 2000, available at http://archives.cnn.com/2000/HEALTH/AIDS/01/31/aids.priests/index.html (accessed September 17, 2006).

145. Greeley (1990), *The Catholic Myth*, pp. 199–225; Gillis (1999), pp. 245–58.

146. Center for Applied Research in the Apostolate (CARA), Georgetown University (undated), "Frequently requested Catholic Church statistics," available at http://cara.georgetown.edu/bulletin/index.htm (accessed May 22, 2007).

147. Dolan (1985), *The American Catholic Experience*, p. 437.

148. CARA, undated, "Frequently requested Catholic Church statistics."

149. Ibid.

150. Gillis (1999), p. 254.

when he wondered aloud if he had made the right choice to become a priest, ultimately realizing the priesthood is indeed where he belongs. Father Leo also took a hiatus from the parish, and Father Eric occasionally reflected upon his own calling, the meaning of priesthood, and whether he was suited to it. *Have Faith* also directly considered the issue in one episode wherein Monsignor Mac's friend from seminary, who has left the priesthood, visited Mac's parish and discussed his reasons for leaving the ministry, including his desire to date women and start a family. The visit led the Monsignor to reveal that at times he himself had had doubts about his calling. Other programs alluded to the issue of the priest shortage, such as when the young, gentle priest from a Mafia family who was sent to train with Father Dowling considered leaving the priesthood; Dowling encouraged him to reconsider, Sister Steve adding "the church needs men like you."

The related issue of the dwindling number of nuns in the sisterhood received scant attention. The number of nuns in the United States dropped from 179,954 in 1965 to 68,634 in 2005 — a remarkable decline.[151] Only *Nothing Sacred* addressed the issue in "A Nun's Story," wherein Sister Maureen's roommate — the last of her order — died and Maureen wondered if she too would die alone, leading her to consider a change of vocation and take a leave of absence from the parish in order to pursue a secular job. *Hack* also included a nun who left her order to lead a secular life. Overall, stories wherein clerics reflect upon their calling not only revealed a growing issue in the Catholic Church but also allowed these programs to highlight dramatic conflict both within a character and between characters, as others comment on the clerics' doubts.

The Catholic Church became more reliant on the laity to assume duties previously undertaken by priests and nuns. Indeed, this was in part the hope of Vatican II, to encourage more shared participation between clergy and laity in the leadership of the church; as one document read, laity should be given "every opportunity" to "zealously participate" in the work of the church "according to their abilities and the needs of the times."[152] This declaration, and the declining numbers of priests and nuns, led to more and more laity filling positions formerly held by clergy.[153] With Vatican II the focus of the ordained ministry increasingly was focused on administering sacraments and saying Mass,[154] leaving the laity to assume other duties. As such, priests have had to learn to share their responsibilities, and as Gillis notes:

> . . . [many] are more than happy to share ministerial responsibilities with the laity. They are not threatened by lay involvement or power. In fact, they welcome it. The more the laity assume ownership for their parishes, the

151. CARA, "Frequently requested Catholic Church statistics."
152. Gillis (1999), p. 27.
153. Ibid., p. 27.
154. Dolan (1985), *The American Catholic Experience*, p. 437.

stronger the parish. These priests and nuns understand their role increasingly as educators and enablers. Their pastoral plan is to hand over to the laity areas of responsibility such as finances, much of the administrative duties, building maintenance and other areas that require time-consuming attention but are ancillary to their central ministry to preach the Gospel by word and action. They also readily share ministerial duties that directly involve pastoral care. Ultimately they remain responsible for proper oversight of all dimensions of parish life, but they need not micro-manage every aspect of parish life and administration. Practicing such a principle of subsidiary frees them to concentrate on aspects of ministry that permit them to serve people in a direct and personal manner.[155]

As another church historian put it, "Post-Vatican II Catholicism has largely become the church of the laity."[156] Given this, it is interesting to compare the depiction of these issues in *Have Faith*, a late 1980s program, with that of *Nothing Sacred*, a program of the late 1990s. Both were set in a parish, but the priests of the earlier program were responsible for virtually all of the church's administrative and service duties, whereas in the latter many responsibilities were performed by members of the laity. Hence, in *Have Faith* priests served as teachers, youth ministers, preaching mentors and the church accountant, all in addition to their duties of counseling, administering sacraments and saying Mass. In *Nothing Sacred*, members of the laity served as youth minister, church accountant, supervisor of preaching and director of education, allowing the priests and nun to focus on counseling, helping the homeless and hungry and visiting the sick, and the priests to administer the sacraments and say Mass. Indeed, even as Sister Maureen took her leave of absence, *Nothing Sacred* introduced Dr. Justine Madsen Judd, a trained member of the laity and graduate of Harvard Divinity School, who came to St. Thomas to serve as director of education and supervisor of preaching.

The role of women and feminist theology developed in the Catholic Church of the period and this was reflected on television in *Nothing Sacred*. Indeed, the issue of women preaching, administering sacraments and being eligible for ordained ministry in the Catholic Church has been the subject of debate around the globe. Official Catholic policy severely restricts women from preaching at Mass and administering most sacraments; women may offer reflections on Bible readings, and administer sacraments in some emergency situations. As Protestant denominations have permitted women not only to preach and participate in all aspects of liturgical and sacramental life but also to become ordained ministers, a growing dissatisfaction has arisen among some US Catholics regarding policies about the role of women in the church.[157] Further,

---

155. Gillis (1999), p. 255.
156. Dolan (2002), *In Search of an American Catholicism*, p. 229.
157. Ibid., pp. 229, 236–7; Dolan (1985), *The American Catholic Experience*, p. 439; Gillis

as the clergy shortage has grown, increasing numbers of Americans have suggested that the church consider ordaining women — a recommendation rejected by Rome.[158] As such, Sister Maureen's invitation to preach at another church, and her leading a gathering in church when all of the ordained men are in jail, touched on issues hotly debated among American Catholics, as did her occasional statements about longing to be ordained. Most pointedly, this occurred in "A Nun's Story," when she said to her principal opponent Father Martin:

> Martin, you are a priest. You know from your experience on that altar that when you participate in that miracle it transcends gender. It has nothing to do with male or female. I know you know this. Why does it make you so angry that I want to participate in that same miracle?

Her dialogues and debates with others in the church about the role of women reflected an important aspect of contemporary Catholicism. So too did her advocacy of feminist theology and her objection to the use of exclusively male language to refer to God. Sister Maureen protested whenever a member of the parish staff referred to God in masculine terms, and the congregation itself used the term "Mother" (in addition to "Father") when referring to God. This behavior emerges from the thought of feminist theologians such as Catholic theologian Rosemary Radford Ruether, who in her landmark book *Sexism and God-talk* (1983) advocated a reconsideration of the exclusively male identity of God. While not all Catholics (or Protestants for that matter) would welcome all that these theologians advocated or its application in liturgy, the issue did emerge in the church of the era and this debate was introduced to television's account of modern Catholicism.

One final area where stories on television programs raised issues of importance in the Catholic church concerns divorce. Official Catholic teaching states that divorce is permitted only if a marriage was never consummated. The Catholic Church does not otherwise grant or officially recognize divorces.[159] While the reality of divorce did appear in Protestant-set programs such as *Good News*, it was more as an opportunity for pastoral care and counseling than as a matter concerning church policy, since Protestant churches recognize divorce. Not so for Catholic settings where, because of official rejection of divorce, far-reaching implications may be portended. Indeed, this was reflected in *Hack* where the priest was disciplined for hiring a divorced woman to work for his parish. Nonetheless, in recent years there has been a changing attitude among Catholic

---

(1999), pp. 239–42.

158. Greeley (1990), *The Catholic Myth*, pp. 141, 214–15, 228; Dolan (1985), *The American Catholic Experience*, p. 439; Dolan (2002), *In Search of an American Catholicism*, pp. 228, 236–7; Gillis (1999), pp. 239–42.

159. An annulment is different and means that the marriage was not valid, for particular reasons outlined by the church.

officials to the growing reality of divorce — an attitude that has "undergone substantial revision" in the church, as Dolan notes, stating that:

> Simply put, a pastoral revolution has taken place. Clergy and bishops are recognizing the reality of divorce among Catholics and have sought to minister to divorced Catholics in a more effective and compassionate manner. In addition, church authorities have become more willing to grant divorce with the right to remarry (i.e., marriage annulments).[160]

Dolan points out the existence of a growing number of pastoral programs and events that cater to divorced people, offering this as evidence of one way the church is striving to respond to a reality facing many Catholics. This reality was reflected on *Nothing Sacred*, when Father Ray helped two people come to terms with the breakup of their marriage, even holding an (unofficial) ceremony to mark the end of their union. Father Ray's handling of his parishioners' impending separation, with a makeshift but poignant ritual, reflects this changing attitude.

Clearly, *Nothing Sacred* juggled a number of ecclesiastic issues that arose during its era, and while it stands out for the salience of these issues, other programs also addressed important concerns of the period, from abortion and the Sanctuary Movement (*Hell Town*, *Nothing Sacred*), to changing demographics (*Hell Town*, *Nothing Sacred*), gang violence and juvenile delinquency (*Hell Town*, *Sister Kate*, *Father Dowling Mysteries*, *Nothing Sacred*, *Good News*), dealing with teenage sexuality, contraception and sexually transmitted diseases (*Mariah*, *Sister Kate*, *Nothing Sacred*, *Good News*), battered women (*Hell Town*, *Hack*), racism (*Good News*), the gay rights movement (*Nothing Sacred*, *Good News*) and the challenge of maintaining qualified people in ordained ministry (*Have Faith*, *Father Dowling Mysteries*, *Nothing Sacred*). In these ways and others, these programs shifted the focus from debating the direction of the church from liberal-conservative viewpoints to how the church can serve the needs of the modern world and remain relevant in it. Some of the already established trends continued, such as the need for fundraising and the Catholic proclivity for business-mindedness. Along these lines, several of the TV parishes featured scaffolding as a permanent fixture in the sanctuary (*Hell Town*, *Nothing Sacred*), bingo remained a cherished money-raiser (*Sister Kate*, *Have Faith, Hack*), and representatives of the church effectively and proudly pressured people to donate money to the church and its mission (*Father Dowling Mysteries*, *M*A*S*H*). While some new ground was broken (for example, a Jewish cleric in *Lanigan's Rabbi*, and African-American and Protestant-set programs such as *Good News*) the overall focus through the 1980s and into the 1990s remained on the Catholic church. This emphasis would shift, however, as Protestant-set programs focusing on families led by clerics would predominate from the mid-1990s on. This, then — the church in the family context — is the

---

160. Dolan (1985), *The American Catholic Experience*, p. 436.

most recent trend in American television programs focusing on the church and its leaders.

Questions for Reflection

1) A number of characters in series considered in this chapter had colorful pasts: *Sarge*'s Father Cavanaugh as a police detective; *Hell Town*'s Father Hardstep as a convict and Sister Indigo as a prostitute; *Hack*'s Liz as a nun-turned-parole-officer; *Father Dowling*'s Sister Stephanie as a juvenile delinquent; even *Sister Kate*'s namesake as a biblical archaeologist. What do you make of this? What does this suggest about the nature of television?

2) In many ways, *Nothing Sacred* is the most realistic program set in the church. Not a zany sitcom, overdrawn drama or sensational detective show, the characters and situations are presented in a more believable fashion. It was also decidedly liberal in its depiction. Was the program unsuccessful from an audience perspective because of its particular politics, or would a program as conservative as this one was progressive have fared the same? Why or why not?

3) Compare television's depiction of church leaders in this era with that in movies, including *True Confessions* (1981), *Mass Appeal* (1984), *Agnes of God* (1985), *The Mission* (1986), *We're No Angels* (1989), *Godfather 3* (1990), *Sister Act* (1992), *Sister Act Two: Back in the Habit* (1993), *Priest* (1994) and *Dead Man Walking* (1995). What similarities and differences arise . . . in the issues addressed? . . . in their representations of priests and nuns?

4) What issues emerge as the most prominent ones facing the churches represented on television shows in this era, and how does this compare with actual issues faced by these churches?

5) Why is it that on all episodes dealing with someone considering taking religious vows or serving in ordained ministry, the focus is on unsuitable candidates who must be talked out of it? What is the impact of having no sincere, appropriate candidates for religious life emerge on these television programs?

Video Sources

M*A*S*H. All eleven seasons are available on DVD. Twentieth Century Fox Home Entertainment.

Good News occasionally airs in syndication on cable television.

Individual episodes are available for screening at the following locations (Library of Congress, Washington, DC [abbrev. LOC]; Paley Center for Media, New York and Los Angeles [abbrev. PCM]; UCLA Films and Television Archives, Los Angeles [abbrev. UCLA]):

    Sarge — LOC

    Hell Town — LOC, UCLA

Sister Kate — LOC, UCLA
Have Faith — LOC, PCM
Father Dowling Mysteries — LOC, PCM, UCLA
Nothing Sacred — LOC, PCM, UCLA
Good News — LOC (UCLA has preservation copies, as yet unidentified
  in their catalog)

Suggested Further Reading

Buhle, Paul (1985), "The Gospel according to Robert Blake." *The Village Voice*,
    September 17, 33–5.
Dolan, Jay P. (2002), *In Search of an American Catholicism: A History of Religion
    and Culture in Tension*. New York: Oxford University Press.
Greeley, Andrew M. (1998), "A *Nothing Sacred* episode you haven't seen." *New
    York Times,* March 1.
Meisler, Andy (1997), "Battling demons (and ratings) at the pulpit." *New York
    Times*, Television, October 26 — November 1.
Seal, Cynthia (1997), "Is nothing sacred? Hollywood's treatment of Catholicism."
    San Francisco Faith, November.

Richard Lewis as Rabbi Richard Glass and Stephen Collins as Reverend Eric Camden, presiding over their children's wedding in *7th Heaven.*

4

THE CHURCH IN FAMILY LIFE

After the first two clusters of church-set programs, a third trend developed focusing on the family life of church leaders. It spotlighted the domestic life of clerics and as such was distinct from earlier programs in that it favored Protestant settings, where parent-child conflicts could arise. That TV series highlighted the households of ecclesiastics is not surprising given how common the domestic situation comedy has become on American television. Producers needed to find innovative family settings for these programs, and turned to the church. Some of these programs focused on traditional nuclear families headed by a cleric, such as *The Family Holvak*, *7th Heaven* and *The Book of Daniel*.[1] Several focused on clerical widows or widowers and their children, such as with *Amen*, *Amazing Grace* and *Soul Man*. Uniquely, *Trinity* spotlighted a Roman Catholic priest and his nuclear family. All of these programs focused regularly and principally on an ecclesiastic (although in *Trinity* the cleric was one of several principal characters).

Before moving on to these, one program that included a cleric as an ancillary character merits brief mention: *The Cavanaughs* (1986–9). This CBS sitcom depicted the family life of a devotedly Irish-Catholic, democratic household, which included a priest as a secondary character. Most episodes focus on retired, widowered 70-something-year-old Francis Cavanaugh, or "Pop," and his relationship with his spunky grown-up daughter Kit, a failed Hollywood actress now living at home. A daily visitor to the home is Pop's grandson — the red-headed, fun-loving Father Chuck Cavanaugh, Jr., whose energetic spirit seems born of his own dreams of show business stardom. In one episode, Father Chuck pitches a priest-detective TV series set in the Bahamas to a Hollywood star visiting the Cavanaugh home, telling him "we'll do lunch."[2] In another, he dreams about a "major musical comedy" based upon the Bible, relishing the chance to direct it.[3] In most episodes, Father Chuck's presence only adds comic religious humor as he reacts to situations facing others. "Gimme Shelter,"

---

1. One other example would have been a Fox network program, developed by renowned executive producer David E. Kelley, called *The Pastor's Wife* (1995), which centered on the family of a Lutheran minister serving a Staten Island parish, but the program never made it past the pilot stage.

2. "Coastal Disturbance." Written by Robert Moloney; directed by Matthew Diamond. Series executive produced by Leonard Goldberg. August 15, 1988. Reviewed at LOC.

3. "Careers." Written by Sam Greenbaum; directed by Matthew Diamond. August 22, 1988. Reviewed at LOC.

however, ties into the trend of TV clerics to question their calling, as it focuses in particular on the priest and his thoughts of leaving his ministry to start his own family.[4]

Father Chuck's homeless shelter has been closed, and he must place all its inhabitants with friends. He asks Pop to take in a young, single woman and her infant son. Father Chuck often visits the two at Pop's house, and Kit and Pop begin to wonder if he is "sweet on" the woman. Father Chuck eventually admits he is thinking of leaving the priesthood to marry. Emphasizing the family drama, Pop tells him that if he stops being a priest he stops being a Cavanaugh, and refuses to talk to him. In the ensuing conflict, the priest's "crisis of faith" leads to occasional references to the post-Vatican II church: Father Chuck jokes that Pop still holds him personally responsible for the proliferation of the folk Mass, "like I invented guitars," he quips; Pop, in turn, grumbles about the demotion of St. Christopher and the lifting of restrictions against eating meat on Fridays. The Bishop gives Father Chuck time off to think about his situation. Chuck confides to Kit that "all priests wonder, they wonder what it would be like to have their own family . . . maybe it's God's will that I give up my time slot and start my own series." In the end, the priest decides he is being selfish, renews his commitment to his ministry, and grandfather and grandson have a touching moment where they apologize for what they put each other through. Somewhat sensational but also touching and timely, the episode demonstrates how the series dealt with situations — including those that touched upon issues related to the church through the role of Father Chuck — in a manner that emphasized the characters' family relations.

This emphasis is indicative of the focus of all of the programs in this grouping. These shows still highlight the life and work of church leaders but now focus on how these affect familial relationships, such as that between a deacon and his daughter (*Amen*), a pastor and his or her family (*The Family Holvak, Soul Man, Amazing Grace, 7th Heaven* and *The Book of Daniel*), or a priest and his parents and siblings (*Trinity*). Though these programs continue to address modern issues and, much less frequently, ideological struggles within churches, the heart of these programs is the relationships among members of each church leader's family.

The Family Holvak

The earliest dramatic series to focus on a minister and his family was the short-lived NBC program *The Family Holvak* (1975).[5] Set in Tennessee during the Depression, the series was an attempt to use the setting of the highly successful family drama *The Waltons* (1972–81) but with a more reasonably

---

4. "Gimme Shelter." Written by Mark Masuoka; directed by Andrew D. Weyman. October 3, 1988. Reviewed at LOC.
5. The series was later were rebroadcast on CBS.

sized family (the Waltons had seven children, the Holvaks only two) and with a pastor as father.[6] Lasting ten episodes, the show took a nostalgic look at a simple family struggling to get by with limited wealth but richly held values. The Holvaks included: Reverend Tom Holvak, a farmer and the town's pastor; his faithful wife Elizabeth, a resourceful, good-humored woman; Ramey, their fair-haired adolescent son, who was as thoughtful and respectful as he was independent and mischievous; and Julie Mae, their inquisitive eight-year-old daughter. Centering more on their family life than on the church, the program highlighted the support the family members offered each other.

The first episode set the direction of the series. Ramey and a friend lounge in a meadow, the friend razzing Ramey that it must be "the Devil's own hell to have a preacher for a pa." Ramey's buddy decides to visit a convict he befriended while hanging around a chain gang. Anxious to prove he is not afraid of mischief, Ramey joins him. The convict asks for the boys' help breaking free, quoting a verse from Isaiah about releasing the unjustly bound and quoting Jesus' proclamation that he came to set captives free. Swayed by his charm and scriptural reassurances, the boys bring him a blade. When another prisoner attacks Ramey, the Bible-quoting convict steps in, hits the other man and "saves" the boy. Unknown to the youngsters, the prisoners staged the attack-and-rescue to gain the boy's trust. The preacher's son thanks the "heroic" prisoner, who asks him to return the favor someday. When the escaped convict later shows up at the Holvak home he claims he was paroled, and asks the boy to tell his family he is a hobo. A bit suspicious but wanting to be hospitable, the Reverend and his wife allow the "hobo" escapee to stay with them. He in return does chores and slowly becomes close to all in the family, especially the boy.

The role of religious faith and the father's vocation feature throughout. Because the convict is staying in the family parlor, the minister must prepare his sermon in his bedroom, and when his wife expresses her displeasure over the situation, Reverend Holvak responds, "Good sermons aren't necessarily written in comfort, you know, darling." Mrs. Holvak's irritation arises from her suspicions about the man — suspicions she later shares with the visitor when privately she advises him not to confuse the family's act of Christian kindness with naïveté, saying, "When someone comes to the door for help, well, we do what we can; but we aren't jackasses, you know." Later, the Reverend debates with a church deacon in the Holvak home about how best to evangelize. The deacon demands that the minister preach on harsh passages from scripture, so that someone will be moved to repent and be saved. This leads the pastor to retort, "You can't scare a man into wanting to be saved," and the deacon to reply, "How many have you loved into wanting to be saved, Reverend?" "Lovin' lasts longer than scarin'," the minister rejoins. Hearing this exchange, the convict remarks that his own father used to throw scripture around like the deacon, thus explaining his

6. Tim Brooks and Earle Marsh (2003), *The Complete Directory to Prime-Time Network and Cable TV Shows 1946–Present*, 8th edn. New York: Ballantine Books, p. 390.

familiarity with the Bible. A day later, Ramey sees the convict in town talking to the prisoner who attacked him. The boy realizes that the attack was a ruse and figures that the two must be planning a getaway. He confesses to his father the truth about their visitor, worrying that his dad will no longer trust him. Aware of the boy's inner struggle, the pastor assures Ramey that he knows the boy did what he thought was right, and commends him for revealing the truth. Calm and understanding, the pastor reassures his son of his love and trust.

The situation comes to a peak that Sunday in the Reverend's church — a simple building with a pulpit, pews, cross, piano and plain windows. The minister and deacon sing a hymn with the choir, after which the Reverend asks if anyone in the congregation "would like to come and take the Lord as their Savior." Seeming genuinely moved and thankful, but also knowing the minister needs to satisfy the deacon, the convict rises and comes forward, leading the Holvaks to look on worriedly, knowing that the sheriff is in the assembly. Outside after the service, the sheriff inquires about the stranger's background, saying officials are looking for two escaped prisoners. Reverend Holvak diffuses his suspicions without lying, assuring the sheriff that the man is staying with them. At their home that evening, the mother, who has grown fond of the visitor, confides to her husband that she hopes he is not thinking of turning the man in. She asks if coming to a minister's house allows the man to claim sanctuary. The Reverend notes a minister's house is not a church. Mrs. Holvak says he is splitting hairs, insisting the escapee is a changed man and that when he stood up in church "he meant it!" She worries what it would do to the man's faith if the minister turned him in. Reverend Holvak reveals that he has been wondering why God led the prisoner to their door, and that he thought he knew why in church, but is no longer sure. The next day the Reverend suggests that the convict turn himself in, saying, "you have me, Elizabeth, Ramey and the Lord Himself standing with you," but when the sheriff's car pulls up outside, the escapee hits the minister, knocking him out, and flees. When the sheriff and his men pursue the convict, Ramey goes after him on his own with a shotgun. He finds the escapee along a riverbank and holds the gun on him, but the prisoner laughs, exclaiming that the "nice, God-fearing son of the preacher Holvak" would not shoot him. As the police approach, the boy slips and falls into the water, and the convict must decide whether to run or save the boy. He does the latter. Later, the sheriff and minister promise to speak on the prisoner's behalf. The convict tells the preacher, "You've had your eye on my immortal soul since the beginning, haven't you?" to which Reverend Holvak replies, "Well, that's my job."[7] The episode shows the Holvak's unconditional love and support for each other. Further, it shows that their religious beliefs are alive but not impractical or overly zealous, and they expect that their faith will be tested, while also believing that with the family's support they will withstand these challenges.

---

7. "The Long Way Home" (Parts 1 and 2). Written by Richard Fielder; directed by Alf Kjellin. September 5 and 14, 1975. Reviewed at LOC.

Some storylines involve the family's faith apart from the church setting, as when Julie Mae must learn to accept death when a pet dies. Some episodes involve almost no religion at all, such as when Ramey develops a crush on his schoolteacher. Other episodes more specifically involve the church.[8] In "Willing Heart," for example, a Ku Klux Klan-styled gang attends services at the Reverend's church. Known for their brutality (they burn barns and whip men who are atheists or adulterers), the robed and hooded "knights" wish to express their support for the restoration of the church, which suffered roof damage during a lightning storm. Reverend Holvak leaves the pulpit to tell them they are not welcome, but they refuse to leave and ask, "Is God's house no longer open to all of His children?" Matters heat up when Ramey sneaks out at night and witnesses the knights flogging the contractor who is asking for too much money to rebuild the roof. When the knights spot the minister's son, they make him swear on the Bible that he will not reveal what he saw that evening lest he be "struck down instantly and suffer hell for all eternity." Ramey later asks his father if a promise made on the Bible is binding if it was coerced, and when the minister says no, the boy reveals what he saw. Learning that the Reverend plans to take his son to the authorities, the knights arrive at the Holvak house with torches burning and set fire to the barn, demanding that the boy come out. The Reverend, having sent the boy to get help, tells them his son is not there, and reaches for a shotgun in the back of a closet. The knights insist that the minister come out. Holvak puts the gun down and leaves his home while his terrified wife and daughter look on. The knights put a hood over his head and threaten him ("I hope you're saying your prayers," one says) just as the sheriff arrives. In the end, the grateful contractor reassesses his arrangement with the church and agrees to work on the roof based solely, as he says, on the Reverend's character as collateral.[9]

Family Holvak was short-lived, failing to live up to the ratings of similar rural family programs such as *Little House on the Prairie* (which debuted the year before) and *The Waltons*. The first television program to feature a Protestant minister, it was also the first to center on a cleric's family life. Its religious themes were not overbearing, as the family dynamic was the prominent feature of the series. A decade later, programs featuring church leaders and their family life reemerged and became a prominent theme in church-set network television programs.

---

8. "First Love" (Parts 1 and 2). Written by Stanley Roberts; directed by John Newland. October 5 and 12, 1975. Reviewed at LOC.
9. "Willing Heart." Written by Preston Wood; directed by Corey Allen. October 19, 1975. Reviewed at LOC.

Amen

The next program to focus on a church leader's family was NBC's successful *Amen* (1986–91). Like *Good News*, it was an Ed Weinberger sitcom. A vehicle for Sherman Helmsley, fresh off his role as George Jefferson on the *The Jeffersons*, the program centered on three main characters: Ernest Frye (Helmsley), an ethically challenged lawyer and widowed deacon at First Community Church in Philadelphia; Thelma Frye, his oft-scorned 30-something live-at-home daughter; and the Reverend Dr. Reuben Gregory (Clifton Davis), a principled man of the cloth who often was at odds with Deacon Frye, and who courted Thelma in an on-again, off-again romance. The series focused as much on the domestic life of the Fryes and the romantic tensions between Thelma and Reuben as it did on the church. In fact, the two main sets for the program were the Fryes' home and the church's office. Other characters in the series included: the sassy and single middle-aged Hetebrink sisters, Casietta and Amelia (the latter played by Roz Ryan — the star of *Good News*), both members of the church's board of directors; Rolly Forbes, an older but lively board member; in early episodes, Lorenzo, the flamboyant choir director; in later seasons, Clarence, a troubled but good-natured teenager assigned to the church for community service, and Inga, the Fryes' Swedish housekeeper.

Amen was the first series to focus on a Protestant parish headed by a single pastor, and as such was able to explore new ground in the form of romantic relationships with the show's cleric. This gave the program the opportunity to develop storylines common to many other sitcoms. Another distinction was that the star of the program was Helmsley, whose character was not only a deacon but also a single lawyer; hence the focus of the program sometimes shifted to his battles in the courtroom, occasionally to save the church from legal action, or his relationship with his daughter or other women. Nonetheless, the deacon's service to the church, the regular church setting and the Reverend Gregory's prominence in the series gave *Amen* a significant and regular focus on the church and its leaders, seen through the Fryes' family life. Sometimes the series focused on explicitly church-related stories; sometimes the religious background provided a setup for less church-focused stories; and sometimes the focus was almost entirely outside the church and its activities, except that the action involved a deacon and minister. This and its lighthearted, often slapstick appeal helped make the show uncontroversial, and hence a successful church-set series.

Compared to earlier church-set programs, the focus on family life in *Amen* was a significant shift in emphasis. Even so, *Amen* did have much in common with other church-set programs, as was clear from the series' pilot.[10] As with *Good News* and *Amazing Grace*, the pilot sees a new minister coming to lead a congregation and, as with those other series, the first meeting with church leadership does not go well, resulting in conflict. The episode opens as Deacon

---

10. "Pilot." Written by Ed Weinberger; directed by Stan Lathan. Series executive produced by Roland Kiddee and Dean Hargrove. September 21, 1986. Reviewed at PCM.

Frye barges into the office of the First Community Church, while the minister is working on his sermon. The deacon reveals his straight-talking, tactless style in his first exchange with the Reverend as he scolds the rather large minister, saying, "It's been six months since I hired you as the pastor of the church, and since that time, our attendance is down 12 percent, our collections are down 33 percent, and your weight is up 250 percent." The Reverend confronts the deacon, saying, "I don't see why my weight is any business of yours," to which the deacon responds: "This church is my business. My father founded this church. Now you're gonna have to do something about yourself. People are complaining you're blocking their view of the choir." After more insults, the minister quits, leaving Frye and the church's board of directors to search for a replacement.

Deacon Frye, the Hetebrink sisters and Rolly assemble to interview their one and only candidate, Reverend Gregory. They ask about his educational background, and he recounts his schooling: he received a master's in religious education from Yale Divinity School and a doctorate in Christian studies from Union Theological Seminary. Given this, the deacon's follow-up question comes as something of a surprise to the rest of the board, as he asks, "Do you believe in God?" The Reverend assures the deacon that, yes, he does believe in God. Startling the board again, the deacon asks if the Reverend has ever been arrested; joining a line of other TV ecclesiastics who were imprisoned for just causes, Reuben says, "Once . . . for picketing against racism outside the South African embassy." The deacon announces he has one last question. The exchange which follows sets up a conflict between the principled minister and the narrow-minded deacon that will last the entire series:

> Deacon Frye: You understand that the board of directors has the last say on all church policy?
> Rev. Gregory: Well, I've always lived according to my own conscience and I don't intend to change that now. I don't think I'd be doing my job if I always pleased the board of directors.
> Deacon Frye: What!?
> Rev. Gregory: Deacon, I'm really here for one purpose only, and that's to serve the Lord.
> Deacon Frye: That is the most narrow-minded view of religion I've ever heard!

The board then asks the minister to step outside so they may deliberate, and vote three-to-one to hire the Reverend, the deacon being the lone dissenter.

The deacon later offers to represent a local high-school basketball player who is being courted by several colleges to play on their team. When the Reverend discovers that the deacon's deal involves under-the-table bribes amounting to tens of thousands of dollars, the minister confronts the lawyer and player with the ethics of their behavior. In a rousing speech to them both at the deacon's house, the Reverend says he believes the young man knows better than to cheat and be a profiteer, for whom money means more than integrity. Pleased when the boy heeds his advice, the Reverend instructs him to stop by the church the next day so they can get him into a good college the legitimate way. The deacon, believing his deal was good, confronts the minister. Reverend Gregory says that it may be impossible for the two of them to work together. After each suggests that the other quit, they reach a tacit agreement to work together for the good of the church.

Conflicts between the minister and deacon are an ongoing theme of the series. Significantly, their differences are not about ideological debates over the direction of the church but personal matters or the deacon's ethics. One example of the continuing friction between the two concerns the Reverend's sermons, which the deacon finds boring. Frye quips after one service, "If we rented pillows and blankets, we'd be millionaires," implying a correlation between the Reverend's sermon and the church's declining collections.[11] On another Sunday, the deacon remarks that he has never enjoyed a service so much, because Reverend Gregory did not give a sermon.[12] The deacon's constant criticism eventually leads Reverend Gregory to accept a call to another church. This occurs in "California Dreaming," when a representative of a Los Angeles parish attends a service, compliments the minister on his "electrifying sermon" and offers him a job that includes a pay raise, funding to build a center for needy children, a parsonage and a car. When Deacon Frye makes his usual remarks about the minister's sermon, and scolds him for considering another position, Reverend Gregory decides to leave. Eventually, Reverend Gregory returns to First Community Church just as they are interviewing new candidates. The minister shares that he remains committed to building a center for needy children, but at their church, and adds: "You'll never be sorry you took me back and I'll never be sorry I came back either, 'cause one thing I've always felt in this church: that's love. The kind of love you can search the whole world over and never find. I realize that now, and I'd like to thank you for your forgiveness, thank you for your kindness, thank you for taking me back into your hearts." The deacon replies, "Welcome back, Reverend. You know, listening to that brought it all back to me. I forgot how boring you are."[13]

Other problems between the deacon and parson arise when Frye tries to make money for the church, such as by turning it into a Las Vegas-style wedding mill in "Wedding Bell Blues."[14] This is one of several episodes that hearken back

---

11. "Deacon's Dilemma." Written by Paris Qualles; directed by Shelley Jensen. February 24, 1990. Reviewed at PCM; also available at UCLA.

12. "Can't Help Lovin' that Man of Mine." Written by William Daley; directed by Shelley Jensen. October 14, 1989. Reviewed off broadcast television; also available at PCM, and UCLA.

13. "California Dreaming." Written by Geoff Gordon and Gordon Lewis; directed by Bill Foster. October 3, 1987. Reviewed at PCM.

14. "Wedding Bell Blues." Written by Jim Wells; directed by Bill Foster. March 12, 1988. Reviewed at PCM.

to Sister Bertrille's money-making schemes and the Reverend Mother's need to step in when matters get out of control, as well as some of the money-making antics in *Have Faith*. The story finds the First Community Church caught up in the deacon's plan, offering a "deluxe wedding package" that includes trained swans (named David and Bathsheba), a Polaroid picture of the groom and bride and a rental bouquet. To have the Hetabrink sisters sing a favorite wedding song costs $20 extra. Even the children of the parish are enlisted to help advertise the venture, as a little girl and boy wear bride and groom outfits and skate about the neighborhood with signs reading "First Community Church, The Chapel of Love." The church's goal is to marry ten couples a day. All this leads the Reverend to express his concern about treating marriage as a commercial venture, but the deacon can see only dollar signs. When a couple whom Reverend Gregory married nearly a decade before come to him for counseling, he advises them to tell each other the truth, and is surprised when the husband confesses to having had an affair. He is even more surprised when the husband later sues him for giving him the advice that led the wife to seek divorce. Worried that he may lose his ministry, Reverend Gregory enlists the help of Deacon Frye, who wins the case on the Reverend's behalf. Even so, the minister learns a lesson, as he professes after the trial:

> I learned something from all of this, deacon. No more quickie marriages. From now on, before I perform a wedding ceremony, I want to make certain the couple understands the kind of commitment they're making to one another. Marriage is a sacrament. It's a holy union performed in the sight of God. It's the very cornerstone of our society. The family unit is a building block of our nation, and we cannot afford to let it crumble without each of us doing everything within our power to strengthen that institution.

The deacon remarks how boring the Reverend is, dismissing his heartfelt religious rhetoric.

The friction between the conscientious minister and conniving deacon is the primary focus of many episodes. In one, the deacon and Reverend have differing goals when a woman considers divorcing her millionaire husband. Frye wants a commission from the divorce, but the minister wants to help her reconcile with her husband.[15] In another, the deacon wants a psychic to invest the church's funds; the cleric finds this "blasphemous." "Why do you insist on bringing religion into everything we do?" the deacon cluelessly asks of the minister. When Reverend Gregory reminds Frye what the Bible says about trusting false prophets, Frye retorts, "I wasn't talking about false prophets; I was talking

---

15. "Deacon Dearest." Written by Eric Cohen; directed by Bill Foster. February 27, 1988. Reviewed off broadcast television; also available at PCM.

about big fat profits."[16] Anything that achieves wealth is above question for the deacon. He once criticizes the minister for exercising too much delicacy in asking for increases in the congregation's offerings, even suggesting Reverend Gregory sermonize about how "the more you give the longer you'll live"; after all, "it works for the Mafia," observes the deacon.[17]

Over the course of five seasons, most of the conflicts in the 111 episodes focus on difficulties arising from character flaws rather than on religious situations. For instance, Thelma's exceptionally bad cooking serves as the basis of an entire episode.[18] A surprisingly large number of episodes involve one of the main characters prematurely considering marriage and being warned by the others about the consequences. Frye's romances or battles in the courtroom are the basis of various episodes. One multi-episode story arch in season four concerns Thelma's enlistment in the army after being jilted at the altar by Reverend Gregory. Much of the humor on the program comprises not smart religious quips (as in other church-set comedies) but physical humor involving the main characters. For example, Deacon Frye courts a talented choir singer from a neighboring parish just to get her to join First Community Church and its choir; when she discovers his deception she wrestles with him all around his living room.[19] To overcome his fear of reptiles, the deacon sees a psychiatrist who leaves him alone in a room with a caged live snake; when the large reptile escapes and wraps itself around the deacon's neck, Frye squirms and winces and flounders about, until he realizes his fear is gone and dances with the viper.[20] After booking Amelia to sing in a sleazy nightclub, where her act follows female mud wrestlers, Deacon Frye yells at an enormous man, telling him to be quiet; the brute picks him up, presses him overhead and throws the deacon into the mud.[21] The church setting of the program is often incidental, taking a back seat to scenarios allowing for slapstick humor involving Frye.

Nonetheless, religious matters do serve as the basis for many storylines. "Sermon from the Cell" involves a number of religious themes, as Reverend Gregory finds himself on the wrong side of the law but for all the right reasons. Government agents arrive at the church to arrest the minister for having provided

---

16. "The Psychic" (Parts 1 and 2). Written by Marshall Karp; directed by Bill Foster. February 11 and 18, 1989. Reviewed off broadcast television; also available at the Paley Center for Media.

17. "The Widow." Written by Barbara Davilman; directed by Bill Foster and Phil Ramuno. February 6, 1988. Reviewed off broadcast television; also available at PCM.

18. "A Star is Burned." Written by Darice Rollins and Allison Abner; directed by John Sgueglia. March 23, 1991. Reviewed off broadcast television; also available at LOC.

19. "The Courtship of Bess Richards." Written by Bob Ellison; directed by Herbert Kenwith. October 4, 1986. Reviewed at PCM.

20. "Snakes Alive." Teleplay by Arthur Julian and Bill Davenport; story by Lisa Rosenthal; directed by Bill Foster. January 2, 1988. Reviewed off broadcast television; also available at PCM.

21. "Sing, Sister, Sing." Written by Marshall Karp; directed by Bill Foster. April 15, 1989. Reviewed off broadcast television; also available at PCM.

shelter to a family of political refugees from El Salvador, similar to an episode of *Nothing Sacred.* Even though the deacon does not understand or take kindly towards the minister's civil disobedience, he agrees to represent the Reverend in court. When the judge says she will suspend the sentence if the minister promises not to engage in such activity again, he respectfully asserts that he cannot make that promise. The judge sentences Reverend Gregory to serve one week in jail. The Reverend's cellmate is Willie — a tough inmate whose nickname is Ice-Pick. On Sunday the Reverend, at first disappointed he cannot deliver a sermon in church, realizes he can still preach to the inmates, but Willie warns him that in prison nobody cares about the Sabbath. "I don't buy that," Reverend Gregory challenges. "See, I've got a calling and this is as good a place as any to follow it." He creates a makeshift podium with a table and stool, and when the other prisoners do not respond, Reverend Gregory preaches directly to Willie. The preacher's enthusiasm and perseverance slowly sway the inmate, as a rousing speech about salvation and responsibility gains Willie's interest. Both swept up in the moment, they yell and, in lieu of a hymn (Willie cannot remember any), sing Patti LaBelle's pop song "I Got a New Attitude." When the deacon arrives to pick up the Reverend, Willie makes the cleric promise to keep preaching as he did, vowing to make the other prisoners listen if the Reverend returns.[22] The episode foregrounds religious activity and the role of a religious leader in reaching out to people in need.

Another episode focusing on preaching is "Dueling Ministers," which features a 12-year-old preacher, Reverend Johnny. When the deacon sees a drop in the attendance of younger congregants, he discovers the parish is losing juvenile members to the First Church of the Reverend Johnny, who has started a ministry in the basement of his parents' house. Going there to investigate, Deacon Frye finds a makeshift church where a few dozen children sit listening to the precocious preacher. The deacon asks Reverend Johnny to bring his ministry to First Community Church. The young preacher agrees, and Reverend Gregory becomes jealous of the success and attention Reverend Johnny enjoys. Ultimately the two preachers find themselves at a wake and try to outdo each other with a more rousing memorial. Realizing he must admit his jealousy to his younger colleague, Reverend Gregory says that even preachers are "vulnerable to the pitfalls of vanity, but it has no place in a minister's life." Reverend Johnny likewise confesses his jealousy of the older preacher, admitting to behavior "unbecoming of a minister." "Let me share something with you that I occasionally have to remind myself of," Reverend Gregory confides, "What we're doing: it's not my work; it's not your work. It's the Lord's work." Finally he adds, "Welcome to the church, son," as the two shake hands and Reverend Gregory puts his arms around Reverend Johnny.[23]

---

22. "Sermon from the Cell." Written by Scott Spencer Gordon; directed by Bill Foster. November 22, 1986. Reviewed at PCM.

23. "Dueling Ministers." Written by Bob Ellison; directed by Bill Foster. October 31, 1987.

In addition to the sermons, wakes and weddings in various episodes, another church ritual features in "The Reverend Ernest Frye," when Reverend Gregory gets the measles and the deacon must assume the minister's duties. Inga, the Fryes' Swedish housekeeper, announces she would like to become a member of the deacon's church. When the deacon tells her she will have to be baptized by immersion, she reveals she is afraid of the water. Although *Amen* does not show a baptismal ritual (unlike *Good News* and *Nothing Sacred*, which did), the program does demonstrate the deacon's effort to help Inga overcome her fear by taking her for a swim in the church gymnasium's pool. Here the episode turns toward slapstick, as Inga pulls the deacon into the water, suit and all.[24] Upstaging a rite for farce, the episode nonetheless hints at the place of religious ritual in the church.

Most often, it is the pretense of doing something on behalf of the church that serves as a setup to a non-church-focused episode. Hence, in one episode a spiritual retreat turns into a cat-and-mouse chase between Deacon Frye and a recently released inmate — a former client whom the deacon thinks is trying to kill him, until Frye discovers the man is there to thank him for changing his life.[25] In another, the deacon's effort to save money by fixing the church's plumbing leads to chaos when the church hosts an interfaith fellowship dinner outdoors. All is well until a broken water pipe drenches the church grounds so much that as the Reverend prays, the attendees sink into the muddy ground up to their necks, the preacher comically repeating his admonition to "Lift us up Lord, please, Lord, lift us up!"[26] Often the church's money problems force the church leaders to engage in some caper, as when the church is willed a restaurant. The church members want to sell it to pay off the church mortgage; however, due to the unusual terms of the will, they are forced to run the restaurant poorly, in order to gain the right to sell it. The congregants give comically bad service to the restaurant's unsuspecting patrons.[27] Other fundraising episodes find the church members staging talent shows, where they perform skits, comedy acts and songs for the entire program to raise money for the church.[28] Here again, although tapping into a long-standing tradition of programs featuring church

---

Reviewed off broadcast television; also available at PCM.

24. "The Reverend Ernest Frye." Written by William Daley; directed by Shelley Jensen. January 28, 1989. Reviewed off broadcast television; also available at PCM.

25. "Retreat, Heck!" Written by David Lloyd; directed by John Robins. November 15, 1986. Reviewed at PCM.

26. "The Minister's Wife." Written by Eric Cohen; directed by Bill Foster. November 22, 1988. Reviewed at PCM.

27. "Maitre D'eacon." Written by David Lloyd; directed by John Robins. November 29, 1986. Reviewed at PCM.

28. "First Community Talent Show." Written by Kathleen McGhee-Anderson; directed by Bill Foster. April 1, 1989. Reviewed off broadcast television; also available at PCM; "The Talent Show." Written by Paris Qualles; directed by Shelley Jensen. February 12, 1990. Reviewed at PCM; "Deliverance" (Parts 1 and 2). Written by Jim Geoghan (Part 1) and Bob Illes and James R. Stein (Part 2); directed by John Sgueglia. May 4 and 11, 1991 (5–21). Both parts reviewed off broadcast television; part two is also available at LOC.

fiscal problems, the focus is more on slapstick comedy and the quirky characters than on church operations or rituals.

One episode that involves a ritual of the Black Holiness and Pentecostal church tradition is "Casting the First Stone."[29] The Reverend suggests that at an upcoming gathering the congregation should try "testifying," which he explains is the old and not often practiced exercise of standing before a group, confessing a temptation or sin and explaining how faith in God led the speaker back to righteousness. At that event, held in the church fellowship hall, something unexpected happens: the church choir director, Lorenzo, confesses to having had an affair with a woman in the room, but that his faith in God brought him back. Thereafter, rife with rumors and suspicions, the congregation nearly comes undone as the members accuse various women of being the woman in question. The tensions peak at an Interfaith Brotherhood Council dinner where the members of First Community, who are hosting the event, slam plates, destroy the cake and ultimately wrestle with each other. To help the parishioners mend their relationships, various women come to Reverend Gregory, claim to be the woman in question, and ask for another testifying event so they can confess and end all the disputes. As the testifying session begins and the Reverend asks for the woman involved with Lorenzo to stand up, all are surprised when every woman in the room rises to her feet. Impressed with their selflessness, the Reverend remarks:

> My friends, you and I have witnessed something really remarkable. A dozen women were willing to stand up and accept undeserved shame in order to help put this church back together again . . . a dozen women who were more interested in healing our wounds than preserving their own reputations. I'd call that kind of courage, that kind of unselfishness and sacrifice and love . . . well, that's remarkable, and I'd just like you to know I feel blessed to be in the same church with each and every one of you. God bless you all.

As the congregation leaves, Lorenzo and Amelia exchange looks and comments that reveal it was she with whom he had the affair.

This episode's focus on sexual ethics and the congregation's willingness to look the other way instead of demand penance is contrary to the rather strict sexual ethic that runs through the rest of the series. For example, in one episode Thelma moves out after a fight with her father and asks the Reverend to take her in. He reluctantly agrees, fearing his congregation will assume the worst. Although he sleeps on the couch while Thelma sleeps in the bed, the church

---

29. John Michael Spencer (1993), "The ritual of testifying in the black church." In *Celebrations of Identity: Multiple Voices in American Ritual Performance*, edited by Pamela R. Frese. Connecticut: Bergin & Garvey, pp. 61–74. "Casting the First Stone." Written by David Lloyd; directed by John Robins. February 7, 1987. Reviewed at PCM.

board jumps to conclusions and, fearing the scandal of two unmarried people living together, discusses how to force the minister to resign. The situation is only resolved when Thelma moves out.[30] Similarly, Rolly courts a widow who fears she will lose a trust fund if she remarries. He says if they cannot marry she should simply move in with him, which she does. The board members are concerned that the two are "living in sin." Rolly offers his resignation from the board, which the Reverend accepts, saying, "I cannot condone a man being on the church board when he's living with a woman without the benefit of clergy." The dilemma conveniently resolves itself when Frye informs them that the clause in the will cutting off the widow's funds if she remarries in invalid. Rolly and the widow are married the following episode.[31] Likewise in "Thelma's Handyman," a 19-year-old maintenance worker develops a crush on Thelma (who is 34 years old) and gossip spreads that they are involved. Reverend Gregory discusses the situation with the deacon's daughter, saying he has heard of "misconduct about a woman in my flock." The Hetabrink sisters remind the deacon that as a member of the church board he should be concerned with the "disgrace" of the deacon's daughter being involved with an unmarried, younger man. In the end, Thelma makes it very clear to all that she has no interest in the young man and the matter is resolved.[32] All of these episodes highlight the series' conservative sexual ethic.

That the church members, and the Reverend in particular, would hold such conservative views in this area reflects trends in African-American church leaders of the time. A survey of black ministers sponsored by the Lilly Foundation in 1992 considered a broad range of issues reflecting respondents' moral attitudes, including those related to sexuality and the family. Writing about the survey, noted professor of ethics and black church studies Richard Franklin summarized that, "in general, the responses on sexuality issues suggest that black clergy continue to be conservative in areas of family values and sexual ethics," and that "at the same time as they express these views, they seek to exhibit love, mercy and patience toward those at odds with cherished moral precepts."[33] These attitudes surely are expressed in an episode of *Amen* which touched on an issue upon which the survey found the most strongly held position, and on which most clergy had preached a sermon — premarital sex.

The episode where this conservative sexual ethic is most present is "The Deacon Delivers." It is also noteworthy for its apparent reference to a well-known PBS documentary about African-American families that aired not long before.[34]

---

30. "The Housekeeper." Written by Arthur Julian and Terry Hart; directed by Bill Foster. November 26, 1988. Reviewed at PCM.

31. "Rolly's Proposal." Written by Arthur Julian and Bill Davenport; directed by Bill Foster. November 21, 1987. Reviewed off broadcast television; also available at PCM.

32. "Thelma's Handyman." Written by William Daley; directed by Bill Foster. December 3, 1988. Reviewed at PCM.

33. Robert M. Franklin (1997), *Another Day's Journey: Black Churches Confronting the American Crisis*. Minnesota: Augsburg Fortress, p. 80.

34. "The Deacon Delivers." Written by Peter Noah; directed by Lee Shallat-Chemel.

In the story, a young woman who grew up in the church returns and asks the deacon and Reverend if she may rejoin the congregation and become a member of the choir. They welcome her back, until she removes her oversized coat to reveal that she is pregnant. In a rare moment of agreement between the minister and deacon, they tell the board they cannot allow her to sing in the choir. "We are a forgiving church," the Reverend explains, saying that he has promised to help her with expenses and does not wish to drive her away, "but in her present condition, I'm afraid I have no choice but to ask her to leave the choir, at least for a while." Reverend Gregory later sits down with the young woman, saying, "The church really wants to help you, but we can't condone an unwed mother setting an example for the rest of the youth of our congregation." The woman accepts the restriction and in an ironic twist comforts the distraught minister. Later, the deacon himself helps deliver the woman's baby in his living room, just when the infant's irresponsible father shows up. When the deacon informs him that his child is born, the young man prances about declaring, "I'm the man, I'm a king!" This phrase directly references an infamous scene from Bill Moyer's well-known January 1986 television documentary *The Vanishing Family: Crisis in Black America*, in which a cavalier, out-of-work father behaves similarly after the birth of his latest son, the third child by one mother, adding to three by other women. In *Amen*, Deacon Frye scolds the young man for his attitude:

> You know what your problem is? You have no idea what being a man is about. Being a man is not scoring every chick you ever see. It's not about making babies you don't want to support, and it's not boasting and bragging and running away. It's standing up and standing by your family, 'cause that's what they are now, your family.

After the boy's baptism in a later episode (where the ritual is not shown), the deacon tries talking the young father into marrying the mother of his child. The man is moved when later he hears someone his own age talk about growing up without a dad, and asks the mother of his child to marry him. She, in turn, asks the deacon to give her away at the wedding ceremony.[35]

Other episodes also focus on helping a young man do the right thing in life, highlighting the importance of education for African-Americans. During the third season, "A Mind is a Terrible Thing to Waste" finds a young man contemplating forgoing college. The boy's mother, fearful he will fall in with the wrong crowd, asks the male leaders of the congregation to talk him into continuing his schooling. One by one, the Reverend, Rolly and Deacon Frye consider what their lives would be like had they not gone to college. Ultimately, Reverend Gregory warns

---

November 1, 1986. Reviewed at PCM.

35. "Yes Sir, That's Your Baby." Written by Bob Ellison; directed by Lee Shallat-Chemel. February 14, 1987. Reviewed at PCM.

the young man that he might end up in jail if he does not go to college and challenges him to have a "hunger" for knowledge. This sways the boy.[36] In the same fashion, a similar decision faces a would-be rapper named Clarence, a young character who joins the cast in the fifth season. Clarence had been involved with gangs, which got him in trouble with the law, and now is performing his requisite community service at the church. The experience transforms the flashy, charismatic youth, who begins to admire the dedication of the church leaders, especially the deacon. Nonetheless, the lure of a rapper's lifestyle leads him to consider dropping out of school. It is only when the Reverend arranges a surprise meeting between Clarence and famed rapper MC Hammer that the young man begins to understand the importance of having an education. Hammer advises Clarence that he must have knowledge in order to have something to rap about. Clarence decides to stay in school.[37] In these instances, the series focused on the importance of higher education to African-Americans.

Beyond Clarence's storyline, the issue of gang violence and the black church's response to it is also considered in one episode. It begins with the Reverend recounting to church members how he tackled the knife-toting leader of a local gang that has been terrorizing the neighborhood, holding him until police arrived. As the church members discuss the situation, the deacon enters and announces that he has arranged with the local cable television company to televise their Sunday services, starting that Sunday. The deacon is excited about the prospect of making money for the church off the venture. At the worship service that Sunday, all is well until a threatening note from the street gang arrives, wrapped around a brick thrown through a stained-glass window. Deciding not to cancel the remainder of the telecast, the Reverend says "this means too much to the church," and proceeds to deliver the following sermon over the airwaves, addressing his message to the gang:

> We shall not be moved. We will not be held hostage by your intimidation. We shall not run and hide while your drugs and violence rob us of our children. We shall not be moved. But let us not forget, you too are our children. We're not each other's enemy, but circumstance has made us enemies of one another, but we are brothers and sisters of each other's flesh. Blood of each other's blood, bone of each other's bone, and in the desert of your anger, of your anger and despair, let this church be an oasis of hope and redemption. Stop the threats. Stop the killing. Come through our doors, not through our windows. We need you here. Come and share our joy, share in our work. We've got a church to build. We've

---

36. "A Mind is a Terrible Thing to Waste." Teleplay by Arthur Julian, Terry Hart and Marshall Karp; story by William Davey, Kathleen McGhee-Anderson and Paris Qualles; directed by Bill Foster. April 22, 1989. Reviewed at PCM.

37. "Three Men and a Hammer." Written by Robert Illes, James R. Stein, Barry Gurstein and David Pitlik; directed by John Sgueglia. February 23, 1991. Reviewed off broadcast television; also available at LOC.

got a community to embrace. We've got children to nurture and we've got a gospel of life to fulfill, and together we can say as one people: We shall not be moved. We shall not be moved!

Later at the deacon's house, the gang comes to confront the Reverend and church members. In the end, after some initial tension and delicate diplomacy, the gang and church leaders shake hands, smile and make peace.[38]

Apart from the Reverend and deacon, another ongoing conflict that sustains the series is that between Thelma and Reuben, and their on-again, off-again engagement. Over the course of the program, the Reverend's response to Thelma turns from disinterest to flirtation, courtship, intense attraction, engagement and marriage. The series ends, in fact, with the birth of the couple's child, a baby boy. This fifth season storyline and a series of guest stars were an attempt to save the series from falling ratings. Nonetheless, after placing 13th in the Nielson ratings during its first season, 15th in its second, and 25th in its third, *Amen* fell below the top 30 programs for its final two seasons and was canceled.[39] Even so, the program was popular enough to enter syndication and be rebroadcast years afterward. Strong on character humor and physical comedy, the program was in fact one of the highest rated comedies in television history focusing on church leaders. Conflicts did not so much concern debates over the direction of the church as personal issues between the characters. Zaniness was more the rule than controversy. Occasionally social issues were addressed, such as on episodes dealing with gang violence, ministering to those in prison and encouraging minority enrollment in college. By and large, the focus of the program was on the deacon, his home life and his efforts with other congregants on behalf of the church. Overall, *Amen* was significant for a number of other reasons: it was the first successful program to be set in a Protestant church; the first church-set program to feature a mostly black cast; and the first of a cluster of programs from the late-1980s onwards focusing on the family life of church leaders. This trend would continue in earnest in the mid-1990s and beyond.

Amazing Grace

The next program to focus on the family life of a church leader was the drama *Amazing Grace*, starring Patty Duke. The first series to focus on a female minister, *Amazing Grace* was a bold, short-lived program that aired on NBC in April of 1995. Controversial in many ways — including the main character's background, her activist ways and left-leaning outlook — the show failed to attract audiences. The program centers on Hannah Miller, a former nurse who has a near-death

---

38. "TV or Not TV." Written by Wanda Griffin and Dexter Griffin; directed by Shelley Jensen. November 4, 1989. Reviewed off broadcast television; also available at PCM and UCLA.
39. Brooks and Marsh 2003, Appendix 3: "Top-rated programs by season."

experience and becomes a minister in an unspecified Protestant denomination. Breaking even more ground, Reverend Miller is a divorcee and recovered drug addict. Her home life centers on her two children, Jenny, an agnostic, and Brian. Also involved in her life is Harry Kramer, a lawyer with whom she is close. Unaccustomed to the potential restrictions of her new profession, Harry once catches himself in a potential faux pas when he gives her a kiss, and then asks, "Am I still allowed to kiss you?" Good-natured but blunt, Hannah replies, "I became a minister, Harry, not a monk." Her other acquaintances are friends at the local hospital, where she worked as a nurse and now serves as chaplain. Seeing Hannah in her clerical collar, a nurse remarks, "out of one uniform and into another," to which Hannah quips "at half the pay!" When a nurse friend asks, "How's saving souls instead of saving lives?" Hannah responds, "Potentially satisfying — and I won't get blood on my clothes." Caring yet confrontational, sensitive yet strong, Duke's Reverend Miller is in many ways similar to other church leaders featured on TV series.

The series is based on an unaired two-hour pilot, which opens on Hannah (in voice-over) retelling the story of her life. She narrates scenes of her working as a nurse at breakneck pace, downing pills to keep her going, and surprising an armed man stealing drugs from a medicine supply cabinet from which she herself was about to do the same. He shoots her. Brought back to life on the operating table, she shares a vow: "I had to die to get a second chance; they brought me back and I swear to God my life will never be the same." She becomes the minister of a run-down parish no one else wants, while also working as the hospital chaplain. There, Reverend Miller helps a woman she knows from drug rehabilitation by taking custody of her newborn twins to keep them away from her abusive husband. The abusive man threatens Reverend Miller, but the strong-willed minister does not back down. In the end, he holds the mother and Reverend Miller at gunpoint in Hannah's church. Clearly unstable, he fires a shot through the stained glass windows as the police arrive outside. Hannah reasons with him, saying he does not want to make orphans of her kids or his. He starts to cry and insists he does not want to hurt anyone but cannot "make it stop," as he holds the gun to his own head. Gutsy and brutally honest, Reverend Miller notes he can take that option or "take a chance" and get the help he needs and "have a life!" Swayed by her impassioned words, he puts down the gun and collapses sobbing into Hannah's arms. The final scene is of Hannah baptizing the two babies in her newly restored and better attended church.

Apart from the major plot line, a number of secondary stories emerge which help define Hannah and her character. One concerns her daughter Jenny's mourning the loss of her father and first family home. (In the series, Hannah has divorced her husband; in the pilot, he died several years before.) When Jenny goes missing, Hannah figures where to look for her — at their old house, which they left when they moved into the parsonage because they could no longer afford the mortgage payments. Sitting on the curb outside the large home, Jenny reveals her strained faith, saying "if taking daddy is God's will, do you know what I say to that? There is no God. Not for me." Wondering if her mom hates her for what she has just said, Jenny is surprised when her mother admits to similar feelings, saying, "You think I don't know what it's like to hate God? I died twice: once when I was shot and once when your daddy stopped breathing." Jenny asks how she can continue to do the work she does, and how she believes in God's will. Demonstrating the relation of her ministry to her family life, the Reverend answers, "No one, least of all me, knows God's will. I only know my own will, and when I could get past my tears, I could see my will: to keep safe everything your father treasured. That's you and Max. Without you, everything else is nothing." Hannah does not insist her daughter reconsider her doubt about God, but gently strokes her hair and embraces her.

Reverend Miller's ministry extends beyond her family, to all those in her life. A nurse at the hospital sees her ministering to the battered new mother and lashes out at Hannah, revealing a grudge against the church. She warns the minister not to moralize when talking to the mother, using scriptures to keep her "in line." Reverend Miller, not yet recognizing the personal story behind the nurse's admonition, defensively says she did no such thing and believes in people as much as God. The nurse warns her not to tell any pregnant 16-year-olds who come to her for advice that they should be ashamed and no longer belong in the Lord's house, "because that is the church as I remember it!" Moved, Reverend Hannah says she had no idea that her friend had such an awful experience. Hannah also has an impact on the detective investigating the battered woman's case. He criticizes the extent of Hannah's advocacy, leading her to discuss with him the role of the church in the lives of people in their community. By the episode's end, Hannah's own faith and witness leads both the nurse and detective to her church. Standing in the back during a worship service, they are curious observers, touched enough by Hannah's ministry to reconsider their feelings about religion.

Her own controversial background relates to another character whose life Hannah touches: Vincent, an aloof, artistic homeless young man whom Hannah spots stealing drugs from the hospital. She reassures him she will not turn him in, and gives him her business card, saying, "I'm a junkie too." The young man later breaks into the church basement and secretly lives there, repairing various items in the church, while also beautifying the basement by painting it. When Hannah discovers he is there and is responsible for the repairs, she allows him to stay and asks him to create a new stained glass window to replace one that broke earlier, when part of the church roof collapsed. She resourcefully enlists the help of many in the community to restore the run-down church. Amidst all this, Hannah even helps her son with his schoolwork in the waiting room of the hospital, her son commenting, "Since you've become a minister, we have to do homework in some really weird places." The final scene, in a renovated, packed church, shows the minister giving the sermon she has been having difficulty finding time to write.[40] Reverend Miller has successfully restored the church, brought in new members, witnessed to doubters, and fulfilled her duties as worship leader — all while maintaining her commitment to her family.

Reverend Miller's identity as a recovering drug addict ties in to a history of television portrayals of clerics. To make them colorful and interesting, they are given surprising backgrounds, ones which seem at odds with their current religious profession. Including ex-convicts, former prostitutes, retired police officers and (in the case of the soon-to-be discussed *Soul Man*) former motorcycle gang members, the ranks of TV's clergy seem prone to personal histories atypical of what most would expect. It is as if their unusual backgrounds are expected to lend them credibility by virtue of their vices. Reverend Miller's experience as an "ex-junkie" fits in line here. As with similar ecclesiastic characters, her own redemption from a troubled past informs her ministry, ironically constructing her (and others) as a realist for having such an improbable past. While these colorful personal stories of deliverance are intended to make the characters more interesting, viewers seem unswayed; most such characters do not draw audiences to their programs, the more successful shows involving clerics with more traditional, innocuous pasts. In this light, the story of Hannah Miller's fall, rebirth and salvation may involve religious themes one would expect to resonate with audiences attracted to a church-set program, but in a context which proved problematic in attracting many viewers.

The series continues the focus on Reverend Miller's ability to balance ministry and family, even as it taps into themes established in earlier church-set TV programs, such as the friction between a new minister and members of the church leadership. The first episode, in fact, opens with Hannah seated before a church council interviewing her for an interim minister position. Listening attentively with her hands folded, she responds to the chairman's pointed questions with courage, spunk and humor. Clearly not taken with Hannah, the chairman declares, "There are things in your background I find very disturbing: your divorce; your pill addiction. There are others — those are the only ones I wrote down." Responding to his question as to why she became a minister, she quips, "I needed structure and a captive audience. The truth is I love stained glass — always have." Unimpressed with her wit, the chairman declares, "I think we've heard enough," to which Hannah responds, "We're not finished gentlemen." "Excuse me?" the chair retorts, surprised. "I have a few questions of my own," Reverend Miller announces, and takes out a writing pad, readying to interview *them*. Clearly, this is a woman who, though inexperienced, will stand up to authority. Later, when the council offers her the position, despite the chairman's objections, the edge between Reverend Miller and the lay leader comes into stark relief:

---

40. "Wing and a Prayer." Written by Deborah Jones; directed by Arthur Allan Seidelman. Executive produced by Bonnie Raskin. Unaired. Reviewed at UCLA.

Chairman: I wanted to welcome you — as our *interim* minister.

Reverend Miller: And I am grateful to the board for giving me this opportunity.

Chairman: Call me old fashioned but in my day we didn't take our spiritual guide from people who used to be pill addicts.

Reverend Miller: . . . at least not the ones who were honest about it.

Hannah then enters the sanctuary alone. She spins about, ascends to the pulpit and stands silently, looking up in reverence at the stained glass windows. She smiles and closes her eyes for a long time, taking in the moment. Reverend Miller is not simply a gutsy radical, but a woman who loves the church and takes her commitment seriously.

The focus of the episode is on Reverend Miller's attempt to help a family reconcile. Noticing that a nurse seems distracted, Hannah, as hospital chaplain, offers counsel: "I don't want to pry, but if something is bothering you — this collar is more than a fashion statement." The nurse confesses that, years before, she ran away from her husband with their son. Hannah tries to help the nurse locate the father and asks her lawyer friend Harry to look into the matter. To find inspiration, the interim minister goes to a secluded lake to talk to God. Amidst softly falling snow, Hannah asks God if she is ready to handle this situation, mentioning her near-death experience, when she stopped breathing and was brought back to life:

Why couldn't you have started me off with a nice simple problem? Like a demonic possession. You know I'm just learning how to do this. It's hard to be wise. How'm I doing? Am I doing okay? Yeah, I know, you don't give hints. All I can do is try to hear you, listen to my heart and do the best I can. I hope you aren't sorry that you didn't let me stay dead on that operating table.

Her challenges increase when a detective learns Harry is making inquiries about the boy's father, and questions Hannah about the situation. This forces the nurse to go into hiding with her son.

Hannah's willingness to stand up to authority is reiterated when the detective confronts Hannah about her involvement in the case, doing so at her church just as she is about to give her first sermon. The detective is accompanied by armed police, and Reverend Miller makes it clear that anyone coming to a house of worship must come inside and participate, and not stand outside in the narthex. She notes that "the street is public property, but *this* is God's house." Unsure if they will take her offer to come in and worship, she adds a moment later: "One more thing — God's house is a gun-free zone." Ultimately the police exit the church, leaving Hannah momentarily victorious in the confrontation. Notably, the TV audience never hears her first sermon. In the end, the family is reunited. Reverend Miller has worked on behalf of the family, doing all she could to fight the system and bring them together. She has accomplished this while also running her own family household, including her rebellious teenaged daughter's budding relationship with an unkempt boyfriend named Link. At the conclusion, Hannah and her congregation are in church singing the hymn "Amazing Grace," and on the line "I once was lost but now am found," Hannah herself is shown in close-up.[41] So ends her first foray into ministry at her new congregation, as a success story.

The story of Reverend Hannah Miller, her family and ministry was brief. *Amazing Grace* was the lowest-rated program on NBC that season, ending its run after four weeks.[42] Daring in many ways while bland in others, one critic wrote that the series was undergoing constant tinkering by the network but that in the end the plots were often "as thin as a communion wafer."[43] The liberal leanings of the program — from Hannah's attitude towards authority and guns, to her drug-addicted past and very identity as a female pastor — may have contributed to making the show controversial for some viewers; while many Protestant churches were by now ordaining women, others were not. Nonetheless, *Amazing Grace* is noteworthy for its focus on a female minister, making it the only program of its kind in the history of television shows featuring ecclesiastics.

Trinity

Another dramatic family-set program that did not achieve much ratings success was *Trinity*, which first aired on NBC in 1998–9. It focused on the lives of an Irish-Catholic family, the McCallisters, living in and around Hell's Kitchen in New York City. Most of the focus was on the lives of the family's grown children — three young men and two young women.

First among the men is Kevin, an ivy-league trained Catholic priest now serving a local parish, Trinity Church. A graduate of Columbia University, Yale Divinity School and St. Joseph's Seminary (a fellow minister calls him 'Phi Beta Priest'), the handsome Father McCallister provides a contrast to his two younger male siblings: Bobby, a short-tempered police detective whose dedication to his job causes friction with his wife; and Liam, a womanizing labor union leader who discovers his office is involved with organized crime. The focus on the contrasting lives of the sons is apparent from the opening scenes of the first episode when various family members are shown at their morning routine, preparing for work. Kevin and Bobby provide the starkest contrast: waking and dressing, they are shown in crosscuts as one reaches for a policeman's badge and gun, and the

---

41. "The Fugitive." Written by Shelley List and Jonathan Estrin; directed by Rick Rosenthal. Series executive produced by Jonathan Estrin and Shelley List. April 1, 1995. Reviewed at LOC.

42. Alex McNeil (1996), *Total Television: The Comprehensive Guide to Programming from 1948 to the Present.* New York: Penguin, p. 35.

43. Bonko, Larry (1995), "Duke has an 'amazing' new role: *The Virginian Pilot*," *Television Week*, April 1, 1.

other for a priest's collar. Adding to the diversity are the two sisters: Fiona, a high-powered stock broker; and Amanda, the grunge-styled youngest and only child still living at home. Amanda must deal with conflicting advice from her family when she finds she is pregnant and uncertain of who is her baby's father. At the head of the family are Eileen, a simple housewife with empty-nest syndrome, and Simon, a transportation worker and bar owner. Although the series focuses on all of their separate lives, the bonds among the McCallisters are evident at their weekly Sunday suppers together at the parents' house.

The series regularly focuses on Father Kevin McCallister and his parish, or his advisory role in situations facing his siblings. In particular it features his efforts to help Amanda with decisions regarding her pregnancy, which at times require him to balance his roles as brother and priest. At the end of the pilot, it is to Kevin that Amanda first confides her situation. Knowing he has been covering for her absenteeism at Trinity parochial school, where Amanda works as a teacher's aide, she waits for Kevin outside their parents' house before their weekly dinner. They discuss the hard time she has been having lately, Kevin asking if she is undergoing an "existential crisis." Amanda speaks to him from behind the bars of a fence, which simulates the look of a confessional, and confides that she is pregnant. Reacting more as a brother than a cleric ("I just want to kick this guy's ass" is among his first comments), Kevin eventually refocuses on his sister. She admits that she is not sure who the father is and what she should do. Not wanting to keep the rest of the family waiting, they go inside. At dinner, Kevin's blessing includes a petition that discretely references a number of family problems that have emerged, among them Amanda's; he prays, "although we may fall short, we do our best to do thy will, and thank you for this time together and for this wonderful and decidedly imperfect family."[44]

In the subsequent episode, Kevin meets Amanda at the parochial school, inquiring about whether she has stopped drinking and smoking, and asking if she has begun prenatal care or had the pregnancy confirmed. He escorts her to Planned Parenthood, where he sees a parishioner and nervously loosens his collar. A test confirms Amanda's pregnancy, and she confides that she does not think she wants the baby. When Kevin asks her to meet with a woman who counsels unwed mothers, Amanda suspiciously asks if she is with the church. Kevin admits she is a former nun who is married and has children herself. Amanda begrudgingly agrees to meet her, but stands her up and takes a road trip with members of a local rock band, one of whom may be the father.[45] In a later episode, when Amanda finally confides her situation to Fiona, the older sister reveals that she had an abortion in college but felt bad about it afterwards because of "all that stuff from church" in their upbringing. Fiona discusses the

---

44. "Pilot." Written by Matthew Carnahan; directed by Michael Caton-Jones. Series executive produced by John Wells. October 16, 1998. Reviewed off broadcast television; also available at LOC and UCLA.

45. "In a Yellow Wood." Written by John Wells; directed by Rod Holcomb. October 23, 1998. Reviewed off broadcast television; also available at LOC.

situation with Kevin, who is surprised to hear that Amanda is still considering an abortion. Saying that their sister probably told Kevin only what he wanted to hear because he is a priest, she accuses him of stating his own opinion as if it were "the gospel truth." Kevin argues that if their sister has an abortion it will teach her to take the easy way out of problems. "My feelings about abortion aside, the church's feelings aside," Kevin begins (Fiona interjecting "fat chance"), "there are consequences to her behavior and Amanda needs to learn that." Fiona asserts that a baby is not a consequence, to which Kevin proclaims, "No, you're right, it's not. It's a human life." Here, the series falls in line with other Catholic-set programs in its focus on a cleric's response to abortion.

Father Kevin continues to argue his conscience, emphasizing his brotherly point of view without ignoring that of the church, when he later confronts Amanda about her decision to have an abortion. Asking if she has already made an appointment, he pleads with his sister, saying, "It's wrong. You know that Amanda." Amanda responds, "Because the church says so?" Kevin replies, "Well, I happen to agree with them on this one." The pregnant sister argues that the church is not familiar with her life and does not know her, but Kevin continues to plead his case, saying, "No, but I know you. And I know that you could love this baby, this tiny bunch of cells that are growing and growing and are gonna be my niece or nephew one day . . . Mom and Dad's first grandchild. You could be a great mother, Mandy." Later, at their parents' house, Kevin greets Amanda outside and continues his brotherly discourse, telling her, "We're not always gonna agree on everything. What you do and who you are, those are two different things, and I may not be thrilled with everything you do all the time, but I'm always gonna love you, no matter what." She says that she may still have an abortion, but as yet has not. Kevin is glad and makes her promise to speak with him if she ever reconsiders.[46] The series ends before the audience learns the fate of Amanda and her child. Nonetheless, the storyline and the family focus are noteworthy for how they challenge Father Kevin McCallister to articulate his own point of view as a brother apart from that as a priest, even if in this case both perspectives agree.

Other storylines also depict Father Kevin's challenge to offer his own perspective rather than simply state the orthodox view when counseling parishioners, somewhat similar to Father Ray of *Nothing Sacred*. In the pilot, Father McCallister counsels a lifelong friend, a married man, who has begun a homosexual affair. Kevin tells the man he is there as a friend and later asks him, "Do you want the church's take on this or do you want mine?" The man replies that he already knows the church's perspective on the situation. Kevin suggests he tell his wife the truth so she can be involved in deciding what they should do about the situation together. Later, Kevin's superior, Father Terry, summons him

---

46. "No Secrets." Written by Lisa Melamed; directed by Christopher Misiano. October 30, 1998. Reviewed off broadcast television; also available at LOC.

to the office to tell him that the wife called to say that her husband left her, and to issue a complaint about Father Kevin's advice. "It seems," Father Terry says somewhat glibly, "you told her husband to go find his bliss and be a fag." Kevin assures the elder priest that this is not an accurate depiction of what happened, but Father Terry remains concerned because the woman has threatened to go to the church hierarchy to get an explanation, and maybe even to the press. Kevin explains:

> Father Kevin: Look, I wasn't there as a priest.
> Father Terry: Oh, really.
> Father Kevin: Yeah, I was there as a friend. I've known this guy his whole life.
> Father Terry: So what did you do with your vows during that period, Father?
> Father Kevin: Come on, Terry, save it for the press conference, okay?
> Father Terry: What do you think, you get to choose when you're a priest?
> Father Kevin: Look, she's pissed off at her husband, not the church.
> Father Terry: (sternly) Do you hear me, Father McCallister?

Kevin later tries to comfort the angry wife, who is upset because her husband left her and their daughter. He says he only told her husband to talk with her about his situation, to which she asks if he considered what might arise if her husband took the priest's advice. Crying and blaming the situation on Kevin, she protests, "Son of a bitch, Kevin, I'm a better Catholic than you are."

While this example may suggest that Father Kevin McCallister is a committed dissident, he is less of a maverick than a dutiful ordainee who allows his familiarity with people around him to influence his advice. Passionately loyal to family and friends, he is a caring man who in some ways is a McCallister first and a Catholic priest second. One example of this occurs in an episode where Kevin counsels a man who confesses to having molested young neighborhood children for years and threatens to commit suicide.[47] Set on Thanksgiving Day, Kevin visits the man, Tim, in his rooftop garden. Tim asks for last rites because he plans to kill himself. Assuming the man must have a terminal illness, Kevin offers somewhat clichéd advice, until the man reveals he does not have an illness, and asks Father Kevin for absolution. Father Kevin begins counseling for depression, saying it can be treated. Finally, the man reveals his sin: that when neighborhood children come to his garden to help care for the plants, he molests them. "God is the easy part," Tim says. "It's man that won't forgive me." The gardener's behavior has gone unreported for years until that morning, when one child told his father, who threatened to go to the police. Shaken but

---

47 ". . . To Forgive, Divine." Written by Edward Allen Bernero; directed by Christopher Misiano. December 27, 1998. Reviewed off broadcast television; also available at LOC.

undaunted, Kevin continues, a bit more poetically: "There's no dark place that God's love cannot touch." Tired with all the talk of God's love, the man reminds Kevin that his brothers used to come to the roof to help tend the garden, and asks if he could forgive him if the victims included his own brothers. Almost in shock, Father Kevin turns away, begins to breathe heavily and appears to understand for the first time the man's claim that he has no alternative but to take his own life. People will not be able to forgive him, Tim says, regardless of what Kevin says of God's forgiveness. The man notes that even his own priest cannot look at him. As police cars pull up to the building, Tim pulls out a gun and shoots himself in the head. In a hospital, Kevin learns that Tim just grazed his skull and that had the priest not been there to stop the bleeding he would have died. Kevin goes into Tim's recovery room and begins saying the Hail Mary when Tim apologizes to the priest and assures him he did not molest his brothers. The two then continue saying the Hail Mary together. Overall, this storyline centers around whether Father Kevin, faced with offering somewhat abstract advice to a confessing sinner, can reconcile his own personal involvement as a person affected by the man's sin with his role as a priest who must extend God's forgiveness to those seeking it. Having apparently done just that, Kevin joins his family for their Thanksgiving celebration, a plate of holiday dinner leftovers serving as his reward.

Compared to *Nothing Sacred*'s Father Ray, another thoughtful young priest from a Catholic-set drama, *Trinity*'s Father Kevin reads more as a native son come of age, who must learn to deal with how his new responsibilities and identity as a priest influence his relationships with those with whom he grew up, including his family and parishioners. Less self-assured and mature than Father Ray, the depiction of Father Kevin's ministry is mitigated by how his grown-child relationships with others affect it. Stories reflect more his unique, lifelong personal relationships with those he counsels, rather than how a priest in general might grapple with questions of ministry, as in the case of Father Ray. As such, Father Kevin's story is bound to that of his family, in a manner that makes it somewhat idiosyncratic; it is so interwoven with that of his family members that many of the challenges he faces as a priest are often conflated with those of being a McCallister brother or son.

For example, Kevin's vocation involves him in the lives of his family in the pilot, when he hears the confession of a man who has been ordered to commit murder and must decide whether or not to honor the secrecy of the sacrament (similar to *Have Faith*). The hit man reveals to the priest the time and place that the killing is to happen. Saying it has been 14 years since his last confession, he requests absolution for the forthcoming murder. Father Kevin says that granting the man's request would be tantamount to giving him permission to kill, and so he refuses and assures the man that there are alternatives. The man abruptly leaves. Going to his brother Bobby, the detective, Father Kevin reveals the man's confession and shares his own inner struggle with doing so: "This is a grey area for me . . . I'm breaking a sacrament." Feeling guilty about violating his oath, Kevin later asks Bobby not to investigate, but Bobby refuses, saying if he does not it is he who will be violating an oath. Meanwhile the third brother, Liam, gets a tip that the confession is a setup — that the confessor is a criminal out for vengeance on Bobby and used Father Kevin to lure Bobby to a deserted street to kill him. Liam pages Bobby just in time for him to escape. Though he compromised the sacrament, doing so saved the life of his brother. Here again Father McCallister's duties as a priest are shown in their relation to how they intersect with his family life.

Later episodes of the series find Father Kevin in a ministry completely unrelated to his family.[48] Kevin is a youth minister and coaches a "midnight basketball" team to keep inner city boys out of mischief. One of the boys he coaches, Tommy, is clearly troubled by something. Father Kevin catches him stealing from the church, warns him against showing up for basketball practice drunk, and calls Tommy a "stupid ass" when the youth jumps another player — a comment for which the priest later apologizes. Telling Tommy he is always available to listen and help, Father Kevin learns that the youth's family life is the cause of his problems. His father committed suicide and his stepfather hits him. At one point during counseling, Tommy sarcastically asks Father Kevin "Is this the part where you try to molest me?" Father Kevin is committed to helping Tommy despite the youth's attempt to anger him with backtalk. Tommy also tries testing the priest by admitting to beating up kids for money. The priest remains unconditionally committed to helping Tommy and says to the young man, "If you're trying to get me not to like you, it's not gonna work. I'm gonna care about you no matter what you tell me." After Tommy steals a garbage truck and is released to the priest's custody, Father Kevin tries to involve the boy's parents, but finds they are not interested in helping their troubled son. In the end, Tommy runs away. The storyline remains unresolved (like Amanda's pregnancy) due to the cancelation of the series. Nonetheless, Father Kevin's unconditional promise to help and love the boy is evidence of his suitability for ministry.

As with other television programs focusing on ordained people, another ecclesiastic issue dealt with on *Trinity* concerns the nature of vocation and a priest's calling. Father Kevin does not so much question his suitability for ministry as reexamine the gifts he brings to it. The arrival of a priest whose strengths seem to reveal Kevin's weaknesses arouses these reflections. When Father Peter joins the church staff, Kevin is surprised by what he discovers about his fellow cleric.[49] A widower with one child in college, he became an alcoholic after his wife's death. His calling came in prison after he was arrested for driving under the influence. Dedicated to sharing the love of God he discovered while locked in his cell, Father Pete went to seminary and became a priest. When Kevin

---

48. "Hang Man Down." Written by Natalie Chaidez; directed by Darnell Martin. December 27, 1998; and "Breaking In, Breaking Out, Breaking Up, Breaking Down." Written by Terri Kopp; directed by Alan Taylor. February 28, 1999. Both reviewed off broadcast television; also available at LOC.

49. "No Secrets."

asks his superior about Pete's past, the elder priest notes how impressed he is that Pete is so open about his personal history. An accomplished cook and experienced handyman, Father Pete is able to help out around the church in ways that Kevin cannot. When Pete is offered a chance to preach ahead of Kevin, the young McCallister feels slighted and inquires about his superior's decision. Father John, the head of the parish, tells Kevin that while he brings many assets to the church (he mentions that he is good with administration and working with kids), there are areas where he is not yet fully developed. Father John counsels Kevin, saying, "The priesthood is a vocation, it's a calling. It's not a career. I put Father Peter up there because he was ready." When Kevin insists that he is ready, Father John continues: "No, not yet. It's up here for you," he says, gesturing to the younger priest's head. "It's gotta come from here," he continues, gesturing to his heart. Ultimately, Father Peter addresses Kevin's jealousy when he gives the sermon and speaks about envy, noting how he envies "this guy" who envies him. As Kevin and Pete catch eyes during the sermon, Father Pete lists all of his friend's strengths (including his education and loving family), finally acknowledging that they both sin by envying each other because "it keeps us from seeing God's light in each of us."[50] As did priests in *The Cavanaughs*, *Hack*, *Have Faith*, and *Nothing Sacred*, *Trinity*'s Father Kevin thus confronts doubts about his calling.

Much like other programs focusing on Catholic ecclesiastics, another aspect of the priest's vocation addressed on *Trinity* is celibacy. Here, this concerns how to deal with attractions to and by women. Indeed, when they have their first private conversation, Father Pete confides in Father Kevin, "I don't know how you young guys manage the celibacy thing . . . I know I couldn't." The issue is explicitly addressed in an episode where Kevin — in athletic wear — literally bumps into a woman while skating through Central Park. Allowing her to flirt with him for a while, Kevin ultimately fesses up to his vocation, admitting to the woman that he was enjoying their conversation and "kinda" led her on. Later, at a poker game with other priests, Kevin shares details of the encounter, claiming that although he let the conversation go on for too long, it was not because of "the sexual part." The others challenge Kevin's claim, and he admits he knew that the woman would treat him differently as soon as she discovered his vocation. The priests then share similar stories of how they handled flirtations from parishioners, one saying that a woman once admitted to loving him in the confessional. Bemoaning that people do not see a priest as a person when he wears the collar, Father Pete says how fortunate they are to have "poker and group therapy." Father Kevin responds, "I guess no matter how old you get or what you do for a living, it always comes down to talking about girls."[51] *Trinity*, like other programs, thus

---

50. "In Loco Parentis." Written by Matthew Carnahan; directed by R. W. Goodwin. November 6, 1998. Reviewed off broadcast television; also available at LOC.

51. "Breaking In, Breaking Out, Breaking Up, Breaking Down."

considers challenges faced by ecclesiastics, including those related to a priest's celibacy.

Furthermore, *Trinity* shows Father Kevin McCallister engaged in the duties typical of a parish priest. From helping to supervise the church school and coaching the parish midnight basketball team, to counseling parishioners in and out of the confessional, *Trinity* shows its featured priest engaged in the everyday activities of a minister, emphasizing how he balances these with the demands of his family life. One episode that is noteworthy in this regard is the final one, where Kevin is offered the honor of being celebrant and preacher at Midnight Mass on Christmas Eve. He is shown throughout the episode trying to prepare his sermon; having a hard time, he is frequently interrupted. One such interruption comes from his sister-in-law, who asks Kevin to come to the hospital where she works to baptize a baby girl who was abandoned and is struggling for life. Baptizing her with the name Faith, Kevin must return to the church, somewhat unprepared, to lead the service and give his sermon. In a touching series of crosscuts between the church and the hospital, the sister-in-law reads a Prayer to St. Jude, the patron saint of hopeless causes, as Father Kevin delivers his sermon. Preaching about how Christ entered the world as an infant "powerless and dependent" and "at our mercy," like the baby in intensive care, Father Kevin invites the assembled congregation to be like Christ and "put ourselves in God's hands." As his sermon ends and the choir sings, Kevin walks to the congregation to begin lighting parishioners' candles. He starts with his mother, who in turn passes the light down the pew to the rest of the McCallister family. At the episode's end, the McCallister clan is assembled at the parent's home, a round of applause greeting Kevin when he arrives. The family dances and shares hugs as Kevin plays "Oh Come, All Ye Faithful" on his violin.[52]

This final episode is a good illustration of the overall focus of the series: while showing its cleric involved in everyday activities of a priest, from sermon preparation to hearing confessions and counseling youth; and while showing him face the challenges of the priesthood, from celibacy to renewing his dedication to serve others; the series evenly balanced this with the young priest's family life, which often became entangled with his minister's duties, and always served as much as his center as did the church. In the end, the program performed dismally in the ratings, perhaps in part owing to too many storylines involving too many McCallisters. It also — like other unsuccessful church-set TV series — involved its share of controversial storylines. Nonetheless, it is one of several network programs of the late 1990s that focused on the family lives of clerics, this one distinguished by its focus on a Catholic priest and his siblings and parents.

---

52. "The Patron Saint of Impossible Causes." Written by Matthew Carnahan; directed by R. W. Goodwin. Unaired in the series' original run; first aired in syndication. Reviewed off broadcast television; also available at LOC.

Soul Man

Another program of the late 1990s to focus on the home life of a minister was *Soul Man* (1997–8), an ABC series that was a showcase for its star and executive producer Dan Aykroyd, of *Saturday Night Live* and *Blues Brothers* fame. In fact, the character he plays, a widowered Episcopalian priest trying to raise four children, is styled after his Blues Brothers character. As quirky as the *Have Faith* gang, the minister's religious awakening came after he broke into a church and stole the offering money, with which he partied for weeks, until he crashed his motorcycle into a telephone pole on which he says he saw the face of God, and felt loved — whereupon the pole fell on top of him.

Formerly a member of a motorcycle gang called the "Blacktop Vampires," where he was known as "Wild Child," the Reverend Mike Weber (Aykroyd) constantly lets his past show by wearing blues band T-shirts, biker boots (even when wearing shorts or a bathrobe), and donning an ankle-length leather raincoat. In his home office hangs a picture of Elvis, carefully placed next to a picture of Jesus Christ; Weber explains ". . . we have 'the King' up there next to the King of Kings."[53] The opening sequence also establishes the Reverend's hip past, beginning with a shot of Weber pulling up on a motorcycle outside a quaint suburban church. As the song "Soul Man" plays underneath, Reverend Weber bops up the stairs, takes off his leather jacket to reveal his clerical collar, and enters the sanctuary. Inside he dances and "rocks" the congregation as spotlights flash around him, with shots of the remainder of the cast interspersed, including his children sitting in the pews and the Bishop at the organ.

Set at St. Stephen's Church in Royal Oak, most of the program takes place in the parsonage, where Reverend Weber lives with his four children: the oldest boy, Kenneth; the middle boy, Andrew; the youngest boy, Frederick; and a daughter, Meredith. The only other character who remains for the entire series is Bishop Peter Jerome, who performs his supervisory role over Reverend Weber with good humor and occasional frustration. In early episodes, Weber has a flirtatious relationship with a newspaper reporter, Bridgette. By the program's end, two other regular characters join the cast: Reverend Todd Tucker, a serious devotee of the church who is the Bishop's nephew and serves as Reverend Weber's assistant; and Glenda, the Webers' housekeeper.

The Webers' family life often revolves around the kind of activities one might expect of a family with a cleric head-of-household. For example, the Reverend gathers his family in the living room around a box marked "Mission Drive." He hopes that his children will learn to give to the less fortunate, but finds he needs to encourage his children to be more generous as he examines their offerings, which include old underwear and a used toothbrush. "Didn't I say giving a gift

---

53. "Communion Wine and Convicts." Written by Carmen Finestra, David McFadzean, and Matt Williams; directed by Andrew Tsao. Series executive produced by Carmen Finestra, David McFadzean, Matt Williams, Elliot Shoenman and Dan Aykroyd. April 22, 1997. Reviewed at PCM.

to the poor is like giving a gift to Jesus?" he mildly scolds his children, and encourages them to do better next time.[54] Even moments not revolving around explicitly church-related activities, such as nightly rituals between parent and children, reflect the ecclesiastic setting of the program. Once, Reverend Weber tries to get his two youngest children to sleep in their own beds, instead of his. When he discovers them hiding in his sheets, he kicks them out, and does not notice their return as he catches his oldest son trying to sneak out of the house. Acting innocent, the boy claims, "I was about to go out to church and pray," to which the Reverend responds, "Pray for a dumb father" as he gestures for his son to about face. Returning to his bed, Reverend Weber discovers his persistent, disobedient children under the sheets. He looks up to the heavens and quotes the Bible, saying, "I have reared children and brought them up and they have rebelled against me"; half asleep, his children recite in unison: "Isaiah. Chapter 1, verse 2." The Reverend nods in approval.[55] In another episode, one of the children comes to the Reverend to confess that he broke a prized Elvis snow globe from their father's collection. The child admits to the wrongdoing in a mock confession, in which Reverend Weber sits next to the boy as a priest receiving an admission of sins. When the act of contrition is over, the boy quips that as his minister Reverend Weber cannot tell the boy's father, whereupon Reverend Weber (now playing the role of the father) makes his own confession: that he was eavesdropping on the conversation with the minister and heard the whole thing.[56] Thus, *Soul Man* establishes a household where church and family life intermingle.

"Communion Wine and Convicts" highlights how Reverend Weber is an effective father when he confronts his oldest son, Kenny, for stealing a bottle of communion wine. The Reverend discovers the 14-year-old's mischief when his middle son tattles, having found the empty bottle in his room. "You think he'd steal better stuff than that," the boy quips. When Kenny comes home, Reverend Weber offhandedly reports that he noticed a bottle of wine missing and asks if he took it. When the teenager denies the charge, the Reverend says, "Son, if there's one thing I hate, it's a liar." Kenny continues his denial, going so far as to request an apology from his father. The Reverend then reveals the empty bottle, and the boy fesses up. Later, Kenny defies his father, saying he will not go to his dad's church for a concert being given by a choir of inmates from a local prison, called the "Joyful Jailbirds." When the Reverend notes that his son's behavior reflects on him and his job, whether that is stealing communion wine or attending a church event, Kenny exclaims he does not like being a role model because he is the son of a minister. Reverend Weber realizes it is best not to pressure his son and tells the boy he does not have to attend the concert.

54. "Mike's Awakening." Written by Tom Leopold; directed by Andrew Tsao. September 30, 1997. Reviewed at PCM.

55. Ibid.

56. "Urges and Lies." Written by Carmen Finestra, David McFadzean, and Matt Williams; directed by Andrew Tsao. April 15, 1997. Reviewed at PCM.

Nonetheless, while the Reverend is introducing the choir to the congregation, his son walks through the church door. Their eyes meet, and the Reverend thanks the congregation for coming, with words also directed at his son, as he says, "it means so much to me that you are here."[57]

Making this story of a minister and his children one about a single father and his family ties in to a long history of such programs in TV history. Running the gamut from *My Three Sons*, *The Andy Griffith Show*, *Family Affair* and *The Courtship of Eddie's Father* to *Full House, My Two Dads* and *Blossom*, single father shows have been a mainstay in television programming. The allure is that these shows maximize storylines, from ones in which dad must learn to nurture his children or balance family and work life, to ones allowing him to develop romances.[58] Indeed, the season *Soul Man* began, some six new programs featuring single fathers were in development;[59] and up to about that time, while more than 70 programs had featured single parents, nearly two-thirds of these focused on male heads of household.[60] Having a man learn to care for children and clumsily pursue romances is more "quirky," adding to a sitcom's appeal;[61] that Aykroyd's single dad was not only a zany father but also a minister maximized the opportunity for unconventional behavior on the show, and hence its whimsical appeal.

In addition to being an effective father, the series also demonstrates how Reverend Weber is an effective church leader, as he goes about the everyday duties of a minister. During the series, the minister is shown sermonizing, leading church gatherings, discussing a soup kitchen, and preparing for mission drives and senior center visits. Like earlier sitcom clerics, the effectiveness of his ministry is based on his quirky personality. In one episode, he counsels a couple whose marriage is in trouble, using sensational methods. Weber, frustrated by the couple's obstinacy, handcuffs the husband to a door to keep him from leaving. Inviting them to recall their first date, he also helps the couple rekindle their romance. The Reverend assists their reminiscence by recreating the mood — turning down the lights, describing the scene, and singing "Natural Woman" à la Aretha Franklin. Ultimately, the couple reconciles.[62] In another episode, Reverend Weber ministers to a grumpy old hospitalized woman, whom he describes as the "most mean-spirited person" to whom he has ever ministered. Realizing she is this way because she is lonely, Reverend Weber visits her at the hospital. The two test each other's will before he confronts her for being so mean. Eventually they develop a mutual understanding and appreciation, the

---

57. "Communion Wine and Convicts."

58. Noel Holston (1992), "Portrayal of single parenthood lacking." *St. Petersburg Times*, August 28.

59. T. L. Stanley, "Father shows best." *Mediaweek*, March 24, 27.

60. Holston (1992).

61. Jennifer Harper (1992), "Single parents have been multiple in TV history." *Washington Times*, September 21.

62. "Communion Wine and Convicts."

woman expressing this with suggestive romantic comments to the minister, who quickly retreats from her room.[63]

This last episode also touches on one of the constant themes in church-set television programs: the church's concern with raising money. In *Soul Man*, this concern is most often expressed by Bishop Jerome, who merely tolerates Reverend Weber's unorthodox style and methods. Hence, the Bishop dispatches Reverend Weber to the hospitalized old woman, insisting that he personally see her because she has asked for him. The Bishop is concerned with the woman's state of mind, saying that she is not thinking clearly. Reverend Weber observes, "You're worried she's not going to leave her money to our church," to which Bishop Jerome replies, "I'm worried she's going to leave it to her dog. Don't get me wrong, I care about her soul too . . . but the youth center needs a new roof. Let the poodle work for the summer house." Similarly, when Reverend Weber sponsors the inmate choir concert at St. Stephen's, the Bishop worries about how the event may affect church finances and his own commemoration by the diocese. He says that when he was at the country club someone was carrying on about the appropriateness of a choir of inmates appearing at the church. The Bishop confides that this man is the largest donor in the district and asks Reverend Weber to cancel the performance so as not to alienate this wealthy parishioner, adding, "before I die I would like to have my name on just one building in this diocese."[64]

Like previous programs focusing on church leaders, *Soul Man* considers the sexuality of ecclesiastics. Having established that Reverend Weber is a widower, the series allows him a flirtation or two, as well as occasional moments of outright lust. Much of this centers around a character who appears in the early episodes — Bridgette Collins, a reporter. Once, the reporter unexpectedly comes to his house, saying she is interested in writing an article about the church's mission drive. The minister is concerned with how he looks, as he greets her wearing a blues festival T-shirt under a short-sleeved jean shirt, shorts and biker boots. While the reporter waits outside, Andy asks his father if he thinks Bridgette is attractive, to which his father responds yes, she is very attractive, and he glances at her through a window. Noting that Bridgette is bent over, the child asks, "isn't it lust if you look at a woman's butt?" to which the father defensively responds, "I only glanced. It would be lust if I looked again." As Andy leaves, the boy turns to catch his father looking through the window once more, leading the child to yell "Lust!" at the top of his lungs before running away.[65]

Reverend Weber meets Bridgette in an earlier episode when she visits the church to write a story on his innovative sermons. While talking at his home, the minister makes her laugh with a few church jokes. She says that she is surprised that his personality is different from what she expected of a minister.

---

63. "Mike's Awakening."
64. Ibid.
65. "Communion Wine and Convicts."

Sitting with his hands between his legs, the Reverend quips, "I know what you mean: boring, pious, asexual." The conversation continues:

> Reverend Weber: Ministers have the same feelings other men do.
> Bridgette: Oh? You have . . . urges?
> Reverend Weber: Of course. I'm human.
> Bridgette: How about sex?
> Reverend Weber: No thanks.
> Bridgette: You're really uncomfortable talking about this, aren't you?
> Reverend Weber: No, I'm perfectly comfortable talking about my sexuality.
> Bridgette: Okay, Weber, is that an urge that you have?
> Reverend Weber: Yeah, but I'm not married.
> Bridgette: So?
> Reverend Weber: So, I believe that that degree of intimacy should exist only within the bounds of marriage.

Thus expressing an orthodox view, the minister shares that his wife passed away three years ago. Bridgette is surprised, asking, "So, you are telling me in three years you haven't, as it says in the Bible, 'known' a woman?" The minister responds, "Three years, no knowing." The flirtation continues as she asks if he can kiss and touch women. The minister responds that yes, he can, it just depends on what part of the body she means. She plays along, saying she will point to a part of her body and he should say if he can touch it. She touches her head, shoulder and leg, but when she points to her breasts, Reverend Weber gets up and recites, "Warning! Warning!" She asks if he could ever touch them, and he responds yes, "If they were on fire, I could put them out."

The next day Bishop Jerome stops by and asks Reverend Weber if he has seen the morning's paper. He shows Mike a three-page story with a front-page headline reading "Sex and the Single Priest." The Bishop says the article describes his "passions and urges," to which the minister exclaims, "This is a disaster!" Defending himself, Reverend Weber notes that the article was supposed to be about the inspiration for his sermons, to which the Bishop retorts "obviously Sodom and Gomorrah." The Bishop continues, saying his wife was "furious" about the article. Reverend Weber asks if she was offended, to which the Bishop responds, "No, she wanted to know what happened to *my* urges." Bridgette later explains why she did what she did, that it made for a good story. Reverend Weber protests that he was not speaking to her as a reporter but as an "attractive woman." He reveals that for the first time in three years he feels himself "potentially attracted to someone." The reporter is confused and a bit shocked. Feeling awkward, Bridgette leaves. She returns to apologize for the story and confesses that she is attracted to him. She adds, however, that her career comes first, and she only has time for casual relationships — so she suggests they just be friends. They shake hands and part.[66] Thus *Soul Man*, like other television programs featuring church leaders, dealt with an ordained person's sexuality.

Soul Man also addressed the relationship between modern- and tradition-minded church leaders. To a certain extent Bishop Jerome plays Reverend Mother Placido to Reverend Weber's Sister Bertrille and has to deal with the impact of the younger ecclesiastic's modern style and methods. Even so, Reverend Weber is a seasoned minister, not a novice, and the Bishop can only express his concerns, leaving Reverend Weber free to lead his congregation as he sees fit. Significantly, the most tradition-minded character is Bishop Jerome's nephew, Reverend Todd Tucker. Tucker is Weber's assistant, and his straitlaced style and by-the-book methods are subject to constant critique from the more down-to-earth senior minister. Reverend Tucker's absolutist approach to separating the traditions of the church from those of the modern world surfaces in a Halloween episode in which Reverend Weber dresses as chef Julia Child. On seeing this, Reverend Tucker protests, "I don't think that a minister should be taking part in a pagan holiday. I mean, there's God and there's evil, and on Halloween you take the — D from 'God' and put it on 'evil' and you've got 'Go Devils'." The young minister's serious attitude towards the church apparently began as a child. This is revealed when he criticizes Reverend Weber for letting one of his kids trick-or-treat as a dinosaur:

> Reverend Tucker: If you're gonna put him in a costume, why couldn't he go as one of the twelve apostles?
> Reverend Weber: Todd, I don't think there's a kid in the history of trick-or-treating who's ever gone as an apostle.
> Reverend Tucker: No, I did. I went as a different one every year.
> Reverend Weber: How many times you get beat up?
> Reverend Tucker: Twelve.[67]

Once, Reverend Tucker begs Weber for "another" chance to teach Sunday School. Reverend Weber is concerned that Tucker's last lesson was "a touch boring." Reverend Tucker challenges, "You consider St. Augustine's interpretation of the sermons of Ambrose boring?" "To a five-year-old, that's boring," Weber replies, adding, "To God, that's boring." The senior minister advises him to entertain the children. He suggests impersonating Arnold Schwarzenegger as the "Terminator" playing Jesus, using an Austrian accent to deliver the line: "I'll be back." Later, Reverend Tucker proudly tells Weber that he told one of the children the Noah's Ark story as Captain Kirk of *Star Trek*, imitating William Shatner's voice as he says, "Captain's log: it's been 40 days and 40 nights of

---

66. "Urges and Lies."
67. "Trick and Treat." Written by John Pollack; directed by John Pasquin. October 28, 1997. Reviewed at PCM.

rain." Impressed, Reverend Weber lets him teach Sunday School again.[68]

The series certainly made the religious setting entertaining. Reverend Mike Weber's disposition saw to that. Nonetheless, the program was subject to constant retooling, with various characters being retired and introduced over the course of its run, including Bridgette, Nancy (the parish secretary), Glenda (the housekeeper) and Reverend Tucker. Similarly, the actor playing the youngest boy was changed during the series. Critics charged that the kids on the program were less-than-charming; one remarked that working with children did not seem to be Aykroyd's strong suit, saying of the show that it "plays its premise with a distinct lack of soul. Safe and indistinct, the 'sincom' uses stereotypes and stock characters to mine its undersized laugh quotient."[69] As a late-season replacement, the program at first showed promise, but on subsequent seasons dropped in the ratings as it was moved around and even removed from the schedule for a while. All this contributed to the program's downfall, despite its having been developed by the same team that produced the successful family sitcom *Home Improvement*. That program's star, Tim Allen, even made cameo appearances on *Soul Man*, and the two shows aired on the same ABC evening lineup. Despite this, *Soul Man* was canceled in 1998, becoming renowned as one example of a midseason start-up that initially performed well but in subsequent seasons suffered in the ratings.[70] The show may also have suffered in comparison with another program airing in the same era that also focused on the family life of a cleric — the long-running and very successful *7th Heaven*.

7th Heaven

Of all prime-time network programs that focused on the lives of clerics, the longest-running by far is WB's (and later CW's) *7th Heaven*, the first to feature a married minister. Beginning its run in the fall of 1996, this family drama ran for 11 seasons, achieving the distinction of being the longest-running family drama in television history, beating such classics as *The Waltons* and *Little House on the Prairie* (both of which lasted nine seasons). With famed television industry magnate Aaron Spelling (of *Dynasty* and *Melrose Place*) serving as executive producer, *7th Heaven* attracted a devoted audience. Set in Glen Oaks, California, the program focused on the family life of the Camdens. While the father, Reverend Eric Camden, was the first cleric introduced on the program, he was by no means the last: during the series, daughter Lucy decides to enter the seminary to become a minister; the Hamiltons, family friends of the Camdens, are likewise headed by a father who is a minister; in later seasons, Reverend Camden is assigned an associate pastor, Reverend Chandler Hampton, who joins the congregation to help run the church while Eric recovers from an illness;

---

68. "Mike's Awakening."
69. Ray Richmond (1997), *"Soul Man"* (Review). *Daily Variety*, April 22.
70. Michael Schneider (2002), "Late season entries fizzle in fall." *Variety*, March 25–31, 27.

and towards the end of the series, Sandy Jameson, a friend of the Camden's who joins the congregation, decides to attend seminary and become a minister.

Even so, with all the ministers in the series, the focus is clearly on the family lives of the characters. That the family is the focus is made clear from the lyrics accompanying the program's opening credits: "I know there's no greater feeling than the love of a family; where can you go when the world don't treat you right?; the answer is home — that's the one place that you'll find: 7th Heaven." In fact, in the first episode the audience is introduced to the Camden family at their home, where Eric and his wife and children are introduced one by one, with no mention of the father's vocation. It is not until after the first commercial break, and lots of family-focused drama, that the Camdens are shown sitting in a pew at church, and the camera follows the feet of a minister as he walks up to the podium, panning up to reveal his clerical robes, and finally his face: it is Eric Camden, who bids his congregation "Welcome."

This first episode introduces the seven members of the Camden family: Eric; Annie, his resourceful wife, a homemaker; Matt, the oldest, a heartthrob, who is 16; Mary, a 14-year-old basketball player; Lucy, a sensitive, conscientious 12-year-old; Simon, the witty and insightful ten-year-old; and Ruthie, the cute but precocious five-year-old.[71] As with all episodes, the first focuses on the challenges facing each family member and how the Camden clan supports each other. It begins with Eric and Annie sharing a glass of wine, looking very much in love as they prepare the family dinner and bring it into the dining room, where the rest of the Camdens are seated. Simon is anxious to say the prayer: "Dear God, thank you for this food. And if there really is a God, God I know you'll find a way to get me the dog I've been wanting. Amen." The kids chuckle. Eric assures his son there is a God and humorously scolds him for "going over our heads to get what you want," wishing him luck on his request. For the remainder of the evening, the Camdens share their problems and try to help each other. Mary confides in Matt that because she is so tall she has trouble getting a date and still does not know how to kiss, and asks for Matt's advice. Mary catches Matt smoking a cigarette, as does Eric, who calmly registers his concern to his son and asks for his allowance money, since he does not want to finance his son's bad habit. Lucy is worried about not yet having had her first period and is horrified when her dad discusses puberty with her; she is much more responsive to a talk with her mother, who quotes from Ecclesiastes to assure her daughter that "to everything there is a season." Eric reminds Simon of his unsuccessful history in taking care of pets, agreeing that if a dog happens to wander into the yard he may keep it. This prompts Simon to tell God it is now up to Him to get a dog to wander onto their property. Finally, Annie receives

---

71. Although the female Camden children would marry and take on other last names, "Camden" is used as their surname throughout to avoid confusion. This should be pointed out for Reverend Lucy Camden in particular, who in later episodes goes by her married name, Reverend Lucy Kinkirk.

a call that her parents are coming from Arizona for a visit, and is curious about why.

Throughout the episode, the church or God are involved here and there. When the family attends church on Sunday, Eric quotes the verse from Ecclesiastes Annie used to reassure Lucy; thinking her dad is about to reveal her prepubescent concerns to the assembly, Lucy runs from the church, followed closely by her concerned mother. Lucy tells Mary she is so embarrassed by her behavior that she may never leave the house again, prompting Mary to remind her sister that the house belongs to the church. Eric gets Matt a job as caretaker for an aging congregation member to help him recoup his lost allowance, wagering six months of church attendance if his son loses the job. Simon faithfully continues to request God's intervention to bring him a dog. Despite these references to church and God, the focus remains on the family. When Eric confides to Annie his disappointment that Lucy does not wish to discuss the "perfectly normal and wonderful process of becoming a woman," Annie gently scoffs at her husband's failure to realize that "it's not all that wonderful, it's also scary and embarrassing and awkward." Later, Eric understands that the women of the house may be better suited to understand Lucy when he finds her elated over her first period. He offers the women money to treat themselves to a private celebratory dinner. Eric is not without parental wisdom, however, as is made clear when Matt discovers that the woman for whom he is caring lost a lung and is on a respirator because she used to smoke. When Matt refuses to buy cigarettes for the woman, who is in on the minister's ploy, Matt loses his job, learns a lesson . . . and owes his father six months of church attendance. Mary dates one of Matt's friends, causing minor friction between the siblings until she agrees not to rush into kissing. All along, Annie and Eric discover their need to keep each other apprised of their children's problems and discuss how best to handle them.

The end of the episode emphasizes the family focus, while also touching on religion. The latter is accomplished when, lo and behold, Simon spots a dog on the property and yells, "It's a miracle!" and "There is a God! There is!" His faith is undeterred when Annie reveals she got the dog at the pound and brought it home to save it from being put to sleep. In response to Eric's assurance that there is a God but He had nothing to do with the dog, Simon responds, "Of course He did! You think mom would've done this on her own?" The parents exchange an impressed look. The importance of the family is spotlighted when Annie's parents arrive, and her mother reveals she has acute leukemia and has decided to spend her final days with family. Keeping the news to themselves, the adults share hugs and tears. The final image is of the entire family on the lawn in front of the parsonage, the adults looking on as the children play with the dog, whom they name "Happy."[72]

---

72. "Anything You Want." Written by Brenda Hampton; directed by Sam Weisman. Series executive produced by Brenda Hampton, Aaron Spelling and E. Duke Vincent. August 29, 1996. Reviewed off broadcast television; also available off commercial DVD and at LOC.

The subsequent episodes maintain the balance established in the first, centering on the family but prominently featuring the church. For example, Matt uses the family car to sneak out and help a girl whom the family discovers is pregnant and has been disowned by her father. Eric restricts Matt's car privileges but notes how proud he is of Matt for being a friend to someone in need. Reverend Camden facilitates a reconciliation between the girl, her father and her child's father, all of whom come to church on Sunday to hear the girl sing in the choir.[73] In another episode, Matt schemes a way around his car restriction by delivering food for the church's "Meals on Wheels" program, only to use the delivery van for a date. His scheme collapses when he gets into an accident in the van, his date at his side. Later, Annie's mother helps Eric and Matt to reconcile only hours before a sleeping Annie has a vision of her mother saying goodbye, and awakens to discover that her mother has passed on.[74] In another story, Simon consults various family members as he tries to figure out where heaven is so he can picture his grandmother there. He is dissatisfied with all the answers he is given (including Eric's, who tells him heaven is a "great and glorious mystery") until the youngest Camden, Ruthie, tells him his grandmother is living in his heart.[75] Sentimentally, the program balances church and family life.

Sometimes these are explicitly interrelated, as when members of the family help people they know from church. For instance, Reverend Camden helps a young boy he previously counseled about drug abuse realize he still has a problem, and facilitates his reconciliation with his parents.[76] Reverend Camden helps an organist who has lost her musical touch achieve a graceful retirement.[77] Matt tries to help an aging parishioner with daily chores, until it becomes clear that her needs exceed his abilities. Reverend Camden convinces the woman to hire an out-of-work contractor, who is moonlighting as the church's fix-it man, to help her. Reverend Camden's ingenuity becomes clear when the woman offers the handyman's family a place to stay in her home until he finds work, solving both of their problems.[78] Sometimes those whom the Camdens help are families of the children's friends. For example, in one episode Matt's girlfriend spends too

73. "Family Secrets." Written by Brenda Hampton; directed by Mark Sobel. September 23, 1996. Reviewed off broadcast television; also available off commercial DVD and at LOC.

74. "In the Blink of an Eye." Written by Catherine LePard; directed by Duwayne Dunham. September 30, 1996. Reviewed off broadcast television; also available off commercial DVD and at LOC.

75. "No Funerals and a Wedding." Written by Molly Newman; directed by Mark Jean. October 7, 1996. Reviewed off broadcast television; also available off commercial DVD and at LOC.

76. "Saturday." Written by Jack LoGiudice; directed by David Semel. November 4, 1996. Reviewed off broadcast television; also available off commercial DVD and at LOC.

77. "See No Evil, Hear No Evil, Speak No Evil." Written by Catherine LePard; directed by Harry Harris. November 18, 1996. Reviewed off broadcast television; also available off commercial DVD.

78. "With a Little Help from My Friends." Written by Brenda Hampton and Jack LoGiudice; directed by Burt Brinckerhoff. January 13, 1997. Reviewed off broadcast television; also available off commercial DVD.

much time with the Camdens because her estranged parents are ignoring her, until Annie and Eric intervene and confront the parents about their behavior.[79] Similarly, Eric discovers Lucy's schoolmate is living in poverty because her parents divorced, and he convinces the father to offer more support.[80] In later seasons, Ruthie befriends a young man whose estranged father is a recovering alcoholic and who is being raised by his mother. Sometimes others learn from the Camdens' devotion, as when Eric allows two of Lucy's ex-boyfriends to follow him around for a school project in order to learn what a minister does. Calling themselves "Ministers in Training," they follow Eric to the hospital, nursing homes, church services and counseling sessions at his office, often frustrating Eric with their lack of appreciation for all he does. In the end, the boys share how they admire Eric for how much he cares about people. "It's the job," Eric offers, whereupon one of the boys responds, "Maybe. But we think it's the man."[81]

Several episodes from the first season of this landmark program merit discussion because they not only focus on the church and its values but also exemplify themes that continue over the course of the series. In "Faith, Hope and the Bottom Line," Reverend Camden attends a community job fair looking for an office assistant for the church. He interviews Ron, who not only can type but also plays the organ. What surprises Ron is that Eric remains interested in him even after he reveals he received some of his office skills while in a correctional facility. Others at the church are against hiring an ex-convict. Lou, the head of the church vestry, opposes the idea, and Annie, although not entirely opposed, notes she understands the others' concerns. A debate over church values and priorities follows. The church board must decide how to spend its limited funds: either to install a security system in the church (which Eric opposes), or hire the ex-con as an office assistant and organist and give him a second chance. Lou is not only concerned about hiring a former criminal but also with protecting the church by installing the security system. "The church is wide open!" Lou argues to Eric. "That's the difference between us, Lou," says Eric, "I think people should always have access to what is inside." The tension between them comes to a head in the Reverend's office one night when they argue about Ron:

Reverend Camden: Knowing the man he is today, I can't go with a security system over a human being. I just can't.
    Lou: I know, and that's what makes you a wonderful, compassionate

---

79. "Now You See Me." Written by Charles Lazer; directed by Harvey Laidman. December 16, 1996. Reviewed off broadcast television; also available off commercial DVD and at LOC.

80. "Brave New World." Written by Catherine LePard; directed by Harvey Laidman. February 17, 1997. Reviewed off broadcast television; also available off commercial DVD and at LOC.

81. "Boyfriends . . ." Written by Brenda Hampton; directed by Burt Brinckerhoff. May 4, 1998; and ". . . and Girlfriends." Written by Catherine LePard; directed by Burt Brinckerhoff. May 11, 1998. Both reviewed off broadcast television; also available off commercial DVD and at LOC.

minister, and a lousy business man.

Reverend Camden: (wryly) Thanks, I think.

Lou: (sarcastically) See, I just thought that you were supposed to represent your parishioners and their values.

Reverend Camden: No, my job is to represent the church and its values to the best of my ability. Now most of the time I do that with the support of my parishioners; sometimes I do that in spite of them. But that's my job as minister of this church.

The debate ends when Lou makes a veiled threat to remove Eric as the church's minister if he jeopardizes the church's well-being.

This being *7th Heaven*, the situation at church influences the family as well. At that moment Annie is serving as the church treasurer and the decision over whether to use church funds to hire Ron or install a security system ultimately hinges on her recommendation. Annie thoughtfully considers each side. At times, she is not pleased with Eric's apparent lack of faith in her. Eric suggests the vestry made Annie treasurer only so she could influence him to support the installation of the security system. Their conflict over the situation climaxes at home in the kitchen, when Eric says, "Faith without risk is easy," to which Annie responds, "and risk without faith, your kind of faith, is scary." The two kiss and make up, Eric telling Annie he loves her and that the church is lucky to have her as its treasurer because of her wisdom. Annie finally addresses the church board, who are assembled in the pews at church, along with the Camdens. She speaks very professionally from the altar, proclaiming that the church budget represents the church's values and that ultimately they are in the business of compassion and should invest in people. Her speech impresses the board members. At the following Sunday's church service, Ron is shown playing the organ as the choir sings. Eric ascends to the pulpit and, seeing his family gathered in the front pew, exchanges a gesture of acknowledgment with his wife.[82] The episode demonstrates the series' somewhat progressive social agenda, where helping those in need is valued over worries of how society at large may respond. While some episodes could be rather conservative, especially where matters of sexual activity are concerned, nonetheless the Camdens emerge as an open-minded family who know their values and stand by their convictions.

Another trend that originates in the first season is the Camden's openness to people of different racial or cultural backgrounds, and their willingness to take a stand against social injustice. For example in "The Color of God," a local African-American congregation's church is burned to the ground by a hate group. The Camdens not only get involved but also learn important lessons. Reverend Camden went to seminary 20 years earlier with the other congregation's minister,

---

82. "Faith, Hope and the Bottom Line." Written by Catherine LePard; directed by Burt Brinckerhoff. April 21, 1997. Reviewed off broadcast television; also available off commercial DVD and at LOC.

Reverend Morgan Hamilton. The loss of the house of worship is a personal matter for Reverend Hamilton because it was his grandfather who built the church. The following Sunday both congregations worship together, intermingling in Eric's church. A gospel choir sings from the altar, and Simon follows the lead of a black woman sitting next to him after she yells "Amen!" during the sermon. Reverend Hamilton addresses the assembly, thanking them for sharing their "grief and anger," warning all not to fight hate with hate, and asking them to consider the direction of the country and whether it is caught in a "vicious circle." "I want each of you," he continues, "to ask yourselves: what are we teaching our children today that will make things better tomorrow?" The answer is explored when the Hamilton family, whose parsonage may be the next target, shares quarters with the Camdens. Prejudices are examined when Mary asks her houseguests if they want to play basketball, and John (the oldest Hamilton boy) accuses her of stereotyping them, until Keesha (the oldest girl) reminds him Mary is on the varsity basketball team and tells him to "give her a break." Lucy befriends Keesha, who helps her wear African braids and beads in her hair and teaches her about their significance. The two also discuss Rosa Parks and listen to hip-hop music. Mary seems annoyed at this until Keesha confronts her, and Mary reveals her attitude is not based on prejudice but on Keesha's taking her little sister away from her. Keesha and Mary bond by discussing what it is like to be a big sister, much as the moms bond by discussing the hardships of being a minister's wife. Meanwhile the two ministers' sons, Matt and John, learn from each other. Matt begins to understand what life is like for John when a security guard harasses John for no good reason. John, on the other hand, learns from Matt that he must learn to control his short temper.

The younger children have the simplest response to the situation. They get along immediately, playing with each other and discussing why someone would want to burn down a church. When the youngest Hamilton boy, Nigel, explains people have been trying to scare them that way for a hundred years, Simon notes that the "bad people" should have learned that their actions are not working. When Nigel and Simon are playing in the schoolyard, a bully calls Simon a "nigger lover." Simon confronts the bully. Despite Nigel's advice that "You can't fight ignorance with violence," Simon hits the bully. Although Simon is suspended, his parents admit they cannot help being proud of his actions. In the end, Eric organizes support for the Hamiltons and their congregation by inviting members of all the areas religious groups to attend services at the site of the burned church. At the ecumenical gathering of Jews, Muslims, Catholics and Protestants, Reverend Hamilton says, "I had no idea I had so many friends," to which Eric replies, "We just wanted you to know we stand by you and will continue to stand by you." When Reverend Hamilton ascends the burned pulpit, broken stained-glass windows behind him, he greets everyone and echoes the words his youngest son used to say grace at the Camden house: "Please, God, stop the fires."[83]

---

83. "The Color of God." Written by Brenda Hampton; directed by Burt Brinckeroff.

The ending of this episode shows another way in which the Camdens emerge as progressive — their acceptance of members of other religions. Theirs is an ecumenically minded church and open-minded family. This is most noticeable in later seasons, when Matt courts, proposes to and marries a Jewish woman in an interdenominational wedding ceremony. Even in the first season, however, this open-mindedness is apparent in "Choices," wherein the church's former associate pastor visits as Lucy is starting confirmation classes. He tells Lucy that choosing one's religion "is one of the most important choices you'll ever make," and shares that he himself considered "every possible choice" before he committed to his church. Lucy says she never realized she had a choice, and the minister advises her that, "it's a lifetime decision you're being asked to make. It shouldn't be entered into lightly." Lucy asks her father for books on various religions. Unconcerned, he gives her books on Judaism, Catholicism, Hinduism, Sufism and Buddhism. When Lucy asks her father if her exploring other religions is okay, he responds, "you should know something about other religions." In confidence, Annie asks Eric if he is really as easygoing about Lucy's explorations as he seems. He says he does not want his daughter to choose their religion just to satisfy them, adding that he thinks Lucy should continue to attend confirmation classes while exploring other faiths.[84]

The themes introduced in the first season continue through *7th Heaven*'s long run, the program continuing to focus on the everyday lives of the Camdens while also focusing on the church, the family's values, and various social issues, often in storylines in which all of these intersect. For example, Reverend Camden helps a friend of Simon's leave a gang, alerts Simon to the dangers of "hugging" (sniffing paint fumes to gain a high) so he can help stop his friends from engaging in the practice, and intervenes with a girl's parents when he discovers a friend of Lucy's is "cutting" herself to change emotional problems into physical pain.[85] Other examples of the many issues facing teenagers and society taken up by *7th Heaven* include drunk driving, excessive alcohol drinking, condom use, the need to talk about sex with one's children, and misogynist lyrics in rap songs and how they affect men's attitudes towards women.[86]

October 14, 1996. Reviewed off broadcast television; also available off commercial DVD and at LOC and UCLA.

84. "Choices." Written by Sue Tenney; directed by Kevin Inch. April 14, 1997. Reviewed off broadcast television; also available off commercial DVD and at LOC.

85. "Girls Just Want to Have Fun." Written by Catherine LePard; directed by Joel J. Feigenbaum. November 3, 1997; and "Who Nose?" Written by Suzanne Fitzpatrick; directed by Harvey Laidman. November 29, 1999; and "Cutters." Written by Sue Tenney; directed by Anson Williams. October 5, 1998. All reviewed off broadcast television; also available off commercial DVD and at LOC.

86. ". . . and Expiation." Written by Catherina LePard; directed by Tony Mordente. November 15, 1999; and "Drunk Like Me." Written by Carol Evan McKeand and Nigel Evan McKeand; directed by Joel J. Feigenbaum. September 28, 1998; "Sweeps." Written by Brenda Hampton; directed by Joel J. Feigenbaum. February 19, 2001; and "Tunes." Written by Brenda Hampton; directed by Tony Mordente. November 27, 2000. All reviewed off broadcast television; only the first two are also available off commercial DVD and at LOC.

Several storylines and episodes focus on single-parent families. For example, Mary refuses to accept an achievement award for high-school sports when she discovers the award committee passed over one of her competitors because she is a single mother. At an assembly, Mary graciously gives the reward to the young woman, who had a baby at 14 years old and balanced her duties as a mother with those of a student athlete, saying she is the real role model.[87] For a number of episodes, Mary dates a responsible, single young man, Wilson, who is raising a son. Later in the series, Reverend Camden calls upon Wilson to speak with an unmarried young man who is a nervous new father and worries about whether he can handle the responsibility. Wilson shares his own experiences with the young man, explaining that the first few weeks of fatherhood are difficult but that "the baby needs you, and the baby's mom needs you, and they're always going to need you" and that "if children have their fathers in their lives they're better off; we're all better off."[88] In a similar situation developed throughout season ten, Simon introduces an old girlfriend, Sandy, to a buddy; she becomes pregnant and has their baby out of wedlock.

Some episodes reference specific world events or issues directly, emphasizing the family's reaction. For example, in "Yak Sada [a.k.a. With One Voice]," the Camden women participate in protests against the Taliban and its practices against Afghani women. Discussing how Afghani women can be beaten for laughing in public or wearing noisy shoes, and how their health is jeopardized by medical restrictions, Eric tells Annie that while the Taliban claims their treatment of women is rooted in Islamic tradition, most agree it is not. In the episode's conclusion, Annie addresses the congregation about women's rights in Afghanistan, while the television audience sees images of Afghani women in heavy robes with their faces covered. In contrast, the episode demonstrates that the Camdens themselves are not given to strictly defined gender roles: Ruthie plays football, Eric takes care of the family's new baby twins and does the laundry, and Matt and Simon clean house and help prepare dinner. In a related story, Eric counsels a couple who wishes to be married, until the woman breaks off the engagement because her fiancé's attitudes about women are based upon a strict interpretation of the Bible, including that women should serve men and stay home to raise children while men should make all the family decisions.[89] Several post 9/11 episodes deal with issues facing the nation: by e-mail, Ruthie befriends a marine serving in Afghanistan, who is later killed; the Camden family helps Muslim-Americans facing discrimination; the family debates the merits of the United States' war in Iraq; and in season eight, a young

---

87. "With Honors." Written by Sue Tenney; directed by Harvey Laidman. October 18, 1999. Reviewed off broadcast television; also available off commercial DVD and at LOC.

88. "Fathers." Written by Jeff Olsen; directed by Harry Harris. October 18, 2004. Reviewed off broadcast television.

89. "Yak Sada (a.k.a. With One Voice)." Written by Elizabeth Orange; directed by Bradley Gross. October 4, 1999. Reviewed off broadcast television; also available off commercial DVD and at LOC.

man stays with the Camdens while his father is serving in the military in Iraq.[90] Other world events are also referenced in the series. In "Lost and Found," the Camdens meet refugees from civil war in Sudan and become aware of the plight of "The Lost Boys," young men who survived attacks on their villages by fleeing the violence.[91] "Can I Just Get Something to Eat?" considers the genocide in Darfur when Ruthie and a friend work on a paper on the subject, causing all around them to discuss the situation and how to respond.[92] In "Teased," Simon discovers that a bullied classmate has brought a gun to school, as at Columbine High School in Colorado.[93]

Given that *7th Heaven* tackled so many subjects, the absence of a number of prominent issues in the 11-season series is worth noting, particularly since these issues were addressed in several other church-set television programs. For example, while other programs included episodes about abortion, the issue is not directly addressed on *7th Heaven*. The closest it comes is to highlight the admirable efforts of single teenaged parents to raise children in spite of the hardships involved. Likewise, the series never features a gay character or considers issues regarding gay people, as did other programs. These absences likely result from the primary target audience for *7th Heaven* — teenaged girls — and the producers' effort to avoid subjects that might compromise the "family values" appeal of the program. Such absences likely helped the program avoid controversy and achieve its unusual success.

As to the ecumenical trend, it is featured several times over the course of the series. In one episode, Ruthie and Simon feel guilty because they did not forewarn their parents about a troublesome situation involving one of their siblings. Fearing they may be "going to hell," the children visit clerics of various religions and ask for advice. Each cleric, in turn, discusses with the children his religion's approach to sin and forgiveness. The children enter a confessional in a Catholic church where a priest, figuring they are not Catholic, assures them that if they ask for God's forgiveness, He will give it. The priest also suggests that they perform an act of contrition, which he explains is "a task that will help you get back on the right track." He reminds the children that one of the Ten Commandments is to honor one's mother and father, and encourages them to talk with their parents. When the children are ready to leave, the priest blesses

---

90. "The Known Soldier." Written by Brenda Hampton; directed by Burt Brinckerhoff. May 6, 2002; "Suspicion." Written by Elaine Arata; directed by Joel J. Feigenbaum. January 21, 2002; "Getting to Know You." Written by Sue Tenney; directed by Harry Harris. November 3, 2003; and "Healing Old Wounds." Written by Brenda Hampton; directed by Harry Harris. February 3, 2004. All reviewed off broadcast television; the first two also available off commercial DVD and at LOC.

91. "Lost and Found." Written by Paul Perlove; directed by Harvey Laidman. May 3, 2004. Reviewed off broadcast television.

92. "Can I Just Get Something to Eat?" Written by Chris Olsen and Jeff Olsen; directed by Harry Harris. January 14, 2007. Reviewed off broadcast television.

93. "Teased." Written by Brenda Hampton; directed by Tony Mordente. October 1, 2001. Reviewed off broadcast television; also available on commercial DVD.

them, and listens to Ruthie's complaints about the size of the confessional and suggestion that they make it larger. But the children still feel guilty, so they visit a nearby Jewish synagogue where a rabbi explains that Jews do not believe in hell and atone for their sins on Yom Kippur, which has already passed. He too suggests the children should talk to their parents. Still not satisfied, Ruthie and Simon head to a Buddhist temple, where they are told to meditate on how to live better lives, and hear about the Buddhist goal of attaining enlightenment. They are told that since all things and beings are interconnected, they should talk with their parents. The two finally go to their father, whereupon Ruthie explains, "We went to a bunch of God's people and tried to do what they said, so God would know we were sorry and maybe make us feel better." Eric reveals that he knew of their search for repentance, since the people the children went to were all his friends and let him know where his children were and what they were up to. As all of the religious leaders had advised, Ruthie and Simon discover that what makes them feel better is talking things over with their parents.[94] Once again, though religion is featured, the family is central.

Perhaps the foremost occasion for exploring ecumenism occurs when Matt decides to marry a Jewish woman whose father is a rabbi. The story develops over multiple episodes, when Matt meets another pre-med student, Sarah Madison, and the two consider getting married. They discuss how successful their marriage would be, given their different faiths. Ultimately, Matt proposes and Sarah accepts. They elope to City Hall but do not tell their parents that they already are married. The announcement that they intend to marry sets off mixed emotions among all involved, in particular the couple's fathers. Sarah's father, Rabbi Madison, is upset that his daughter will be marrying outside of the faith. To make things easier, Matt offers to convert to Judaism, a decision which upsets Reverend Camden.

When the two families share their first dinner at the Madison home, the occasion serves as a primer on Jewish traditions. During a Shabbat dinner, the group discusses Jewish dishes, blessings, holidays and traditions. A lighthearted moment occurs after Matt reveals his decision to convert to Judaism and Ruthie asks about circumcision. Over the course of the couple's short engagement, many difficulties arise. At the height of the conflict, Reverend Camden refuses to attend his son's wedding, and Rabbi Madison refuses to perform the ceremony. Ultimately, the fathers come to accept the marriage, due to their wives' pleas and scheming. The cleric-fathers co-officiate the wedding, the Rabbi offering explanations of the Jewish parts of the ceremony. Eric expresses the ecumenical sentiments of the storyline when he addresses the temple congregation after hearing his son's intention to marry and convert. Rabbi Madison invites him to speak after a service, when Reverend Camden shares the following thoughts:

Even though there are many differences between our religions, there are

_____

94. ". . . and Expiation."

also things that unite us that are universal and transcend churches and temples and faiths of all kinds — and the one transcendent thing that jumps to my mind right now is love: love for family, love for friends, and the love that two young people feel who know that, together, they can overcome any obstacles that life puts in their way.

The Reverend then wishes all "Shabbat shalom," a salutation echoed by all in the synagogue, including the Camden clan.[95]

The focus on the church and family continues in later seasons. When it is time for her to pursue higher education, Lucy decides to enter the seminary to prepare to be a minister. When Eric undergoes double bypass heart surgery, his church hires Reverend Chandler Hampton, a young, single minister, to serve as its associate pastor. In addition to seeing Reverend Hamilton perform pastoral duties, such as counseling and leading church services, the series also focuses on his family life as he reconciles with his dying father (who disowned him when he decided to attend seminary), dates several women and adopts a young boy. One episode features a conversation between Chandler and Lucy in an empty church where they share their reasons for being interested in church work. Lucy's reason is that studying religion and being involved in the church "makes me feel whole." Meanwhile, as on other television programs focusing on clerics, Eric undergoes a vocational crisis and considers leaving the ministry. "The God business is just not working for me so well anymore," he explains.[96] Saying he is tired of helping others and wants to try other vocations, what brings him back to the church is not a renewed sense of service or calling, but Lucy's request that he officiate at her upcoming wedding. Similarly, Reverend Morgan Hamilton admits to annual thoughts of leaving the ministry, but adds that these are always fleeting and he never seriously considers them.[97]

A trend of the later seasons is to introduce somewhat more edgy storylines. Several of these involve Simon. For example, Simon must deal with feelings of guilt after he kills someone in a car accident. He also becomes sexually active, considers getting birth control pills for a girlfriend, and has sex with a young woman whom he later discovers has a sexually transmitted disease (unspecified), which forces him to undergo tests and nervously await the results. When he calls his father to discuss his worries, just before the minister is to give a sermon, his dad tells him he loves him and they can discuss any problem he has. While awaiting the test results, Simon reads the Bible and prays, saying, "God, if everything is okay, if I turn out okay, then I promise I won't ever have sex again until after I'm married, I promise I'll start going to church again, and I

95. "Lip Service." Written by Paul Perlove; directed by Joel J. Feigenbaum. April 15, 2002. Reviewed off broadcast television; also available on commercial DVD and at LOC.

96. "Lost Souls." Written by Brenda Hampton; directed by Harry Harris. November 18, 2002. Reviewed off broadcast television; also available on commercial DVD.

97. "High Anxiety." Written by Sue Tenney; directed by Joel J. Feigenbaum. February 23, 2003. Reviewed off broadcast television; also available on commercial DVD.

promise that I'll just try to be a better Christian."[98] After he discovers that he is in fact okay, he wears a cross as a reminder of his promises.

Simon's sexual activity leads Reverend Camden to a renewed conviction that the church must emphasize the importance of sexual abstinence for teenagers. In fact, he asks his new Associate Pastor Lucy to teach a sex education class at church that emphasizes this point of view. Lucy agrees on the condition that the class does not restrict itself to teaching abstinence.[99] Lucy delivers a sermon on the subject and cites the Song of Solomon to argue that young people (especially young women) should take time to get to know themselves and pursue their dreams, and consider not getting sidetracked by things like sex.[100] At the beginning of the tenth season, Lucy's sermon about working mothers' ability to balance work and childrearing gets her in trouble with the congregation and members of her family.[101] This sermon, together with "other" issues (a hint at her gender), leads some in the congregation to seek to oust Lucy as associate pastor.[102] Although only implied in this episode, challenges to the authority of women to serve as church leaders are raised explicitly elsewhere, as in an episode where Reverend Lucy Camden hears this opinion outright. In response to these attitudes and the efforts by some to get rid of Lucy, Eric Camden confides the following to his daughter: "Women are essential to religion, all religions; and throughout history, women have been good for religion, but I'm not sure that religion has been good to women in return. We can change that, starting with you and me and our church." Reverend Eric Camden, as the final authority in the parish, decides his daughter will remain a pastor in the church.[103]

From the beginning, *7th Heaven* excelled in placing the church and religion at the center of the Camden family life. The Camdens successfully balanced religious idealism with the practicalities of everyday modern life. Some episodes explicitly grounded themselves in church life. Others touched on religious activity in passing, such as when family members said a prayer in times of trouble. Still other episodes barely involved the church or religion at all (apart from the fact that the family was headed by a minister). Sometimes God was discussed in a lighthearted way. At other times, when the gravity of a situation facing a member of the Camden clan warranted, religious moments were treated more solemnly. The Camdens were a family whose attendance at church was as natural a part of their life as going to school, basketball practice or work; and as with those

98. "Leaps of Faith." Written by Jeffrey Rodgers; directed by Ron High. May 9, 2005. Reviewed off broadcast television.

99. "The Best Laid Plans (a.k.a. This is Going to Kill Mom)." Written by Brenda Hampton; directed by Harry Harris. September 20, 2004. Reviewed off broadcast television.

100. "The Song of Lucy." Written by Sue Tenney; directed by Joel J. Feigenbaum. September 27, 2004. Reviewed off broadcast television.

101. "It's Late." Written by Brenda Hampton; directed by Harry Harris. September 19, 2005. Reviewed off broadcast television.

102. "Home Run." Written by Brenda Hampton and Chris Olsen; directed by Harry Harris. September 26, 2005. Reviewed off broadcast television.

103. Ibid.

other everyday activities, their degree of enthusiasm for attending church activities fluctuated, given the circumstances. In short, the role of the church was presented as a normal, everyday part of the Camden family life — one that influenced their understanding of themselves, their world and their family, if often in simplistic ways.

The Book of Daniel

In contrast to the Camden's sentimental household was that of Reverend Daniel Webster, an Episcopal priest at the center of the short-lived, decidedly liberal-leaning NBC dramedy *The Book of Daniel* (2006). Four hour-long episodes aired on NBC, with several unbroadcast episodes available as webcasts on the network's website, and the whole series later available on DVD. Starring Aidan Quinn as a suburban minister, and film star Ellen Burstyn as his boss and bishop, the program focused on Reverend Webster's family and how it affected his job as a church leader. Given that the Webster's family problems exceeded those of most afternoon soap operas, the challenges facing the minister quickly added up.

To begin with, the Reverend's daughter Grace is caught selling marijuana; not a regular user of the illegal drug, she nonetheless pushes pot to raise money to buy computer programs she needs to create a comic strip journal of her life. The Reverend's son Peter is openly gay to all of his relatives except Reverend Webster's father, a bishop. Peter is perhaps the most well-adjusted of the children yet, in an effort to conceal his sexual identity from his girlfriend-pushing grandfather, he winds up having sex with a young woman who happens to be the niece of his father's boss, Bishop Beatrice Congreve. Bishop Congreve is alternately supportive and critical of Daniel's job performance. She is having a secret adulterous affair with Webster's father, Bishop Webster, whose wife suffers from Alzheimer's disease. Daniel's mother's confusion and insanity strain the family. This and the loss of Peter's twin to leukemia years before lead Daniel's wife Judith to guzzle martinis throughout the day. Her drinking increases after her brother-in-law steals money from the church's building fund and dies on the run, apparently while having sex with a woman who now lives with her widowed sister as her lesbian lover. The sister, her husband and this other woman had had a threesome prior to his running off with the church funds. To help recover the missing stolen money, Reverend Webster enlists the help of an Italian Catholic priest who introduces Daniel to mobsters. The mobsters offer their assistance in exchange for the minister's promise that he will award their Mafia-connected construction company the contract for the building project. Meanwhile, the Reverend's adopted Chinese son Adam, a confident, smart-mouthed jock, is sneaking around having sex with the daughter of a churchwarden whose wife reveals the racist reason they object to the relationship: "I have no intention," the warden's wife tells Judith, "of watching little Oriental children running around my Christmas tree." To round things off, Grace discovers that the Webster's housekeeper has been stealing her marijuana and smoking it in hiding to ease pain caused by her diabetes. A sympathetic Grace offers to get her more pot. Finally there is Reverend Webster himself, a devoted and level-headed minister who is addicted to Vicodin. He speaks to Jesus quite literally as the Savior appears to him and rather casually offers insight, advice and occasional wry commentary.

While the over-the-top plot twists border on satire, the series was grounded enough in both issues of faith and Reverend Webster's internal struggles to keep the emotional aspects of the show fairly authentic. The pilot episode, "Temptation," serves as an example. It opens with Daniel Webster and his wife retrieving his daughter Grace from a police station, where she has been charged with marijuana possession. They arrive at their house at dawn, when Daniel tells the women to go inside and get ready for church. Alone in the car, Daniel reaches into the glove compartment where he finds a bottle of Vicodin. He pops a pill in his mouth. In voice-over, Daniel says, "Temptation: is it really a bad thing? I don't think so . . ." And with that, the show cuts to Daniel in a green and white chasuble standing at a pulpit in an ornate, Gothic church, saying just those words as he preaches a sermon.

Daniel, whom the audience now knows is a minister, continues: "What I mean is if there were no temptation how could there be redemption? If we never did anything bad, how could we repent and be stronger for our weaknesses? Doesn't good need evil in order to be good?" The Bishop, seated across the altar wearing her cape and miter, bristles; her eyes widen and she coughs self-consciously, sending a message to the preacher. Reverend Webster looks at her and tries to clarify his point, only digging himself deeper into trouble. The sermon over, Reverend Webster leaves the pulpit and crosses paths with the Bishop, who mutters, "we need to talk." Later, outside the church, Reverend Webster comforts a parishioner whose mother is hospitalized and on life support. The woman informs Daniel that she will make the doctors "turn off those damn machines" that night, and Reverend Webster asks if he can be present. Meanwhile, a contractor informs Daniel that there is a problem with the start-up money needed to begin construction on a new school building for the parish; the fund, which should have over three million dollars, is empty. Reverend Webster withdraws to his office where he finds the Bishop, who scolds him for his permissive sermon. Daniel retorts that he was the one giving the sermon and is entitled to his interpretation, apparently at ease enough with his superior to have a debate on the subject. The exchange continues as the Bishop refers to the headquarters of the worldwide Anglican community, saying, "Canterbury has publicly spanked the US Episcopal for its liberal policies. We're a church in crisis." Reverend Webster responds, "We're a country in crisis," to which the Bishop retorts, "And in such a climate, do you really think it's wise to validate the inevitability of sin?" The minister quotes Corinthians as the Bishop says "Please, don't quote the Bible to me" and reminds him of her credentials, which include a doctorate in theology and a faculty position at Yale Divinity School.

Reverend Webster wonders about the sensibility of expecting people not to give into temptation, the Bishop ironically responding, "and yet, Daniel, that's the business we're in!" Daniel says he has to run and leaves.

Back home, college-bound Peter informs his father and their housekeeper that he has decided to enter the field of cancer research. Peter notes that he thinks he owes it to his brother, who died of leukemia. When Peter mentions his brother's name, his jittery mother drops a plate, which breaks. Recovering from the incident, they all enter the dining room, where a young Asian man greets them in mock Japanese, bowing to each and saying: "Papa-san, mama-san . . . gay-son." Peter smirks at the jibe and the brothers begin a witty exchange about politically correct ways of identifying "queers" and "Orientals." They call to Grace, who is in her bedroom hiding marijuana in a teddy bear. She joins the family as they are singing grace. As dinner begins, the youngsters good-naturedly snipe at each other until mom, unable to handle any tension, gets up and announces she is making herself a martini. Later, the priest and Peter are alone at the table. Daniel humorously inquires as to whether his son has found a nice girl to marry, leading Peter to ask if he will have to "come out" to his dad at every meal. The two smile as the father reaches for his son's arm.

The central gimmick of the series is introduced when Daniel tries to phone his brother-in-law from the car to discuss the missing church funds. When he cannot reach him, he instead reaches for a Vicodin. Suddenly a man with long hair and a beard, wearing a white robe, is seated next to Daniel, and matter-of-factly says, "I thought you were cutting back on those." The Lord Jesus Christ is riding shotgun with the minister. Unstartled, Reverend Webster explains that he has a golf date with a church official and his back is hurting. They discuss the minister's habit of popping pills until Daniel puts the pills back, defensively saying, "I only take them occasionally," to which the Lord Jesus sarcastically responds, "Right!" Daniel asks, "Could you fit more judgment into that 'right'?" Jesus replies, "Yes, I could!" and they both laugh. Daniel begins to discuss his family problems with Jesus, Christ offering some advice but reminding Daniel "I am not a fortuneteller" when the minister asks if it will all work out. Daniel builds up the courage to make an inquiry of Christ:

> Reverend Webster: You know, I've been meaning to ask you, have I been . . . chosen?
> Jesus: No.
> Reverend Webster: Well, why do you talk to me then?
> Jesus: I talk to everybody.
> Reverend Webster: Well, few mention it.
> Jesus: Few hear me. Some hear what they want. Most don't listen. You're tailgating.

And with that, a distracted Daniel narrowly avoids an accident, with the Lord's help.

Back in the Webster's kitchen, Judith and her sister Victoria discuss their inability to reach the missing husband, and Victoria innocently reveals she has also been unable to reach Jesse, his 28-year-old secretary. Judith belittles her sister for not being able to put the pieces together: that her husband, his young secretary and millions of dollars are missing all at once. Daniel walks in and erupts, noting that if anyone is going to be held responsible for the missing money it is he himself. Judith informs him that, in addition to her brother, the secretary is missing. Daniel catches on faster than his sister-in-law and exclaims, "Oh great! Perfect! Just what the diocese looks for when they're naming a new bishop!" Daniel leaves to visit the dying parishioner whose life support is to be turned off. At the hospital he finds a sickly woman on the verge of death, her family gathered around her. Reverend Webster, dressed in black and white vestments, traces the sign of the cross on the woman's forehead and tells her it is okay, that she can "let go" now. The woman smiles, rests her head on her pillow and silently passes on, as her family quietly sobs around her. Outside the hospital later, Daniel gets into his car, where he finds Jesus sitting quietly, faithfully waiting for him.

The next day, Daniel gets a call from a Mafia-connected Catholic priest, who tells him that his "friends" found the missing brother-in-law in a hotel in Daytona, naked and dead of a heart attack, with no money to be found. The Bishop grills Daniel in her office about the dead accountant and missing money. When he informs her he has not yet contacted the police, she "tells" him (in a leading tone) that she does not know about the missing money and will hear about it "for the first time" from the vestry, after he informs them. Luckily, she notes, she will be out of town for the vestry's next meeting, as she has plans for dinner and theater with Daniel's father. She looks uneasy as she reveals this to Daniel. Outside, Jesus stops Daniel from taking a pill, offering him a Lifesavers candy instead. Daniel confides that he likes talking to Jesus and asks what he should do. Jesus says he understands that life can be hard and that is why there is a reward at the end of one's life. "I know that's supposed to be comforting," Daniel replies, "but it's not! Aren't you supposed to comfort me?" "Oh, where did you read that," Christ retorts, "some Episcopalian self-help book?" The two laugh, and Jesus tells Daniel he should laugh more often.

At his brother-in-law's funeral, Reverend Webster officiates. The family gathers around the casket on a bright, sunny day. At the end of his sermon, Reverend Webster quotes Jesus' words about the rewards awaiting everyone at the end of life. The minister invites all to bow their heads in silence, just as a woman in a red convertible pulls up across the cemetery. Victoria whispers "That bitch!" when she recognizes Jesse, the secretary. As the car pulls away, Victoria yells "Somebody stop that bitch!" and runs across the cemetery yelling "Murderer!" as Daniel — in his liturgical robes — chases after her. The next morning Daniel goes to Victoria's home to comfort her. As he rounds the corner, he sees the red convertible and hears women laughing in the house. Peeking inside, he spies Victoria in a nightgown and Jesse in her black funeral dress, the two enjoying a cheerful breakfast together. Jesse tenderly puts her hand on Victoria's. A stunned Daniel backs away from the window and finds Jesus leaning against the convertible. "Boy, you never know, do you?" Christ says, shaking his head and grinning, as the episode ends.[104]

Although the focus in the pilot and subsequent episodes is on the Webster family, *The Book of Daniel* also takes on issues facing the modern church. A right-to-die issue is on the periphery of the first episode, when Reverend Webster prays for a parishioner at the termination of life support. The medical use of marijuana emerges in relation to the Webster's housekeeper. The church's care for those facing other healthcare situations arises when a parishioner comes to Reverend Webster concerned about a lump she has found in her breast. In "Revelations," he suggests she speak with a woman who has gone through the same situation — his wife Judith. Sitting in a church pew with the worried woman, Judith counsels the parishioner about fears of breast cancer; she herself found a lump in her breast while kneeling against the communion rail one day, and coped with her fears until her doctor found that the growth was benign.[105] Another episode, "Forgiveness," addresses the issue of couples living together outside of marriage, as Reverend Webster counsels two betrothed young people about a sexual problem. When the man mentions they are cohabiting, Webster acts shocked and asks if they are "living in sin" together; the man, caught off guard, looks dumbfounded, until the minister smiles and lets him off the hook, saying "just kidding."[106]

The ordination of women (although challenged by some in the Episcopal church) is a foregone conclusion given the Episcopal setting of the series, and *The Book of Daniel* features Bishop Beatrice Congreve as Daniel's cleric-wearing colleague and superior. As if to further underline the difference between Catholics and Episcopalians and forge new territory in church-set programs, Bishop Congreve mentions that she has been married twice before and implies she is not anymore because she was "no good at it."[107] One concludes she is twice divorced, something forbidden for Catholics. When Bishop Webster suggests that they abandon their vocations and pursue their relationship unfettered, Bishop Congreve scolds him for his arrogance.

The series maintains a particular focus on gay characters and the church's acceptance of them, while also acknowledging resistance to this. Hence, Peter's reminiscences about a past boyfriend, his commitment to being "out," and his intimate relationship with Bishop Congreve's nephew (a young man he meets

---

104. "Temptation." Written by Jack Kenny; directed by James Frawley. Series executive produced by Jack Kenny, Flody Suarez and John Tinker. January 6, 2006. Reviewed off broadcast television and commercial DVD.

105. "Revelations." Written by John Tinker; directed by John Fortenberry. Unaired; webcast. Reviewed off commercial DVD.

106. "Forgiveness." Written by Jack Kenny; directed by Rob Thompson. January 6, 2006. Reviewed off broadcast television and commercial DVD.

107. "Assignation." Teleplay by Dava Savel; story by Dan E. Fesman, Harry Victor; directed by Mel Damski. January 20, 2006. Reviewed off broadcast television and commercial DVD.

in the church choir) involve gay storylines. So too does Daniel's effort to tell his father, the conservative Bishop, about Peter's sexuality. Speaking of his father, Daniel remarks, "We have an openly gay Bishop in New Hampshire, for God's sake. It's time he stumbled into the twenty-first century!"[108] Additionally, Judith's sister Victoria is bisexual, but occasionally referred to as "lesbian." Reverend Webster at one point informs the churchwarden that he has an appointment to meet a gay couple wanting to join their parish, to which the warden remarks, "More gays? I should think the seven we already have would be sufficient." Daniel reminds him that all are welcome at their church. When Reverend Webster goes to his office and finds two men waiting for him, he assumes this is the gay couple, only to discover after some conversation that the men are from the Mafia-connected construction company. A further twist comes when one of these men returns to confide to Daniel that he is in fact gay but is worried about what his coworkers and family will think of him. Daniel and the gay mobster, Michael, have the following exchange sitting in the church hallway:

> Michael: Does God think I'm bad because I'm gay? And that I'm evil or gonna burn in hell? Because I've seen these people talk about it on TV and . . . I don't know . . .
>   Reverend Daniel: Being gay doesn't make you a bad person.
>   Michael: You're not just saying that, right? I mean, you've got to mean it because I'm talking to you now as a priest.
>   Reverend Daniel: God loves all his children. "Let he who is without sin cast the first stone."

Michael thanks Daniel for the talk and, referring to his Mafia-related activities, notes that if he does go to hell he is glad it will not be because he is gay. A final surprise comes when Michael informs Reverend Daniel that he thinks the cleric is attractive.[109] A more serious storyline comes in an unaired episode in which Peter is "gay bashed" and nearly dies. The Websters have to face the possibility of losing yet another son. The attack is presented rather dramatically, as images of the beating appear over Reverend Webster's voice as he reads the 23rd Psalm to his mother.[110] Using his underground connections, Michael discovers the identity of one of the assailants and tricks him into meeting the Reverend in his church office. The man calls Webster's son a "fag" who got what he deserved. Confronted by the man's lack of remorse, Reverend Webster beats the man (off camera) and later collapses into Christ's arms, fists bloodied, sobbing, "Don't forgive me!"[111]

---

108. "Forgiveness."
109. "Assignation."
110. "Withdrawal." Written by Tracey Stern; directed by Adam Bernstein. Unaired; webcast. Reviewed off commercial DVD.
111. "God's Will." Written by David Simkins; directed by Michael Fields. Unaired. Reviewed off commercial DVD.

In response to a number of issues arising in his congregation and family — from acceptance of gay people to racism directed at his son — Reverend Webster offers the following sermon as various characters are shown listening from the pews:

> "The Episcopal Church welcomes you." I don't know how many of you have noticed but that's kind of our motto. How do we as a church, as a community of faith, welcome our brethren? Isn't it our jobs as Christians to welcome and accept everyone? Acceptance means not shutting our minds and hearts when we encounter differences in others and it doesn't happen all at once. It's a process. It takes time. But if we can truly open ourselves to others, see the other side of every argument, understand something we thought we could never understand, then we might some-day really listen to one another, learn from one another, love one another, as God designed us, as Jesus asked us.

The choir sings "Just As I Am," including a duet between Grace and Peter's soon-to-be-boyfriend, the Bishop's nephew.[112]

The series bore some resemblance to the ABC hit *Desperate Housewives* in its over-the-top, behind-closed-doors look at modern suburban family life. Clearly liberal in its overall point of view, *The Book of Daniel* introduced a number of firsts to television series focusing on church leaders: the first female Bishop; the first regularly appearing gay, lesbian and Asian characters; the first series explicitly set in the Episcopal Church, wherein the denominational identity is at the forefront and part of the very premise of the series. (In *Soul Man*, the Episcopalian identity is implied but not overtly stated.) Ultimately, the sensational situations depicted in the context of a church-set drama contributed to its downfall. Suffering from low ratings, the series also faced criticism from some religious groups, such as the conservative American Family Association, which cited the show as evidence of the network's "anti-Christian bigotry."[113] Some network affiliates, concerned with the criticism, refused to air the series. In response, the show's creator said he never intended to deride religion but instead show a balance of "humor and grace" in a man's struggle with issues of family and faith.[114] Certainly, even as *The Book of Daniel*'s excessive crises pushed the boundaries beyond what some found appropriate, they also provided an opportunity for Reverend Webster to explore issues of faith and commitment to family. His dialogues with Jesus depicted a man weighing issues and struggling for appropriate, faithful and ethical responses. While this device was often a gimmick, it was

---

112. "Acceptance." Written by Dan E. Fesman and Harry Victor; directed by Perry Lang. January 13, 2006. Reviewed off broadcast television and commercial DVD.

113. Associated Press (2006), "NBC drops *Book of Daniel* from schedule." *ABC News*, January 24: available at http://abcnews.go.com/Entertainment/wireStory?id=1538244 (accessed September 17, 2006).

114. Ibid.

sporadically rendered rather poignantly, as when Daniel learns his son is close to death and Christ is shown nearby, head solemnly bowed.[115] Most often the crises Reverend Webster faced were personal, family predicaments that somehow influenced his role as parish leader. Thus, *The Book of Daniel* is one more program which focused on a church leader in his role as head-of-household as much as cleric, and one more to fold in part due to its controversial approach to religious subject matter.

Discussion

After periods of church-set programs focused on the internal struggles of church leaders, and the church's struggle to remain relevant in the modern world, the most recent cluster of programs focused on clerics in family context. While the church leaders of this cluster certainly dealt with problems at church, a major spotlight was on their home life and how they handled problems within their families. The one Catholic-set program in this cluster, *Trinity*, presented a priest as a dutiful son, devoted not only to serving the church but also helping his parents and siblings with their problems. Of the Protestant-set programs, only the two most recent — *7th Heaven* and *The Book of Daniel* — featured married clergy and dealt with marital issues in addition to parental ones. Nonetheless, all of the Protestant-set shows (including those about divorced or widowered clerics) featured situations arising from child rearing and its challenges. Consequently, whereas many earlier church-set programs may be categorized as workplace-set series (the church here serving as the setting, alongside other programs focused on offices, bars, hospitals and schools), or as belonging to some other TV genre (such as the detective series, as with *Father Dowling Mysteries*), the more recent programs fit an equally well-developed television program type: the domestic comedy or drama. Of course, these programs had to be set in denominational contexts where having a spouse and children are allowed and the norm; hence the Protestant focus of these programs.

Programs focusing on Protestant church leaders and their families also raised the possibility of introducing romantic storylines — ones which went beyond the somewhat sensational episode-specific romantic stories in the Catholic *Father Dowling Mysteries*, *In the Beginning*, and *Hell Town*. For example, a major storyline of *Amen* concerned Reverend Reuben Gregory and his on-again, off-again romance with the deacon's daughter Thelma, leading to their marriage and the birth of their first child. *Amazing Grace* saw divorcee Reverend Hannah Miller not only deal with the aftermath of a failed marriage, but also flirt with an ex-boyfriend, the lawyer who helped her in her ministry, and deal as best she could with her daughter's problematic relationship with a slacker. Reverend Mike Weber's widowered status not only explained his children but also allowed him to flirt with a reporter and church secretary, while his boys' growing interest in girls

---

115. "God's Will."

also provided a focus in later episodes.[116] The long-running *7th Heaven* focused considerable attention on the mature, committed romance between Reverend Camden and his wife, in addition to the children's proliferating relationships — including his minister-daughter's marriage to a police officer. Other ministers of *7th Heaven* involved in marriages or courtship included Reverend Hamilton and his family, and Reverend Hampton, Eric's young associate pastor. *The Book of Daniel* not only depicted Reverend Webster's relationship with his wife, but also an affair between a previously twice-married bishop and another, still-married bishop; all this in addition to showing the sexual lives of Webster's children (one gay) and his "swinger" sister-in-law. Even *Trinity*'s Reverend McCallister, like other Catholic priests before him, had one episode devoted to exploring his sexuality, the remainder of the series focusing on the romantic relationships of his siblings and his role in advising them. (It is noteworthy that *Good News*' Pastor Randolph, a Protestant minister free to explore romantic relationships, chose instead to focus on his pastoral duties and service to the community, even though women expressed interest in him and he in them. This makes *Good News* fit even more into the previous chapter's grouping, as a program focused on the church's effort to remain relevant in the modern world, rather than the church in family life.) Hence, the Protestant focus of most all of the programs in this grouping allowed them to enter new territory, not possible before given the previously exclusive focus on the Catholic Church and its leaders.

This trend was part of a larger American network movement to develop distinctive family programs. The domestic situation comedy has been a staple of the American network lineup since its beginning, and an opportunity to advance the genre into distinct territory by contextualizing the family in a unique way helps set one program apart from others. One way to distinguish a TV family is by means of the occupation of the parents, and comedies and dramas have emerged in which the parents are teachers, politicians, TV personalities, doctors, lawyers, etc. The church as a setting for a parent's employment helps distinguish a family program from others while also providing the opportunity for unique comedic or dramatic situations. Sometimes the church setting introduced unique storylines, such as when Reverend Weber's son raided the communion wine. The parent's leadership role in the church often influenced their response to the children's mischief, as when Reverends Camden, Webster and Weber had to remind their children that the youngster's behavior influenced the parent's image in the community, or when any of the clerics based advice given to their offspring on church-based values. Even when stories focused on situations having little to do with the church, the setting itself provided a sensibility that influenced viewers' responses. Be these part of the single-parent family trend (*Amen*, *Soul Man*, *Amazing Grace*) or a two-parent family (*7th Heaven*, *The Book of Daniel* and even *Trinity*), the search for new and distinct family programs when combined with Protestant settings

---

116. Brooks and Marsh (2003), p. 1102.

allowed networks to develop innovative family programs by setting these in the church.

Significantly, programs set in Protestant churches made a late entrance into popular American television programming. Aside from the short-lived *Family Holvak* in 1975, the first program featuring a Protestant ecclesiastic setting was *Amen* (1986–91), followed by *7th Heaven* (1996–2007), *Good News* (1997–8), *Soul Man* (1997–8) and *The Book of Daniel* (2006). This shift from Catholic-set programs owes as much to the search for innovative family settings as to the Catholic and Protestant churches of the time. Many of the Protestant-set programs do not specify their denominational setting. The one program which labors to specify its context, *The Book of Daniel*, identifies the Episcopal Church throughout, and includes signs, flags and other set pieces to make clear the denominational setting. While the Catholic Church of this period had been dealing with *scandals*, the Episcopal Church had been beset with *controversies* (not unlike those facing post Vatican II Catholicism, when Catholic church TV programs were prominent) and the difference may in part account for the interest in the Episcopal Church as a setting. Although the Episcopal Church did face sexual misconduct scandals, especially in the 1980s, these were not as prevalent or well-publicized as those facing the Catholic Church in the 1980s and beyond, and often involved male clergy misconduct with adult women, as opposed to misconduct with minors as in the Catholic Church.[117]

The Book of Daniel certainly made use of the Episcopal Church's controversial decisions about homosexuals in the church. Episcopal leaders, in particular Newark's Bishop John Spong, were outspoken proponents of a new sexual ethic that did not condemn homosexual people for their orientation, and in fact supported ordination of gay and lesbian people.[118] Similarly, Episcopal leaders have advocated and/or presided over same-sex union ceremonies. The issue reached its peak when Bishop Gene Robinson, an openly gay minister involved in a longtime relationship with a man, was confirmed in 2003 as a Bishop of New Hampshire. The appointment sparked much debate within and outside of the Episcopal Church, a debate which received much news coverage. That a television program set in the Episcopal Church context would be open and eager to deal with conflict in the church in general and issues about gay people in particular is not surprising; it allowed this Protestant-set program to capitalize on well-publicized national church policy debates by way of gay storylines at a time when gay people and issues were receiving more attention in the news and entertainment media, here in a denominational context in which such issues were actually being debated. Of course, the Catholic-set programs of the era also included gay storylines (*Trinity*, *Nothing Sacred*), as did other Protestant-set

---

117. Robert Prichard (1999), *A History of the Episcopal Church*, Rev. edn. Pennsylvania: Morehouse Publishing, pp. 302–4; and Patrick W. Carey (2004), *Catholics in America: A History*. Westport, Connecticut: Praeger, pp. 146–55.

118. Prichard (1999), pp. 286–93.

shows of the era (*Good News*). Nonetheless, as the only Protestant-set program to explicitly specify a denominational context, *The Book of Daniel*'s selection of the left-leaning Episcopal Church as in some ways the "new" Catholic Church for television's programming purposes was not surprising. As such, much as well-publicized debates within Catholicism contributed to the early focus on the Catholic Church as a setting for fictional TV programs focusing on ecclesiastics, so too the increased public attention on internal debates in the Episcopal Church may account for attention on the Episcopal Church as a dramatic setting.[119] In fact, although the series did not principally focus on ecclesiastics, ABC's 2007–8 *Dirty Sexy Money* included as a character an Episcopal minister who was trying to keep his wife from discovering that he fathered a child from another woman — further using the controversy-beset church and its marriage-permissible clergy as a vehicle for a television storyline.

The networks did not abandon the Catholic setting altogether, although its place clearly was displaced by the upsurge of Protestant-set, family programs. The one program that did focus on Catholicism, *Trinity*, continued to highlight controversial issues facing the Catholic Church. There was the abortion storyline, where the priest argued the traditional Catholic stance. Then again, there was the storyline focusing on a gay parishioner and the priest's somewhat unorthodox sympathy for the man's situation. As to the issue of gay priests, this arose only in the unaired episode of *Nothing Sacred*. Notably, one of the most visible issues facing the modern Catholic Church in America, that of the priest child abuse scandals and the church hierarchy's efforts to cover up the extent of the problem, has been virtually ignored by television programs set in the church. Perhaps too much of a hot-button issue, the only reference to it came from the teenaged boy whom the priest of *Trinity* was trying to help and counsel, when the teenager quipped to Father Kevin, "is this the part where you try to molest me?" One would hardly expect a popular fictional TV program to cast one of its regular characters as an abuser, but it is noteworthy that no storylines even acknowledged this well-publicized national story. Although television's reticence to depict such a distasteful subject on these shows is understandable, the subject's absence from such programs is all the more glaring and in stark contrast to the amount of attention the subject has received in the news media. Arising between the mid-eighties and early nineties, the scandals reached their "watershed years" in 1992–3, later culminating in the "shock wave" of 2002, when the full extent of the problem and cover-up became international news.[120] The significance of the scandals went beyond the purely salacious, and compromised the church's very authority to speak on relevant contemporary issues. Dolan characterizes the situation well:

---

119. The election of Katharine Jefferts Schori as presiding Bishop of the US Episcopal Church occurred later in 2006, after *The Book of Daniel* was produced and aired; even so, the publicity and controversy surrounding the election of a woman to this post only strengthens the case for seeing the Episcopal Church as a high-profile denomination dealing with conflict.

120. Peter Steinfels (1997), "Beliefs." *New York Times*, September 20, pp. 40–67.

As Catholicism has become a more public, less insular religion, church leaders have addressed such topics as war and peace, the economy, abortion and the death penalty. By speaking out, they assumed an important moral authority in the public discussion of these critical social issues. The duplicity and cover-up on the part of many bishops has severely damaged, if not destroyed, that authority, and it will take more than just apologies to restore the credibility lost in the revelations . . .[121]

The older controversies concerning the struggle between liberals and conservatives allowed for impassioned dialogue between church leaders representing both sides of issues on fictional television programs. Even the controversial issue of abortion received attention on TV programs. In contrast, the priest child abuse scandals have proven too contentious for church-set television series to date, although they have been the subject of individual episodes of crime dramas such as *Law and Order: Special Victims Unit* ("Silence") and *The Practice* ("The Telltale Nation"), and films such as *Primal Fear* (1996), *Deliver Us from Evil* (2006), and *Doubt* (2008). In fact, the trend away from Catholic-set series may in part derive from the unwanted attention the scandals placed on the Catholic Church.

Other issues facing the church have also been reflected in the latest cluster of church-set television programs. Older, second-career ministers have been an increasing trend in the newly ordained clergy in the United States,[122] and this was portrayed in *Amazing Grace*, *Trinity* (in the person of Father Peter) and *Soul Man*, as well as in *Sarge*. Further, whereas most mainline Protestant denominations had been ordaining women for decades (the Presbyterians and Methodists since the 1950s, the Episcopals and several Lutheran denominations since the 1970s), the first female cleric to be featured in a network television series was Reverend Hannah Miller in *Amazing Grace* (1995), followed by Reverend Lucy Camden in *7th Heaven* (1996–2007), and culminating in Bishop Beatrice Congreve in *The Book of Daniel* (2006). Historically, this is a bit surprising. While the number of female clergy has been steadily increasing over the decades,[123] this trend is only reflected in American TV series of the last decade. Certainly, fewer female clergy than men have served denominations; for example, US labor force data for 2003 found that about 14 percent or one in eight clergy were female.[124] A growing but still small number of women have reached national leadership positions in American churches, and *The Book of*

---

121. Jay P. Dolan (2002), *In Search of an American Catholicism: A History of Religion and Culture in Tension*. New York: Oxford University Press, p. 258.

122. Larry A Witham (2005), *Who Shall Lead Them? The Future of Ministry in America*. New York: Oxford University Press, p. 15.

123. Ibid., p. 16.

124. US Census Bureau (2004), "No. 597. Employed civilians by occupation, sex, race and Hispanic origin: 2003," *Statistical Abstract of the United States: 2004–2005*. Washington, DC: US Government Printing Office, p. 385.

Daniel's depiction of a female Episcopal Bishop reflects this trend. Indeed, the June 2006 election of Bishop Katharine Jefferts Schori as presiding Bishop of the Episcopal Church in America demonstrated the success of women in reaching top church posts, even as it helped mask other problems facing female church leaders. A sizable number of congregants still question women's ability to lead the church, or outright oppose women's ordination; indeed, the election of Bishop Schori led some members of the Episcopal Church to see her appointment as "an affront to others in the denomination who opposed ordination of women," and to wonder how her election would position the US Episcopal Church with the less liberal Anglican Church worldwide, the Vatican, and other more conservative US denominations.[125] Notably, the appointment of women to higher positions of church authority also masks the challenge women face gaining positions in larger parishes, what some call "the stained glass ceiling":

> Whether they come from theologically liberal denominations or conserva-tive ones, black churches or white, women in the clergy still [experience . . .] longstanding limits, preferences and prejudices within their denomi-nations that keep them from leading bigger congregations and having the opportunity to shape the faith of more people. [. . .] It is often easier for women in the mainline churches — historic Protestant denominations like Presbyterian, Lutheran, Methodist, Episcopal and the United Church of Christ — to get elected as bishops and as other leaders than to lead large congregations.[126]

Bishop Congreve's unchallenged authority as an Episcopal Bishop in *The Book of Daniel* therefore reflected one side of the story facing female ecclesiastics — increased visibility in leadership positions of the national church.

Still, their minority status and their congregants' unfamiliarity with their style of preaching and ministry have challenged female clergy. This contributes to dramatic situations which TV programs might use. For example, many female clergy have problems being accepted as authority figures and preachers. Then again, studies show women bring strengths to ministry, such as the ability to build consensus.[127] The challenges to Reverend Miller's authority in *Amazing Grace* surely reflected some congregants' resistance to full acceptance of women in

---

125. Neela Banerjee (2006), "Woman is named Episcopal leader." *New York Times*, June 19, A1, 15.

126. Neela Banerjee (2006), "Clergywomen find hard path to bigger pulpit." *New York Times*, August 26, A1, 12.

127. See for example: Witham 2005, pp. 41–59; Barbara Brown Zikmund, Adair T. Lummis, and Patricia M.Y. Chang (1998), "Women, men and styles of clergy leadership." *Christian Century*, May 6, 115(14), 478–86; Rick Wolff (1988), "Clergywomen: The Lutheran case: an inside look at Lutheran female clergy in America." *The Cresset* (Valparaiso University, Indiana) 51, April, 16–21.

the pulpit, as did her appointment to head a small parish that reportedly no one else wanted. Reverend Lucy Camden of *7th Heaven* shared similar ground with Reverend Miller, serving as a church leader in her childhood parish, although only as an associate pastor. Even so, members of the congregation challenged her after she gave a sermon about working mothers.[128] She also had to deal with those who thought women should not be pastors.[129] Also worth noting is that, unlike Bishop Congreve and Reverend Miller, Reverend Camden doubted her effectiveness in ministry and wondered if she, instead of her husband, should leave her job and be a stay-at-home parent;[130] research suggests that first-career ministers are much more likely than older, second-career clergy to doubt their calling at some point.[131] Beginning with Reverends Congreve, Miller and Camden, the budding, if limited, image of fictional female clergy on television is worth examining as it further develops.

Many modern family television programs, particularly those focusing on European-American characters, have been set in the suburbs. Significantly, many of the Protestant-set family programs have been set in suburban locales, and often have not highlighted the financial plight of their churches as much as the urban-set Catholic programs did. While Catholicism has historically been associated with urban settings — and television programs, including this era's *Trinity* and *Nothing Sacred* have maintained this focus — Protestantism has been just as associated with suburban and rural settings. While the rural church setting has been virtually ignored in church-set television programs (save for *Family Holvak*), the Protestant association with the suburbs has been in evidence in TV programs. The two urban Protestant TV programs had predominantly African-American casts: *Good News*, set in Compton in southern Los Angeles, and *Amen,* set in Philadelphia. This reflects the actual situation facing African-American churches where, after the "largest internal migration America has experienced," black Americans moved from rural to urban settings, establishing places of worship in America's cities.[132] Meanwhile, predominantly Korean churches, mostly Protestant and also largely urban, are on the rise in America,[133] but as yet not represented on television; nor are predominantly Hispanic churches, which also are on the rise, largely urban, and mostly Catholic but with a sizable number in the Pentecostal tradition.[134]

As to the depiction of the African-American church experience, *Amen* picked up on a number of concerns addressed by black churches of its time.

---

128. "It's Late" and "Home Run."

129. "Soup's On." Written by Brenda Hampton and Victoria Huff; directed by Joel J. Feigenbaum. November 7, 2005. Reviewed of broadcast television.

130. "Ring Around the Rosie." Written by Brenda Hampton and Elaine Arata; directed by Michael Preece. October 10, 2005. Reviewed off broadcast television.

131. Witham (2005), pp. 15–16.

132. Ibid., p. 106, quoting Eric Lincoln and Lawrence H. Mamiya (1990), *The Black Church in African-American Experience*. Durham: Duke University Press, p. 118.

133. Witham (2005), pp. 101–3,114–19.

134. Ibid., pp. 101–3, 110–14.

Sociologists Lincoln and Mamiya identified a number of issues facing the African-American community and black churches, including high rates of teen pregnancy, female-headed households, incarceration (especially of men) and gang membership. While teenage pregnancy is not exclusively a problem of the African-American community, the rate of teen pregnancy among blacks is significantly higher than for whites.[135] As such, it is a "major challenge to the traditions of black churches," whose values are often at odds with those of the sexual revolution and its aftermath.[136] Indeed, reflecting on the Lilly Foundation sponsored survey attesting to the conservative sexual ethic of black clergy, Robert Franklin observes, "given the high rates of teen pregnancy and disease, church leaders will need to grapple honestly with strategies for protecting young people from their own irresponsible behavior."[137] Franklin, Lincoln and Mamiya note this is one area in which black churches may take a leadership role in promoting change. Along these lines, it is interesting that in other programs where a young, unmarried woman was facing pregnancy (*Hell Town*, *Trinity*, *Nothing Sacred*) the situation was treated as a personal issue, whereas in *Amen* it was treated as a community issue. Hence, in "The Deacon Delivers," the church leaders did not allow a young, unwed expectant mother to join the choir because they did not wish to condone her behavior, noting in particular the example it might set for the church's youth. Similarly, representatives of the church encouraged the baby's father not to do as others in the community had done and abandon his child, but to marry the mother. The influence of leaders in the black church as role models for young men was a continual theme in *Amen*. Several episodes focused on the men of the congregation counseling a young man about such matters as the dangers of gang membership, criminal behavior or leaving school, and encouraging higher education — all issues facing the African-American community. Indeed, as Lincoln and Mamiya note, "Perhaps one of the most important functions that black churches performed for young people was to provide a place where they could meet older adults, men and women, who could serve as role models for them"; they add that "studies have shown that black pastors and laity have been important role models for black youth."[138] Finally, the depiction of African-Americans as a small portion of the predominantly white denominations depicted in TV programs reflected the reality of the black church experience in the United States. Virtually all of the congregants depicted, from the Catholic assembly of *Trinity* to the Episcopal congregation of *The Book of Daniel*, were white. Having the majority of television's black churchgoers appear in predominantly black Protestant churches, as on *Amen* and *Good News*, reflected actual trends in membership of African-Americans in contemporary churches.[139]

---

135. Lincoln and Mamiya (1990), p. 324.
136. Ibid., pp. 324–5.
137. Franklin (1997), p. 80.
138. Lincoln and Mamiya (1990), pp. 312–13.
139. Ibid., p. xii.

One aspect of modern church life that perhaps has become so commonplace as to no longer receive much attention on church-set programs is the ecumenical movement. Whereas earlier TV programs made reference to the ecumenical spirit facing much of the American religious landscape in the latter twentieth century, only *7th Heaven* reflected this trend in an ongoing way. From the outpouring of support given by a wide variety of churches when a local African-American church was burned down, to the ongoing storyline of interreligious understanding when one of Reverend Camden's children married the daughter of a Jewish rabbi, to episodes where the Camden children visited leaders of other faiths in their worship spaces or otherwise explored the variety of faiths in America, *7th Heaven* maintained a focus on ecumenism as a prominent interest of the contemporary church. What is more, *7th Heaven* highlighted in particular the Muslim-Christian dialogue that has been on the rise in the United States ever since the events of September 11, 2001 focused national attention on Islam — its beliefs, practices and believers. Such efforts to promote increased awareness and understanding of Muslim people, faith and issues were reflected over the years in *7th Heaven*. For example, interdenominational gatherings in episodes of the program, such as at the rally in support of the burned Christian church, included Muslim leaders. A more pointed example of the series' commitment to promoting awareness and understanding of Muslims occurred in an episode airing in January 2002 titled "Suspicion," in which a young Muslim girl and her family were harassed by townspeople because of their religion and ethnicity, and showed how the Camdens came to know and support them. The episode included a visit from Reverend Camden to a Muslim cleric to discuss the situation facing the family. The focus continued in a 2003 episode titled "Getting to Know You," which echoed the themes of "Suspicion," once again highlighting a Muslim girl and her family. In actuality, many local and national churches have begun to promote study of Islam and engage in interfaith dialogue with Muslims. Many major national church bodies in the United States, such as the United Methodist Church, the Roman Catholic Church and the Evangelical Lutheran Church in America, provide parish resources to promote understanding of Islam or have sponsored commissions on Muslim-Christian interfaith dialogue. One example of an institution created for just this purpose is the Center of Christian-Muslim Engagement for Peace and Justice, established in 2006 by the Lutheran School of Theology at Chicago; its stated purpose is to "provide cultural and educational opportunities in which Christians, Muslims and people of other faiths will come together for mutual enrichment, understanding, healing and wholeness."[140] This center joined the Center for Muslim-Christian Understanding at Georgetown University, and the long-established Duncan Black Macdonald Center for the Study of Islam and Christian-Muslim Relations

---

140. Lutheran School of Theology (2006), "Lutheran School of Theology at Chicago establishes a Center of Christian-Muslim Engagement for Peace and Justice." Press release, Office of Communications, Lutheran School of Theology at Chicago, June 6.

at Hartford Seminary, alongside many other interfaith organizations, receiving increased attention and support in recent years for their efforts at promoting understanding and dialogue between Christians and Muslims. Perhaps in part because it was the only successful church-set show that continued past 9/11, *7th Heaven* distinguished itself from other programs not only for its continued depiction of ecumenism in general but also its focus on Muslim-Christian dialogue in particular.

As to the future of programs focusing on the church and its leaders, this may make use of other developing trends in American organized religion as yet not reflected in TV programming. For example, one significant growing phenomenon in the United States is the "megachurch", defined as any congregation with 2,000 or more members. The number of such churches in the United States doubled in the five years between 2000 and 2005, rising to 1,210, while attendance at these churches likewise rose.[141] Beyond this, the visibility of these churches and their leaders has grown; as one study on the megachurch phenomenon reports, "Not a week passes without several stories in the nation's papers, radio or television in which megachurches figure prominently. Megachurch pastors always dominate lists of most influential religious leaders in the country."[142] The rise of these churches is a significant current trend in American organized religion, receiving much attention in emerging scholarship on the church in the twenty-first century, and interest in them may lead to future TV program premises. In fact, at present one of the networks is negotiating with TV evangelist and megachurch pastor Joel Osteen to develop a reality series based at his Lakewood Church.[143] Other areas for potential development that go beyond the groundwork already laid by past church-set television programs would include more programs featuring minority and/or female clergy, and smaller or rural parishes. As is, the church landscape as depicted on American network television programs has focused mainly on suburban white Protestant, urban African-American Protestant and urban white Catholic parishes, most of these led by a male cleric. It is an overall look at these and other trends, past and potential — what accounts for them and what impact they had or may have — that is the final subject of consideration.

---

141. Scott Thumma, Dave Travis, and Warren Bird (2005), "*Megachurches Today 2005, Summary of Research Findings.*" Hartford Institute for Religion Research: available at http://hirr.hartsem.edu/megachurch/megastoday2005_summaryreport.html (accessed October 2, 2006).

142. Ibid.

143. CBS (2008), "Joel Osteen answers his critics." *CBS News*, June 8: available at http://www.cbsnews.com/stories/2007/10/11/60minutes/main3358652.shtml (accessed June 8, 2008).

Questions for Reflection

1) The cleric-led family drama seems to be a phenomenon particular to television. (How many such films can you name?) Why is this? What does this suggest about the nature of television compared to film?

2) Abortion is an issue that television regularly uses to signify the Catholic Church's moral authority and how this affects individual Catholics, from female laity who face it personally to Catholic priests who counsel them. Consider how *Hell Town*, *Nothing Sacred* and *Trinity* treated the issue of abortion. How does each depict women facing the issue, clergy counseling them and the role that official Catholic Church doctrine plays in these matters?

3) Ed Weinberger was a writer-producer for both *Good News* and *Amen.* How do these programs and their depictions of clerics compare? Consider also how these programs fit in with other programs on which Weinberger worked, including the family-set *Cosby Show* (1984–92), the workplace-set *Taxi* (1978–83) and *Mary Tyler Moore Show* (1972–7).

4) Compare television's depiction of church leaders in this era to that of movies, such as *Sleepers* (1996), *The Preacher's Wife* (1996), *Stigmata* (1999), *Keeping the Faith* (2000), *The Order* (2003), *The Exorcism of Emily Rose* (2005), *The Da Vinci Code* (2006), *Deliver Us from Evil* (2006), *Doubt* (2008), *First Sunday* (2008) and *Angels and Demons* (2009). What similarities and contrasts do you see between the two media's portrayals? Consider continuing depictions of spiritual versus worldly concerns, and sensational versus sentimental imagery. Note that while television began focusing on Protestant leaders and their families, most movies continue to focus on the Catholic setting. Why is this?

5) Before reading the conclusion, consider: If one was to take television's depiction of priests, pastors and nuns as accurate, with what activities do church leaders fill their days? What is left out of this depiction? What is the impact of this representation on the image of ecclesiastics in popular culture? In what ways is this constructive? In what ways is it lacking?

Video Sources

7th Heaven. Seasons one through eight available on DVD, with additional seasons forthcoming. Paramount.

The Book of Daniel. All episodes available on DVD. Universal Studios.

Amen and *7th Heaven* regularly air in syndication on broadcast and/or cable television.

Individual episodes are available for screening at the following locations (Library of Congress, Washington, DC [abbrev. LOC]; Paley Center for Media, New York and Los Angeles [abbrev. PCM]; UCLA Films and Television Archives, Los Angeles [abbrev. UCLA]):

   Family Holvak — LOC

Amen — LOC, PCM, UCLA
Amazing Grace — LOC, UCLA
Trinity — LOC, UCLA
Soul Man — PCM
7th Heaven — LOC

Suggested Further Reading

Elliott, Stuart (2006), "Few are booking ads on *The Book of Daniel*." *New York Times*, January 11, C3.

Mason, M. S. (1997), "Religious themes get wider play, more nuanced portrayal in fall shows." *Christian Science Monitor*, October 14, 13.

Steinfels, Peter (1997), "Beliefs." *New York Times*, September 20, A10.

Witham, Larry A. (2005), *Who Shall Lead Them? The Future of Ministry in America*. New York: Oxford University Press.

5

ASSESSING TELEVISION'S PORTRAYAL OF THE CHURCH AND ITS LEADERS

We have watched these people of God, these leaders of the church, for years — decades even. We have seen them perform traditional clerical duties ranging from caring for the sick and counseling parishioners to sermonizing and leading worship. And yes, we have seen them engage in not so traditional tasks as well, from chasing criminals and solving murder mysteries to brawling and flirting in bars, and overcoming gravity. We have seen various types of ministry: leading parishes; running orphanages and missions; serving as chaplains in wartime or correctional facilities; caring for the sick in hospitals. Our televised clerics represent various religious traditions: ten of the featured programs (which focused regularly and principally on church leaders) have Catholic settings and seven Protestant, with brief discussions (of programs including clerics as members of an ensemble) considering five additional Catholic programs, one more Protestant and one Jewish-set program. For the most part, the Catholic-set programs, predominant in the past, have yielded to Protestant-set family programs. Women have risen to positions of leadership in Protestant churches and members of racial minorities have risen in visibility, as have issues of particular concern to their communities. We have seen trends and issues come and go, from a focus on internal debates about the direction of the church to the church's search for relevance in the world, and the struggle of church leaders to balance church duties with family life.

So ran television's depiction of church leaders. Often sensationalized, yet frequently tapping into contemporaneous issues in the life of the church, the view of institutionalized religion on American television was at different times realistic and embellished, accurate and exaggerated, faithful to the church's priorities and faithful to those of the television industry. Indeed, trends in the history of episodic television account for the representations of the church that emerged as much as trends in the life of the church itself. Therefore we now turn to what television historians may contribute to the understanding of why televised representations of the church developed as they did. By fitting depictions of church leaders into the latest programming trends, television's shifting tendencies influenced the kinds of images of the church audiences received. Hence, early in the lineage of historical trends in comedic programming identified by television scholar David Marc,[1] we found a familial, living room centered, comforting milieu established

---

[1]. David Marc (1989), *Comic Visions: Television Comedy and American Culture*, 2nd edn, Massachusetts: Blackwell.

on programs such as *Father Knows Best* (1954–63), *Leave it to Beaver* (1957–63), and *The Donna Reed Show* (1958–66), and this was reflected in the church-set *Going My Way* (1962–3), the priests serving as surrogate fathers for members of their congregation, discussing their problems over dinners in the rectory and passing on paternal wisdom to children and families in their parish. Accounting for the oddities of *The Flying Nun* (1967–70) was its place among what Marc calls the "magicoms" of the late 1960s, where televisual escapism took the form of programs highlighting fantastic "violations of the laws of nature," in shows such as *Bewitched* (1964–70), *I Dream of Jeannie* (1965–70), *The Munsters* and *The Addams Family* (both 1964–6), *My Favorite Martian* (1963–6) and *Nanny and the Professor* (1970–1).[2] The politically aware "litcoms," programs known as much for their socially relevant subject matter as for their clever dialogue, arose in the seventies with shows like *The Mary Tyler Moore Show* (1970–7), *All in the Family* (1971–83), *Good Times* (1974–9), *One Day at a Time* (1975–84), and the cleric-bearing *M*A*S*H* (1972–83).[3] This trend could include the politically charged, sharp-witted dialogue of *In the Beginning* (1978).

Entering the 1980s, a movement away from the litcom legacy led to more morally simplistic, less edgy fare, like *Happy Days* (1974–84), *Who's the Boss* (1984–92), *The Facts of Life* (1979–88), *Growing Pains* (1985–92) and the reliance on physical comedy in shows like *Mork and Mindy* (1978–82) and *Three's Company* (1977–84)[4]; this trend included the one-dimensional, slapstick *Amen* (1986–91) and even the one-dimensional, loony assembly of priests in *Have Faith* (1989). *Soul Man* (1997–8), with its motorcycle riding, leather and boot wearing ex-convict cleric, fit not only into the mainstay of television sitcoms, the domestic situation comedy, but also into the concurrent trend of programs like *Roseanne* (1988–97) and *Grace Under Fire* (1993–8) to focus on working-class families. Outside the purview of Marc's period of analysis, *Good News* (1997–8) followed in start-up network UPN's focus on youthful shows featuring African-American casts, and NBC's *The Book of Daniel* (2006) followed in the footsteps of network programs such as *Desperate Housewives* (2004–), attempting to compete with edgier cable programs such as *The Sopranos*, *Sex and the City* and *Six Feet Under* by pushing the envelope with scandalous, hyper-sexualized depictions of family life in the suburbs. While Marc's study focuses on the television comedy, the remaining non-comedic church-set programs followed similar trends in televised dramatic programming. For example, the sleuthing seniors of *Murder, She Wrote* (1984–96) and *Matlock* (1986–95) gave rise to *Father Dowling Mysteries* (1989–91), and the rural, poverty-stricken, wholesome family life of *The Waltons* (1971–81) was the forerunner of *The Family Holvak* (1975).

Another way to look at how these programs fit in to the trends and priorities of the television industry is to consider how successful they were, according

---

2. Ibid., p. 127.
3. Ibid., pp. 136–64.
4. Ibid., pp. 155, 164–80.

to the industry's standards. Compared to programs focusing on other social institutions, such as those looking at the legal, healthcare and education systems, programs focusing on the church have not fared as well. In both comedic and dramatic forms, programs focusing on other institutions were considerably more successful over the course of television history, assessed both in terms of longevity (number of seasons on the air) and ratings (popularity among television audiences). Shows focusing on the legal system (police and lawyers) have included everything from *Dragnet, The Streets of San Francisco* and *Adam 12*, to *Hill Street Blues, Barney Miller, Night Court, CHiPs, L.A. Law, Hooperman, Ally McBeal*, and the *Law and Order* and *CSI* franchises. All have been successful by television's standards. The healthcare system likewise has enjoyed a ubiquitous presence on American popular television, represented by programs such as *Medical Center, Dr. Kildare, Emergency, House Calls, Nurse, The Nurses, Doogie Howser M.D., Julia, Empty Nest, Trapper John M.D., Chicago Hope, ER, Scrubs* and *Grey's Anatomy*. Educational institutions were also represented by shows such as *Mr. Peepers, Our Miss Brooks, Room 222, Welcome Back Kotter, Square Pegs, Head of the Class, A Different World, Hangin' with Mr. Cooper, Boy Meets World, Boston Public* and most teen-centered series wherein schools figured prominently, from *The Brady Bunch* and *Eight is Enough* to *The Wonder Years, Beverly Hills 90210, My So-Called Life, Dawson's Creek* and *Felicity*. Compared to series set in these institutions, church-set programs were not as numerous or successful.

Using annual season's-end Nielsen rankings of top TV shows, of the programs discussed in depth only *Amen* reached the top 30 programs, doing so three times.[5] *M*A*S*H* and *AfterMASH* also received season's-end top-30 rankings. None of the other programs focusing on ecclesiastics achieved such success in the ratings. Using longevity as a guide, one (*7th Heaven*) reached 11 seasons, one reached five (*Amen*), and only two of the remaining 14 programs reached a third season (*The Flying Nun, Father Dowling Mysteries*). Of the programs discussed in brief, *M*A*S*H* lasted 11 seasons, whereas all the rest lasted only one or two. Most of the programs discussed at length herein lasted only one season. In general, programs focusing on church leaders have not been successful; they certainly have not done as well as programs focusing on people serving other social institutions. Those that have fared better in terms of ratings and longevity have taken a more lighthearted approach to depictions of the church (*Amen, The Flying Nun, Father Dowling Mysteries*) or have been geared towards a youth niche market (*7th Heaven*). Those that have fared the worst have taken a more controversial approach to depicting the church, and include *In the Beginning, Hell Town, Amazing Grace, Trinity, Nothing Sacred* and *The Book of Daniel*. Why should this be?

---

5. Based upon Nielsen rankings appearing in an appendix of Tim Brooks and Earle Marsh (2003), *The Complete Directory to Prime-Time Network and Cable TV Shows 1946–Present*, 8th edn. New York: Ballantine Books.

Taking on controversial material is a hallmark of programs set in other institutions, particularly those set in the law enforcement and healthcare settings, and is part of the reason for their success. The difference is that when church-set programs take on controversy, issues meet with not only civic debate (as on programs set in other institutions) but also ecclesiastic doctrine, which to many viewers is not given to debate. "Cop shows," for example, might involve abortion if criminal behavior is involved, such as rape or the bombing a clinic, and "doc shows" if someone's health is affected by a pregnancy. Such episodes may involve only momentary reflection or discussion of the issue, but the characters in the end will simply do their jobs, and how they respond will not necessarily be a commentary on the state of the healthcare or legal systems. However, if clerics face the issue of abortion (as on *Hell Town*, *Trinity* and *Nothing Sacred*) they are most likely counseling someone about the moral consequences of the act, and their advice is more likely to be seen as a commentary on the church and its beliefs. Similarly, when a cleric struggles with a personal problem like addiction or alcoholism (as in *Amazing Grace*, *Nothing Sacred* and *The Book of Daniel*) this is assessed in relation to idealized expectations of clerical behavior, which are more puritanical than those facing representatives of other professions. Personal problems of featured characters in church-set series are not just personal obstacles to be wrestled with and overcome but considered in relation to strict standards of proper clerical conduct. To many viewers, the sacred — as symbolized in church leaders — is not to be presented as compromised, no matter how realistic or relevant the portrayal. When issues of faith are concerned, televised popular culture is not as able to sustain controversy — at least not to do so and remain successful by television's standards. The programs that have taken a more lighthearted approach to the church setting have proven more acceptable to television audiences.

For many viewers, there is more at stake in the representation of the church on popular television. Programs that depict the church provide a testimony to the sort of behavior and values one hopes to find in the church itself. They do this in their creation of a *mythos* of "the church." Whatever the success of these programs, consideration of the type of "reality" depicted for the church is important. Television imposes a way of viewing reality that is both particular and naturalized; that is, it depicts one specific way of making sense of the real but in a fashion that makes that reality seem matter-of-fact. Realism in this sense, as television theorist John Fiske notes, "does not just reproduce reality, it makes sense of it — the essence of realism is that it reproduces reality in such a form as to make it easily understandable. [. . .] Realism is thus defined by the way it makes sense of the real, rather than by what it says the real consists of."[6] This goes beyond a simple suspension of disbelief, where we accept even the implausible because it is presented as believable. Hence, for example, we accept that a nun can fly because we see her do so, and observe other characters watch

---

6. John Fiske (1987), *Television Culture*. New York: Routledge, p. 24.

and accept her doing so, and we consent to that idea as acceptable within the given narrative system. Likewise, we accept that the zany assembly of priests of *Have Faith*, or the fiercely committed collection of progressive church leaders of *Nothing Sacred*, can and do exist and serve their parishes as they do: the former fighting doubt with good humor, the latter confronting problems with principled passion.

Beyond this, television narrative slips in other aspects of "realism" by means of its form, by "what it does rather than what it is or what it shows (the content)."[7] So, for example, while particulars of each episode might change, an understanding of how the universe of a program operates is instilled in the audience over time. A steady state, or what John Ellis calls a "repetition of a problematic," remains from episode to episode, and reinforces a series' sense of the normal.[8] This in fact distinguishes television from film narrative in that the episodic nature of television demands a form wherein the basic understanding of the narrative world and how it operates is reinforced every episode.[9] The steady state of *Going My Way*, *The Flying Nun* and *In the Beginning* is one wherein conflict between younger liberals and older conservatives is the norm — "just the way things are" in the church — and that while both the maturing progressives and seasoned traditionalists debate their points of view in a heartfelt manner, it is the younger progressives with whom television encourages audiences to identify in their struggles. It does this in various ways: by focusing on these characters in the program opening; by showing these characters as they commit to a plan (such as organizing an event, or helping someone) and then strive to follow through, often by overcoming obstacles or naysaying from superiors; and, if they are overzealous or uninformed of the consequences of their methods, by showing them learning from their mistakes by program's end. Since the depiction of a situation wherein a young liberal and older conservative easily agree is outside the series' normative principle of ongoing conflict, it is not represented as part of their particular reality. What remains, despite particulars of each episode, is the certainty of conflict and the particular relationships among the regular characters.[10] This itself is the "reality" depicted in a series, here influencing the view of the church and its leaders. The other program clusters likewise depict their own steady state as their reality. *Hell Town*, *Nothing Sacred* and others portray a church in conflict with the values of society and struggling to transform these, often by radical means. *Soul Man*, *7th Heaven* and others illustrate how a church leader deals with ongoing conflicts among members of his or her family. Emerging from these depictions of reality is a particular ideology — of progressivism in *Nothing Sacred*, or traditional values in *7th Heaven*. In this way, while developments in church history may have given rise to particular issues

---

7. Ibid, p. 24.
8. John Ellis (1982), *Visible Fictions*. Boston: Routledge & Kegan Paul, p. 154.
9. Ibid., pp. 156–7.
10. Ibid., p. 125.

facing television's church leaders taken up by church-set TV programs — from abortion to the sanctuary movement, from women serving as preachers or bishops to the church's openness to gay and lesbian people — television's form itself influences the depiction of the church and its leaders. It contributes to a popular mythology of "the church" and "church leaders."

What has television contributed to this mythology? In part, it is of a clergy that exhibit a commitment to immerse themselves in helping to solve the personal crises of parishioners and a willingness, perhaps even an eagerness, to fight whatever social or political forces that stand in their way — even when these are forces in the church itself. They are experts at debate and use their verbal skills to challenge those who do not share their values and goals. They accept the challenge to go about their religious, sectarian work in a secular, pluralistic society. They are committed to transforming lives, society and sometimes the church itself. These are professionals who take their vocation seriously, while nonetheless maintaining a distinct sense of humor. Occasionally they struggle with the consequences of how vocation impacts on their lives and vice versa, such as how to maintain celibacy or how addiction affects the image they project. We see them in private moments, from when they pray, face inner struggles or counsel parishioners, to when they clash behind closed doors with other church leaders over commitment, values or proper behavior. Seeing their behavior in private adds to the mythology of ecclesiastics, as television portrayals take us behind closed doors to what media theorist Joshua Meyrowitz (using the language of sociologist Erving Goffman) calls "back region" or backstage behavior.[11] While members of most professions must perform particular socially accepted and expected roles in public (that is, "front region" or onstage behavior), they also must avoid other behaviors in public; backstage behavior is shielded from the public eye. Society knows this back region behavior exists but is protected from witnessing it by well-established customs. While we know ministers must have private doubts, personal struggles, confidential counseling sessions and private arguments, we are not privy to witnessing them. Television exposes these moments in a fictitious but "realistic" form. It allows audiences to witness clerics' ordinarily unseen backstage behavior, exposing their frailties and doubts. In these ways, television contributes to the popular mythology of the church leader and may serve to humanize what otherwise might be the iconic ideal of "the church leader."

What is usually sacrificed on televised portrayals of church life is attention to the contemplative and spiritual. All activity is directed outward as service or debate, towards practical matters, to solve worldly problems; little if any activity is directed inward, towards awareness of the transcendent. Such moments might

---

11. Joshua Meyrowitz (1985), *No Sense of Place: The Impact of Electronic Media on Social Behavior*. New York: Oxford University Press, p. 30. The terms he applies to media studies originated in the classic sociological book by Erving Goffman (1959), *The Presentation of Self in Everyday Life*. New York: Anchor.

come in prayer, meditation or personal reflection. The camera might reveal a person's thoughts in some manner, or audio (perhaps a voice-over) might serve as inner monologue to elucidate a philosophical truth, theological justification or Biblical reference. Church-set television series rarely if ever focus on such inner reflection. All is dialogue about the practical and temporal, to solve the current crisis or interpersonal conflict, upstaging contemplation about the eternal and transcendent. The one series which had a ready-made vehicle to occasion such reflection was *The Book of Daniel*, wherein Reverend Webster's visions of Jesus Christ might have allowed for discussions of the spiritual; however, the banter between the cleric and Son of God was mostly jovial, and did not regularly rise to serious contemplation of the otherworldly. Other programs touched on such matters on occasion, such as "The Window" episode of *Have Faith* and "The Devil and the Deep Blue Sea Mystery" of *Father Dowling Mysteries*. *Nothing Sacred* came closest to regular and serious considerations of the spiritual and Biblical, with discussions of Christ's example and its application in modern life; one episode even depicted a young man having spiritual visions and speaking in tongues.[12] Ironically, other television series, not focused on clerics or the church, have considered the spiritual in various ways. Two relatively recent examples include *Joan of Arcadia* (2003–5), in which God speaks to a teenage girl in the form of ordinary people she meets in everyday situations, and *Miracles* (2003), in which a former seminarian joins a team investigating paranormal, unworldly phenomena. One television series which achieved a regular focus on the contemplative and spiritual was not set in a Judeo-Christian setting but in the Buddhist tradition, as *Kung Fu* (1972–5) followed the wanderings in the nineteenth century American West of a Shaolin monk on the run, wanted for murder by Chinese authorities. The monk's frequent flashback meditations on philosophical truths taught to him by elders at the Shaolin temple grounded the series in the spiritual, even as his regular use of his martial arts training allowed the series to balance this with action sequences.[13] No series set in the Judeo-Christian setting achieved this kind of regular contemplation of spiritual matters and philosophical truths.

Also underplayed is the clergy's regular role in leading the liturgical life of a worshiping community. Some series afforded more attention to this role than others, but most minimized it or showed it irregularly. This is ironic given that leadership in worship is the most regularly visible activity of a cleric in the life of a congregation. *Going My Way* and *Have Faith*, for example, had no such depictions. *Father Dowling* only included liturgy when it played a role in solving

---

12. "Speaking in Tongues." Written by Sandy Kroopf; directed by John Coles. November 13, 1997. Reviewed off broadcast television.

13. As the lead character of *Kung Fu* did not serve a temple as a Shaolin priest, the series was not included for in-depth discussion; nor was the series' spin-off, *Kung Fu: The Legend Continues* (1993–6), which had a similar flashback format to the original but followed the ancestors of the Shaolin monk in a modern day setting. Further, the spin-off was only released in syndication, and never aired in prime time on a broadcast network.

a crime. Other programs, such as *Soul Man*, *Hell Town* and *Amen*, offered occasional glimpses of worship services and sermons. For those programs not set in a parish, such as *In the Beginning*, *Sister Kate* and *The Flying Nun*, it is significant that the characters were never shown in worship. *Good News*, *Nothing Sacred* and *7th Heaven* were the series that regularly offered attention to liturgy and the role of the clergy in leading worship. *Good News* and *7th Heaven* included sermons and hymn singing; *Nothing Sacred* included these and other parts of rituals. Given television programs' need to create and resolve conflict to maintain interest, their lack of a focus on liturgy is not unexpected. Nonetheless, in considering what is and is not reflected in the depiction of the church on popular television series, it is noteworthy that most programs omit this aspect of religious life, making those that do include it all the more significant for doing so.

When all is said and done, the representations of the church and its leaders on prime-time American network programs have had little if any direct effect on actual churches' evangelism, membership, policies or practices. Seeing a "positive" or "negative" image of the church, however one might interpret these, is not likely to encourage or dissuade a viewer from exploring churches in their community. Such images may contribute to what Protestant theologian Martin Marty — writing in his classic 1961 reflection on the mass media and the Christian faith, *The Improper Opinion* — calls "pre-evangelism": seeing characters of a given faith go about their daily lives and living out their faith in their practice of everything from the mundane to the more explicitly religious may raise in viewers a curiosity about that faith — a curiosity which might someday serve as a groundwork for others engaged in more explicitly evangelical efforts.[14] His assertion is that a particular religious faith (his focus being on Christianity) would have a difficult time being considered "proper" or acceptable for presentation over a "mass" medium because the nature of such media is to appeal to as broad an audience as possible. This proved to be prophetic. Marty wrote this assertion a year before the first television program considered herein appeared, as *Going My Way* debuted in 1962, and his perspective may clarify why programs set in the church have been relatively scarce, particularly when compared to programs set in the context of other institutions. Even in those shows that have made it on the air, reference is often made to "God" and "God's" place and impact on the lives of people, as opposed to the more particular "Jesus Christ" (or any other religious figure), reflecting Marty's contention that the less particular the portrayal, the more successful a program would be. Beyond this, the more specifically challenging aspects of a faith, such as Christ's call to abandon all other commitments in service to him, be those to riches or family, are also out-of-bounds for mass portrayal, resulting in what Marty calls "diminution and muffling through the mask of drama" and "the only way of seeing faith at 'prime

---

14. Martin E. Marty (1961), *The Improper Opinion: Mass Media and the Christian Faith*. Philadelphia: Westminster Press.

time' where it really reaches masses."[15] For him, the potential impact of such televised portrayals of religion to bring people to faith or a church is to lay the groundwork for later development. Explicating the term "pre-evangelism," he notes that the most mass media can do to bring individuals to a church is to "merely [prepare] the soil," to "[raise] curiosity"; "it whispers rather than shouts."[16] This is the practical, potential impact of church-set television programs on the life of the church — indirect and uncertain.

What is certain is that there will be an image portrayed of the church in the public sphere, and churches, like any public institution, are concerned with their image. Likewise, producers of programs are concerned with the image of the church presented, as they need not only viewers but also sponsors, and therefore have a stake in making sure their programming does not elicit condemnation or boycotts. This is why many programs, from *The Flying Nun* and *In the Beginning*, to *Amen*, *Nothing Sacred* and *The Book of Daniel*, used consultants from the churches represented, to advise them on matters ranging from the merely technical (such as the proper way to wear clerical attire or behave in rituals) to the more critical (such as in reviewing scripts and advising on controversial storylines). Producers and churches alike are aware that televised images matter. While the producers' concern is for their commercial success, the churches' concern is in their very identity, their public character. Hence, churches take appropriate interest in how accurately and fairly they are portrayed in popular culture. Fictional television programs as part of that culture contribute perceptions of the church and its leaders, and so the image presented on such programs concerns them.

Non-Christian churches have another concern. While Christian denominations must concern themselves with how they are portrayed, non-Christian faiths may be concerned with their lack of representation. The relative lack of programs focusing on rabbis, synagogues and Jewish congregations effectively sentences organized Judaism to "symbolic annihilation," where the absence of representation in popular media indicates cultural indifference, lack of full participation in social consciousness, and in this way nonexistence.[17] Certainly not all Christian denominations are represented, as the lack of programming set in more fundamentalist settings indicates, the networks choosing to focus on mainline churches. Beyond this, entire faiths are not yet represented, as no television programs have focused on leaders in religions such as Hinduism, Buddhism and Islam. *Kung Fu* came closest to a program focusing on a Buddhist leader, albeit one separated from his temple. Given attention to Islam in recent years, one might expect programming set in this tradition to be forthcoming. In

---

15. Ibid., p. 118.
16. Ibid., p. 139.
17. George Gerbner and Larry Gross (1976), "Living with television: the violence profile." *Journal of Communication*, 26, 182. For a general discussion of the portrayal of Jews on American television, see David Zurawik (2003), *The Jews of Prime Time*. Hanover: Brandeis University Press.

fact, the Canadian Broadcasting Corporation developed just such a program in 2007, called *Little Mosque on the Prairie*. It is a comedy which spotlights an imam leading a new, rural Muslim congregation in Saskatchewan, and examines the interactions between members of the mosque and their wary non-Muslim neighbors. The program met with initial success, although the CBC is proceeding cautiously, hiring consultants to stave off potential offense from Muslim audiences.[18] In years to come, American network television programs focusing on leaders of non-Christian faiths may add to the diversity of programming. Until then, these faiths will suffer from a lack of representation, even as Christian churches remain concerned about the portrayals they receive.

As is, that portrayal runs the gamut from comedic to dramatic, Catholic to Protestant, sensational to sensitive, trite to challenging. From programs illustrating a generational ideological conflict in the church, to those depicting the church's struggle for relevance in the world, and finally those showing the challenge of clerics to balance church and family life, television programs featuring church leaders have passed through various eras, reflecting developments in the church and trends in television programming. These portrayals have presented a range of social issues, personal struggles and interpersonal battles for these ecclesiastics to confront. In facing these, the featured church leaders have shown commitment, devotion, courage, weakness, good humor and faith. Their fictional faith is a reflection of actual believers' faith in the church and what it represents. It is for them that the representation of the church and its leaders on American television programs is of particular concern; it presents to the world a popular image of an institution they consider sacred. For this reason, lighthearted, sentimental approaches to the church on television succeed more than controversial ones. Overall, while the church's depiction on television follows trends in church history and developments in television programming, successful programs steer clear of contentious social issues and shortcomings of clerics and instead present a cheery, inoffensive portrait of the church and its leaders. While controversial subject matter helps television programs depicting other social institutions succeed, challenging content in the context of ecclesiastic settings is discouraged. The sacred nature of the church leads the public to expect popular portrayals of the church on television to maintain ideals.

Questions for Reflection

1) Consider television's representation of other professions and social institutions: teachers and schools; doctors/nurses and hospitals; police/lawyers and the judicial system, etc. How do these compare to the representation of priests, pastors, nuns and the church?

---

18. Christopher Mason (2007), *"Little Mosque* diffuses hate with humor." *New York Times*, January 15.

2) What is the image of church leaders left by television's depictions? What impact do these images have on the viewing public?

Video Sources

Little Mosque on the Prairie. Season one available on DVD. Canadian Broadcasting Corporation (CBC) Home Video.

Suggested Further Reading

Marty, Martin E. (1961), *The Improper Opinion: Mass Media and the Christian Faith*. Philadelphia: Westminster Press.

Bibliography

Abi-Nader HM, Jeanette (1978), "Beyond *The Flying Nun.*" *National Catholic Reporter,* September 8, 13.

Associated Press (2006), "NBC drops *Book of Daniel* from schedule." *ABC News*, January 24, available at http://abcnews.go.com/Entertainment/wireStory?id=1538244 (accessed September 17, 2006).

— (2000), "Priests hit hard by hidden AIDS epidemic." Cable News Network report, January 31, available at http://archives.cnn.com/2000/HEALTH/AIDS/01/31/aids.priests/index.html (accessed September 17, 2006).

Banerjee, Neela (2006), "Clergywomen find hard path to bigger pulpit." *New York Times,* August 26.

— (2006), "Woman is named Episcopal leader." *New York Times,* June 19.

Baugh, Lloyd (1997), *Imaging the Divine: Jesus and Christ-Figures in Film.* Wisconsin: Sheed and Ward.

Becker, Ron (2006), *Gay TV and Straight America.* New Jersey: Rutgers University Press.

Bergensen, Albert J. and Greeley, Andrew M. (2000), *God in the Movies.* New Brunswick: Transaction Publishers.

Bonko, Larry (1995), "Duke has an 'amazing' new role: *The Virginian* pilot," *Television Week,* April 1, 1.

Boswell, Parley Ann and Loukides, Paul (1995), *Reel Rituals: Ritual Occasions from Baptisms to Funerals in Hollywood Films, 1945–1995.* Bowling Green, Ohio: Bowling Green State University Popular Press.

Brooks, Tim and Marsh, Earle (2003), *The Complete Directory to Prime-Time Network and Cable TV Shows 1946–Present,* 8th edn. New York: Ballantine Books.

Brown, Donal (2006), "Asian Americans go missing when it comes to TV." *New American Media*, August 28, available at http://news.newamericamedia.org/news/view_article.html?article_id=2187822d260441c3 75f65241320819d0 (accessed September 17, 2006).

Buhle, Paul (1985), "The Gospel according to Robert Blake." *The Village Voice,* September 17,33–5.

Carey, Patrick W (2004), *Catholics in America: A History*. Westport, Connecticut: Praeger.

CBS (2008), "Joel Osteen answers his critics." *CBS News*, June 8, available at http://www.cbsnews.com/stories/2007/10/11/60minutes/main3358652.shtml (accessed June 8, 2008).

Center for Applied Research in the Apostolate (CARA), Georgetown University (undated), "Frequently requested Catholic Church statistics," available at http://cara.georgetown.edu/bulletin/index.htm (accessed May 22, 2007).

Clark, Scott H. (2005), "Created in whose image? Religious characters on network television." *Journal of Media and Religion,* 4, 137–53.

Dart, John (1997), "The 'sacred' debate television: as ABC renews its drama about a liberal priest, Catholics remain divided over the show's intent." *Los Angeles Times,* December 4.

Dolan, Jay P. (1985), *The American Catholic Experience: A History from Colonial Times to the Present.* New York: Doubleday & Company.

— (2002), *In Search of an American Catholicism: A History of Religion and Culture in Tension.* New York: Oxford University Press.

Douglas, John (1992), "Dick York — a farewell interview." *FilmFax* April/May, 57.

Elliott, Stuart (2006), "Few are booking ads on *The Book of Daniel.*" *New York Times,* January 11, C3.

Ellis, John (1982), *Visible Fictions.* Boston: Routledge & Kegan Paul.

Ellis, John Tracy (1969), *American Catholicism,* 2nd edn, rev. The Chicago History of American Civilization series, edited by Daniel J. Boorstin. Chicago: University of Chicago Press, 1969.

— (1970), "American Catholics and intellectual life." In *Catholicism in America,* edited by Philip Gleason. New York: Harper & Row.

Farley, Christopher John (1996), "TV's black flight." *Time,* June 3, available at http://www.time.com/time/magazine/article/0,9171,984646,00.html (accessed May 25, 2007).

Fisher, Ian and Goodstein, Laurie (2005), "In strong terms, Rome is to ban gays as priests." *New York Times,* November 23.

Fiske, John (1987), *Television Culture.* New York: Routledge.

Franklin, Robert M. (1997), *Another Day's Journey: Black Churches Confronting the American Crisis.* Minnesota: Augsburg Fortress.

Fraser, Peter and Neal, Vernon Edwin (2000), *Reviewing the Movies: A Christian Response to Contemporary Film.* Wheaton, Illinois: Crossway Books.

Gallagher, Michael (1985), "*Hell Town* no tribute to inner-city Catholics." *Catholic New Times* (Toronto), 9, October 13, 7.

Gerbner, George and Gross, Larry (1976), "Living with television: the violence profile." *Journal of Communication,* 26, 182.

Gilkey, Langdon (1975), *Catholicism Confronts Modernity.* New York: Seabury Press.

Gillis, Chester (1999), *Roman Catholicism in America.* Columbia Contemporary American Religion Series. New York: Columbia University Press.

Gleason, Philip (1970), "The crisis of Americanization." In *Catholicism in America,* Philip Gleason, ed. New York: Harper & Row.

Goffman, Erving (1959), *The Presentation of Self in Everyday Life.* New York: Anchor.

Greeley, Andrew M (1998), "A *Nothing Sacred* episode you haven't seen." *New York Times,* March 1.

— (1990), *The Catholic Myth: The Behavior and Beliefs of American Catholics.* New York: Simon & Schuster.

Gross, Larry (2002), *Up from Invisibility.* New York: Columbia University Press.

Hamamoto, Darrell Y. (1994), *Monitored Peril: Asian Americans and the Politics of TV Representation.* Minneapolis: University of Minnesota Press.

Harper, Jennifer (1992), "Single parents have been multiple in TV history." *Washington Times,* September 21.

Hennesey, James (1981), *American Catholics: A History of the Roman Catholic Community in the United States.* New York: Oxford University Press.

Holston, Noel (1992), "Portrayal of single parenthood lacking." *St. Petersburg Times,* August 28.

Janosik, MaryAnn (1997), "Madonnas in our midst: representations of women religious in Hollywood film." *U.S. Catholic Historian,* 15(3), 75–98.

Johnson, Ted (1997), "Holy role." *TV Guide,* October 18.

Johnston, Robert K. (2000), *Reel Spirituality: Theology and Film in Dialogue.* Grand Rapids: Baker Academic.

Keyser, Les and Keyser, Barbara (1984), *Hollywood and the Catholic Church: The Image of Roman Catholicism in American Movies.* Chicago: Loyola Press.

Lardner, James (1978), "The new season: I." *The New Republic,* October 7, 27.

Leddy, Mary Jo. (1985), "Enough!" *Catholic New Times* (Toronto) 9, October 13, 7.

Lincoln, C. Eric and Mamiya, Lawrence H. (1990), *The Black Church in the African American Experience.* Durham: Duke University Press.

Lutheran School of Theology (2006), "Lutheran School of Theology at Chicago establishes a Center of Christian-Muslim Engagement for Peace and Justice." Press release, Office of Communications, Lutheran School of Theology at Chicago, June 6.

Lyden, John C. (2003), *Film as Religion: Myths, Morals, and Rituals.* New York: New York University Press.

Lynch, Christopher Owen (1998), *Selling Catholicism: Bishop Sheen and the Power of Television.* Kentucky: University Press of Kentucky.

Marc, David (1989), *Comic Visions: Television Comedy and American Culture*, 2nd edn. Massachusetts: Blackwell.

Marsh, Clive and Ortiz, Gaye (eds) (1997), *Explorations in Theology and Film.* Massachusetts: Blackwell.

Martin, Joel W. and Ostwalt, Conrad E. Jr. (eds) (1995), *Screening the Sacred: Religion, Myth, and Ideology in Popular American Film.* Boulder: Westview Press.

Marty, Martin E. (1961), *The Improper Opinion: Mass Media and the Christian Faith.* Philadelphia: Westminster Press.

Mason, Christopher (2007), "*Little Mosque* diffuses hate with humor." *New York Times,* January 15.

Mason, M. S. (1997), "Religious themes get wider play, more nuanced portrayal in fall shows." *Christian Science Monitor*, October 14, 13.

Massa, Mark S (1999), *Catholics and American Culture: Fulton Sheen, Dorothy Day, and the Notre Dame Football Team.* New York: The Crossroad Publishing Company.

Mayer, Martin (1978), *American Film.* November, 16.

McDannell, Colleen (ed.) (2008) *Catholics in the Movies.* New York: Oxford University Press.

McNeil, Alex (1996), *Total Television: The Comprehensive Guide to Programming from 1948 to the Present.* New York: Penguin.

Meisler, Andy (1997), "Battling demons (and ratings) at the pulpit." *New York Times,* Television October 26 — November 1.

Meyers, Sister Bertrande (1967), "Raise your voice: cast your vote." *Vital Speeches of the Day,* 33, August 15, 662.

Meyrowitz, Joshua (1985), *No Sense of Place: The Impact of Electronic Media on Social Behavior.* New York: Oxford University Press.

Miles, Margaret R. (1996), *Seeing and Believing: Religion and Values in the Movies.* Boston: Beacon Press.

O'Connor, John J. (1985), "TV reviews: Robert Blake as priest in *Hell Town* on NBC." *New York Times,* March 6, C22.

Paitta, Ann C. (2005), *Saints, Clergy and Other Religious Figures on Film and Television, 1895–2003.* North Carolina: McFarland and Company.

Prichard, Robert (1999), *A History of the Episcopal Church.* Rev. edn. Pennsylvania: Morehouse Publishing.

Quill, Erin (undated), "Why there are 'no' Asians on television" (Four part series), Asian American Village at *IMDiversity,* available at http://www.imdiversity.com/villages/asian/arts_culture_media/quill_asian_TVa_0805.asp (for subsequent installments of the series, replace TVa with TVb, TVc, and TVd) (accessed September 17, 2006).

Reinhartz, Adele (2007), *Jesus of Hollywood.* New York: Oxford University Press.

— (2003), *Scripture on the Silver Screen.* Louisville: Westminster John Know Press.

Rich, Frank (1978), "The 1978–79 season: III." *Time,* September 25, 75.

Richmond, Ray (1997), "*Soul Man*" (Review). *Daily Variety,* April 22.

Rios, Tere (1965), *The Fifteenth Pelican.* New York: Doubleday & Company.

Schneider, Michael (2002), "Late season entries fizzle in fall." *Variety.* March 25–31, 27.

Seal, Cynthia (2006), "Is nothing sacred? Hollywood's treatment of Catholicism." *San Francisco Faith,* November, available at http://www.sffaith.com/ed/articles/1997/1197cs.htm (accessed June 6, 2006).

Spencer, Jon Michael (1993), "The ritual of testifying in the black church." In *Celebrations of Identity: Multiple Voices in American Ritual Performance*, edited by Pamela R. Frese. Connecticut: Bergin & Garvey, pp. 61–74.

Stanley, T. L. (1997), "Father shows best." *Mediaweek*, March 24.

Steinfels, Peter (2003), *A People Adrift: The Crisis of the Roman Catholic Church in America.* New York: Simon & Schuster.

Stern, Richard C., Jefford, Clayton N. and Debona, Guerric (eds) (1999), *Savior on the Silver Screen.* New York: Paulist Press.

Sterngold, James (1997), "A Jesuit takes the heat for a gritty TV series about a doubting priest." *New York Times,* October 25.

Stone, Bryan P. (2000), *Faith and Film: Theological Themes at the Cinema.* St. Louis: Chalice Press.

Sullivan, Rebecca (2005), *Visual Habits: Nuns, Feminism, and American Postwar Popular Culture.* Toronto: University of Toronto Press.

Tatum, W. Barnes (1997), *Jesus at the Movies: A Guide to the First Hundred Years.* Santa Rosa, California: Polebridge Press.

Terrace, Vincent (1986), *Complete Encyclopedia of Television Series, Pilots and Specials.* New York: Zoetrope.

"The 1997 TV season: what's black and what's back." *Ebony,* October, 84.

Thoman, CHM, Elizabeth (1978), "What went wrong with *In the Beginning.*" *National Catholic Reporter,* November 24, 14.

Thumma, Scott, Travis, Dave and Bird, Warren (2005), *Megachurches Today 2005, Summary of Research Findings.* Hartford Institute for Religion Research, available at http://hirr.hartsem.edu/megachurch/megastoday2005_summaryreport.html (accessed October 2, 2006).

Tropiano, Stephen (2002), *The Prime Time Closet: A History of Gays and Lesbians on TV.* New York: Applause Books.

US Census Bureau (2004), "No. 597. Employed civilians by occupation, sex, race and Hispanic origin: 2003," *Statistical Abstract of the United States: 2004–2005.* Washington, DC: US Government Printing Office.

Wakin, Edward and Scheuer, Father Joseph F. (1965), "The American nun: poor, chaste and restive." *Harper's Magazine,* August, 35.

Walsh, Richard (2003), *Reading the Gospels in the Dark: Portrayals of Jesus in Film.* New York: Trinity Press International.

Walters, Suzanna Danuta (2003), *All the Rage: The Story of Gay Visibility in America.* Chicago: University of Chicago Press.

Whitney, Dwight (1968), "I didn't want to play a nun." *TV Guide*, March 16–22, 21–5.

Witham, Larry A (2005), *Who Shall Lead Them? The Future of Ministry in America.* New York: Oxford University Press.

Wolff, Richard. "*The Bishop and the Gargoyle*: a study of network-produced, prime-time church-set dramatic old-time radio programs." *Journal of Radio Studies, 72 ,* 428–40.

— (1988), "Clergywomen: The Lutheran case: an inside look at Lutheran female clergy in America." *The Cresset* (Valparaiso University, Indiana), 51, April, 16–21.

Zikmund, Barbara Brown, Lummis, Adair T. and Chang, Patricia M. Y. (1998), "Women, men and styles of clergy leadership." *Christian Century,* 115, May 6, 478–86.

Zook, Kristal Brent (2006), Interview with Brooke Gladstone, "Gentrifying the airwaves." *On the Media* radio program, WNYC — New York Public Radio. Transcript of January 27, 2006, available at http://www.onthemedia.org/transcripts/2006/01/27/04 (accessed May 25, 2007).

Zurawik, David (2003), *The Jews of Prime Time.* Hanover: Brandeis University Press.

Index

Bold type indicates a reference to an illustration.